The Cooking of Scandinavia

Other Publications:

WORLD WAR II

THE GREAT CITIES

HOME REPAIR AND IMPROVEMENT

THE WORLD'S WILD PLACES

THE TIME-LIFE LIBRARY OF BOATING

HUMAN BEHAVIOR

THE ART OF SEWING

THE OLD WEST

THE EMERGENCE OF MAN

THE AMERICAN WILDERNESS

THE TIME-LIFE ENCYCLOPEDIA OF GARDENING

LIFE LIBRARY OF PHOTOGRAPHY

THIS FABULOUS CENTURY

TIME-LIFE LIBRARY OF AMERICA

TIME-LIFE LIBRARY OF ART

GREAT AGES OF MAN

LIFE SCIENCE LIBRARY

THE LIFE HISTORY OF THE UNITED STATES

TIME READING PROGRAM

LIFE NATURE LIBRARY

LIFE WORLD LIBRARY

FAMILY LIBRARY:
  HOW THINGS WORK IN YOUR HOME
  THE TIME-LIFE BOOK OF THE FAMILY CAR
  THE TIME-LIFE FAMILY LEGAL GUIDE
  THE TIME-LIFE BOOK OF FAMILY FINANCE

The Cooking of Scandinavia

by

Dale Brown

and the Editors of

TIME-LIFE BOOKS

photographed by Richard Meek

TIME-LIFE BOOKS, ALEXANDRIA, VIRGINIA

Time-Life Books Inc.
is a wholly owned subsidiary of
TIME INCORPORATED

FOUNDER: Henry R. Luce 1898-1967

Editor-in-Chief: Hedley Donovan
Chairman of the Board: Andrew Heiskell
President: James R. Shepley
Vice Chairman: Roy E. Larsen
Corporate Editor: Ralph Graves

TIME-LIFE BOOKS INC.
MANAGING EDITOR: Jerry Korn
Executive Editor: David Maness
Assistant Managing Editors: Dale M. Brown,
Martin Mann
Art Director: Tom Suzuki
Chief of Research: David L. Harrison
Director of Photography: Melvin L. Scott
Senior Text Editors: William Frankel,
Diana Hirsh
Assistant Art Director: Arnold C. Holeywell

CHAIRMAN: Joan D. Manley
President: John D. McSweeney
Executive Vice Presidents: Carl G. Jaeger (U.S.
and Canada), David J. Walsh (International)
Vice President and Secretary: Paul R. Stewart
Treasurer and General Manager:
John Steven Maxwell
Business Manager: Peter G. Barnes
Sales Director: John L. Canova
Public Relations Director: Nicholas Benton
Personnel Director: Beatrice T. Dobie
Production Director: Herbert Sorkin
Consumer Affairs Director: Carol Flaumenhaft

FOODS OF THE WORLD
SERIES EDITOR: Richard L. Williams
EDITORIAL STAFF FOR
THE COOKING OF SCANDINAVIA
Associate Editor: Jay Brennan
Picture Editor: Donald Hinkle
Designer: Albert Sherman
Assistant Designer: Robert Pellegrini
Staff Writers: John Stanton,
Ethel Strainchamps
Chief Researcher: Helen Fennell
Researchers: Sarah Bennett, Wendy Afton,
Linda Ferrer, Helen Isaacs, Eva Smidth,
Diana Sweeney
Test Kitchen Chef: John W. Clancy
Test Kitchen Staff: Fifi Bergman, Sally Darr,
Joel Levy, Leola Spencer

EDITORIAL PRODUCTION
Production Editor: Douglas B. Graham
Operations Manager: Gennaro C. Esposito
Assistant Production Editor: Feliciano Madrid
Quality Director: Robert L. Young
Assistant Quality Director: James J. Cox
Associate: Serafino J. Cambareri
Copy Staff: Susan B. Galloway (chief),
Florence Keith, Celia Beattie
Picture Department: Dolores A. Littles,
Joan Lynch, Barbara S. Simon
Traffic: Barbara Buzan

CORRESPONDENTS: Elisabeth Kraemer (Bonn);
Margot Hapgood, Dorothy Bacon (London);
Susan Jonas, Lucy T. Voulgaris (New York);
Maria Vincenza Aloisi, Josephine du Brusle
(Paris); Ann Natanson (Rome). Valuable assis-
tance was also provided by: Knud Meister (Co-
penhagen); Lance Keyworth (Helsinki); Caro-
lyn T. Chubet (New York); Arne Bonde
(Oslo); Mary Johnson (Stockholm).

THE AUTHOR: Dale Brown *(above, left)*, a member of the staff of TIME-LIFE
BOOKS and a former editor of *Holiday*, received his introduction to Scandinavian cooking in Denmark in 1953, while studying literature at the Univer-
sity of Copenhagen on a Danish government fellowship. Since then he has traveled throughout Scandinavia a number of times, most recently while gathering
information for this book.

THE PHOTOGRAPHER: Richard Meek *(above, right)*, a member of the original
SPORTS ILLUSTRATED photographic staff, is now a versatile freelance photographer who has covered assignments as varied as the America's Cup races
and the wildlife of the Canadian Rockies. *The Cooking of Scandinavia* is his first
major assignment in food photography, but his interest in cooking goes back
to the days when he worked in his father's bakery in Richmond, Indiana.

THE CONSULTING EDITOR: The late Michael Field adapted most of the recipes
in this book from traditional Scandinavian sources. One of America's first-rank
food experts and teachers of cooking, he conducted a school in Manhattan and
wrote many articles on the culinary arts for various magazines. His books
include *Michael Field's Cooking School* and *Michael Field's Culinary Classics and
Improvisations*.

THE CONSULTANTS: Pernilla Tunberger *(above, left)*, food editor of the Stockholm Dagens Nyheter *(Daily News)*, has been influencing Scandinavian cooking habits for more than 30 years. Her food guides for diabetics and heart pa-
tients have been praised by leading medical authorities. One of her many
cookbooks, *The Novice at the Range*, is the basis for a Swedish radio program on
cooking. Paula Peck *(above, right)*, author of *The Art of Fine Baking*, gave
special guidance on Chapter VIII.

THE COVER: Glassblower's herring *(recipe, page 98)*, a Swedish favorite, mari-
nates in a jar of Finnish design, ready for serving with aquavit in a Norwegian
glass, and with Swedish bread and Danish cheese.

The text for the chapters of this book was written by Dale Brown, the picture essays and
appendix material by the staff, the recipes by Helen Isaacs and Miriam Ungerer.

Contents

The Recipe Booklet that accompanies this volume has been designed for use in the kitchen. It contains all of the 93 recipes printed here plus 13 more. It also has a wipe-clean cover and a spiral binding so that it can either stand up or lie flat when open.

Introduction: A Cuisine Built on Nature's Simplest Foods

It has been said that the only thing we Scandinavians will own up to, in the name of fellowship among our countries, is the Vikings. True enough, the Vikings are part of the common cultural heritage of Scandinavia, but they are by no means the only part. Ever since the earliest settlements in these lands, food and customs have intermingled among the countries and, blended with influences from foreign shores, have created a cuisine and a culture that take second rank to none. In 1247, when Cardinal William of Sabina made the long trip to Norway to crown Haakon Haakonsson, the papal legate told the court that he had been warned against making the journey to the barren lands of the North, where there would be little bread, the drinks would be limited to water and milk, and the people would behave like animals. Instead, the cardinal informed his delighted hosts, he had found a great assembly of people of excellent manners and an abundance of fine food and drink. Even at that early date, the cardinal stood before people who knew how to set store by food and drink after the European fashion.

On a map of the world, the greater part of Scandinavia looks like a group of frozen, forbidding clumps of earth and mountain, and its history is as rough as its terrain. This corner of the globe has known a stormy past, but out of it has come a remarkable unity. We have today something singular, a kind of interdependence and mutual trust not common on this planet. Clear boundary lines between the countries are difficult to define. As far as food is concerned, we share a special culinary tradition. Something remarkable has occurred: an inter-Nordic kitchen has appeared—and we share the delights of it among ourselves. We feel at ease at one another's tables.

Through the ages we have had a varied diet, but it has always been down to earth, plain and simple. It has sprung out of nature itself, and bears traces of the rhythm of the seasons. The underlying principle is simplicity, and the guiding thread—as Dale Brown points out in this volume—is the natural taste that soil, climate, mountain and lake have produced. Thus, our dishes are uncomplicated, varied and in harmony with nature.

While it is true that this inter-Nordic kitchen shares in the European tradition, as does the American kitchen, some of the dishes and culinary customs that are presented in this book may at first seem strange to people under other skies. When the late Norwegian painter Edvard Munch invited artist friends to parties, it is said that he often served vintage Champagne with a dish of beef and onions. It is not unusual in Scandinavia today to drink red wine with boiled cod and roe. It is, of course, an affront in some other lands to dare to combine the freshest of cod boiled in salt water with hearty red wine, or to serve Champagne with beef and onions. Nonetheless, we make such robust combinations, however little they agree with other traditions. We also like to precede or accompany our food with strong aquavit and beer, and do not concern ourselves overmuch with cocktails. To us, and now I am speaking with a Norwegian tongue, beer is one of the finest of drinks. It goes with the fare that is our own, and emphasizes its goodness. If we eat herring, or flat bread with salted butter and cheese—good, everyday food—we give little thought to a drink other than beer.

To amplify this point, one does not find in our latitudes what might else-where be called the sophisticated kitchen, the classic *grande cuisine*. Such a cuisine derives partly from another time—the time when with culinary artifices one tried to conceal the taste of the raw materials because, in all likelihood, their freshness had disappeared in the long journey from source to kitchen. Of primary importance to the modern culinary art is the freshness, cleanliness and genuineness of the raw materials. Today these qualities can, of course, be preserved by technological means. Nowadays, the natural taste is characteristic of our kitchen. The goal is always the unassuming, the uncomplicated.

If the word gastronomy is mentioned in Scandinavia today, there are many who think of an ideal of refinement from the gilded 1880s. They are in a sense right; the word does not really belong to our time, but to an age of tranquillity and gentility. But to me, gastronomy is still alive to the highest degree in Scandinavia.

Gastronomy, by my definition, is culinary art closely connected to a living tradition. We ourselves do not give our living gastronomy much thought, because it is an integral part of our everyday life. Only when it is called to our attention do we stop a moment and meditate on it a bit. That is why Dale Brown's book is so welcome and so valuable.

—*Hroar Dege, chef, author, and Director, Norwegian Food Center, Oslo*

I

A Taste
of Nature

The Scandinavians are widely known as brilliant designers, and much of what they have designed, crafted and sent out into the world for the past three decades has been for the beautification of the table—porcelain, silverware, crystal, linen. It is not so widely known that they are excellent cooks as well. It should stand to reason, however, that a people who could care so much about the way a table looks would also care vitally about food, and the Scandinavians do.

Why, then, with the exception of the *smörgåsbord,* is their cooking relatively unknown? The Scandinavians are in a way themselves to blame. They are all too shy about it. Having industrialized late and thus begun to emerge from a background of rural poverty only within the last century, they still tend to see their wonderful native cuisine in humble terms. Besides, for generations their aristocrats, intoxicated by all things Gallic, had pounded home the idea that the only real cooking was French. Still influenced by this tradition, Scandinavian restaurants go on serving somewhat gallicized dishes to foreign guests, while the Scandinavians keep hidden in their kitchens those they like best and are best at preparing.

What is Scandinavian food? It is many things: fish, of course, but pork and poultry as well; beets, potatoes, cucumbers; dill, parsley and horseradish; apples and almonds; cream and that golden product of cream, butter. The cooking is pure, and it is simple. Foods taste of themselves in the North: they smack of the sea, or a fresh-water lake, or even the earth. And some, like the garnet lingonberry or the sand-colored mushroom, are not only born of the forest, but bring a breath of pines or birches to the table

Scandinavia's finest fish, the salmon, commands respect and receives it. Here a freshly hooked prime Norwegian specimen lies garlanded with snow buttercups and Arctic harebells, signifying that a woman caught it. This one will be poached— although it could as easily be broiled, baked, smoked or cured with salt, sugar, white pepper and dill.

with them. It is this palatable communion with nature that makes Scandinavian food appealing.

I know, having once been, a rather long time ago, a very skinny student in Copenhagen—a Danish hostess' dream, someone to fatten up. Whenever I have returned to Scandinavia since then, I have never failed to eat well, and have never ceased to be amazed that so much freshness and naturalness can still exist in the world. On my last visit, with my wife and year-old daughter, I felt myself undergoing the same mental and physical refreshment I had experienced in previous stays, and this despite the fact that we had come to Scandinavia in midautumn when the afternoons were shrinking into darkness. Each day the sky seemed to descend a little lower, a blind being inched down toward the horizon. And everywhere we went rain fell. A depressing time of year—and yet not really; it is the time of year in Scandinavia when people go back inside their homes, when friends and food and entertaining are much on their minds. Wheeling our daughter in her stroller along the darkening streets, we seemed forever to be passing through delicious aromas—invisible ribbons curling out of unseen kitchens, trails we wished we could have followed, invitations we wanted to accept.

Scandinavian food is romantic. There is something about it of the fairy tale—curds and whey, porridge, fruit tarts. The distant past clings to it. Many of the foods and some of the dishes the Vikings ate are still consumed by their descendants. The Vikings loved oysters and mussels; they savored mutton, cheese, cabbage, apples, onions, berries and nuts, and all these continue to be staples of the Scandinavian diet. The Vikings raised chickens and geese, and they hunted wild birds, elk, deer and bear, just as their modern counterparts do. Even a few of the more esoteric tastes of the Vikings live on. The Norwegians insist that a whale steak properly marinated and broiled can taste as good as beef; some Swedes rave about smoked horseflesh, which they refer to as "hamburger" and buy thinly sliced.

Hospitality in a hallowed tradition

Moreover, the Vikings were great hosts. The thread of hospitality in Scandinavia has never been broken, and it shows no signs of fraying. The conditions for entertaining were laid down by the god Odin, and his admonition to his people rings out in a poem called "Hávamál," the Viking code: "Fire he needs who with frozen knees / Has come from the cold without; / Food and clothes must the farer have, / The man from the mountains come. / Water and towels and welcoming speech / Should he find who comes to the feast." And it was long the custom for a Norwegian farm wife to hang under the roof of her storehouse a basket with folded flat bread, a butter box, and cured meat and sausage, with a white tablecloth draped over everything—just in case somebody dropped by.

To cook is to tell a story; to cook the Scandinavian way is to re-create the past. For hundreds of years many of the recipes being used today were not written down but handed down, like folk ballads, mouth to mouth, memory to memory. Who can begin to trace the evolution, much less approximate the age of a dish like herring salad, eaten for so long and so thoroughly enjoyed that it is now found not only throughout Scandinavia, but wherever Scandinavians have gone? How many of us, setting out to make it for the first time *(page 26)*, will even know that its basic ingredient is one of Europe's oldest foods? Herring bones turn up in kitchen middens of Denmark dating from the early Neolithic period, when Europeans were giving up their nomadic way of life for a more settled existence in coastal areas close to a ready source of food.

There are several reasons—fascinating and again romantic—that so much that is old should survive in the cookery of modern Scandinavia. One important factor is the area's relative geographical isolation from the rest of Europe *(map, page 13)*; only the peninsula of Jutland, part of Denmark, is joined like an outthrust thumb to the continent proper. Finland and Norway abut on Russia, but this is as good as facing a wall—a barrier of enmeshed pine trees, over which can come not much more than icy winds as ferocious as a raging bear. The three northern countries in turn are cut off from Denmark by water, and, in part because of this, they preserve an even older food culture. And Iceland, adrift in the mid-Atlantic many miles away from everything, is in its isolation like a reservoir of the Viking past.

If there is any convenient way to characterize the 485,000-square-mile area of Scandinavia (excluding Greenland), it is in terms of water. The Baltic washes the coasts of Denmark, Sweden and Finland, offering up its shoals of herring to the tables of each, while to the west rolls the much saltier and bigger North Sea, with its own locker of well-chilled fish and crustaceans. And here too the silver-blue herring dominates.

When seen from the air, as from the eyes of a seagull, Scandinavia looks as though it were melting; the coastlines seem to be crumbling into the seas, and the islands offshore to be dissolving. Even granitic Norway erodes under the salty thrust of the waters that penetrate its heart through countless fjords. Sweden and Finland lie puddled with some 150,000 lakes. And across much of the rumpled surface of this lake-dotted landscape sweeps yet another kind of sea—the forest, spreading northward into Lapland at the top of the world, there to thin out and disappear into a wasteland of tundra, snow and ice.

To the watery geographic isolation of Scandinavia should be added a second formative influence—the human isolation, until a century ago, of most Scandinavians from each other. Distances to this day remain long in the underpopulated countrysides of Sweden, Norway and Finland. What could they have been like 100 years ago? The way out of a Norwegian farm was often only by water, down long fjords and along coastal channels. In northern Sweden even churchgoing could mean traveling miles and miles, and many of the far-flung parishioners of the city called Luleå actually owned second homes, cottages adjacent to their central place of worship. Thus, instead of spending only an occasional hour or so in the presence of God whenever weather and time permitted, they could sleep and eat in the cottages and soak up enough religion in the church next door to last them all through the winter, when snowed in back home.

Such isolation inevitably helped spawn many local dishes and traditions. Out of the far North has come one of the greatest Scandinavian delicacies, cured salmon *(page 27)*. Prepared with sugar, salt, white pepper and dill, this moist, tender, springlike dish is now also relished in Denmark, and such is the character of its sweet, clean-tasting appeal that undoubtedly, in years to come, it will spread far beyond Scandinavia to wherever fresh salmon can be found. The Swedes call it *gravlax*. *Gravlax* is Scandinavia. Its preparation can be an introduction to the region, as well as to the foods. It seems to bring together, in the orange-pink flesh of the spawning salmon, two of the major components of the area, salt and fresh water. The feathery tufts of dill used for flavoring are a reminder of the short summer's rich green grass; the salt and sugar sprinkled over it speak of the frost and the long winter's snow. Its affinity to nature at large is beautifully suggested in the recipe of a Swedish sportsman who says that *gravlax* should be made in silence, in coolness and in shadow. He has a point, but none of these is actually necessary. All that is needed is a weight to put on top of the salmon to act as a press during preparation, and a little daring—for *gravlax* is served uncooked, although well cured, with a sweet-sour mustard-dill sauce *(Recipe Booklet)*. The timid can take courage from the fact that pickled herring is not cooked either.

Superb as *gravlax* is, there are some other locally invented Scandinavian dishes that only a native brought up on them would take for granted. *Svartsoppa*, or black soup, is one—a November specialty of Sweden's most southerly province, Skåne. The soup is brownish, as thick and as smooth as velvet, rather sweet, quite spicy—made of a mixture of goose and pig's blood that has been constantly stirred in the cooking pot to keep it from coagulating on the bottom. *Svartsoppa* is of course a pagan dish, one that originated with the brawny, hard-sinewed Vikings a thousand years or so ago. The Vikings were by no means above eating their meat raw, and drinking their blood warm—and liking it.

As served at the Savoy Hotel in Malmö, however, *svartsoppa* displays the many civilized touches that it has picked up since the Viking days. These additions, which go a long way toward disguising the soup's basic ingredient, include a little sherry, port, Madeira and Cognac, some red wine and some white, a jigger of gin, prune juice, pinches of thyme and marjoram, some salt and pepper, cinnamon, ginger, cumin and bay.

Just as many old dishes survive in Scandinavia, so do old ways of preparing food. Again in Sweden, but this time to the north in the beautiful prov-

The map of Scandinavia *(opposite)* includes the nations of Finland, Norway, Sweden and Denmark. (The island republic of Iceland, also often considered Scandinavian, lies some 600 miles to the west, in the North Atlantic.) Symbols on the map show some of the major food products of each country. As the symbols indicate, Denmark and Sweden are larger agricultural producers than the other nations, although Finland also obtains rich harvests. Finland in addition takes a variety of fish from its numerous lakes. Norway is a great fishing nation; fleets from such ports as Ålesund and Stavanger bring in seafood for sale at home and around the world.

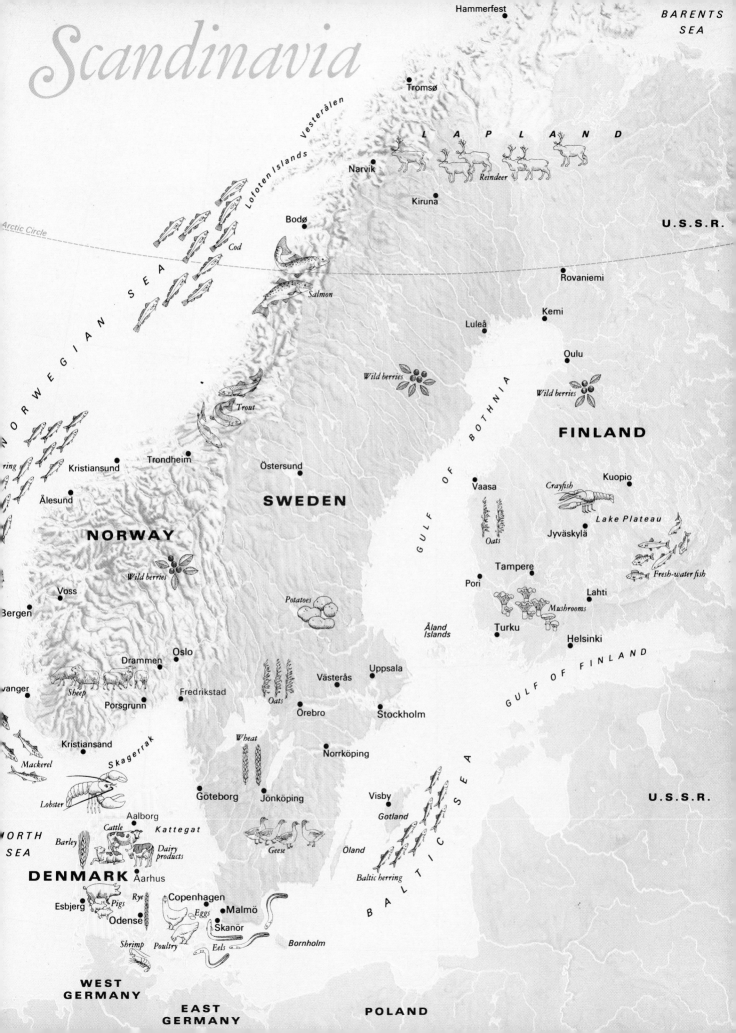

Scandinavia

BARENTS SEA

Hammerfest

Tromsø

LAPLAND

Reindeer

Narvik

Kiruna

U.S.S.R.

Bodø

Cod

Arctic Circle

Rovaniemi

Salmon

Kemi

Luleå

Oulu

Wild berries

Wild berries

FINLAND

Trout

NORWEGIAN SEA

Östersund

SWEDEN

Kuopio

Crayfish

Vaasa

Kristiansund

Trondheim

Lake Plateau

Jyväskylä

ring

Ålesund

Oats

Fresh-water fish

NORWAY

Wild berries

Tampere

Pori

Lahti

GULF OF BOTHNIA

Voss

Mushrooms

Bergen

Potatoes

Turku

Oslo

Åland Islands

Helsinki

Drammen

Sheep

Porsgrunn

Fredrikstad

Uppsala

GULF OF FINLAND

vanger

Oats

Västerås

Örebro

Stockholm

Kristiansand

Wheat

Norrköping

Mackerel

Skagerrak

Visby

Lobster

Göteborg

Jönköping

Gotland

Öland

BALTIC SEA

U.S.S.R.

Aalborg

Cattle

Kattegat

NORTH SEA

Barley

Dairy products

Geese

Baltic herring

DENMARK

Aarhus

Esbjerg

Pigs

Rye

Copenhagen

Eggs

Malmö

Odense

Skanör

Shrimp

Poultry

Eels

Bornholm

WEST GERMANY

EAST GERMANY

POLAND

ince of Dalarna, I watched an elderly man and three middle-aged women in aprons and bandannas make another food, simpler than black soup and no less venerable: flat bread, which by the time they were through was as thin as parchment and as big and round as a wagon wheel. They worked quickly and efficiently in a sun-filled, whitewashed room in an anachronistically modern farmhouse. Each had a task to perform. The man prepared the dough, following a casual recipe: a barrel of potatoes, boiled, peeled and mashed, a fistful of salt, some barley flour and enough water to allow the mixture to be squeezed through a ricer to produce a mass of what looked like congealed spaghetti.

Now it was the women's turn, and the flash of their hands soon told me that despite the apparent imprecision of the recipe, this would not be crude bread—and that it would be bread I had never before seen. One woman had already taken a lump of the yellowish dough and fashioned it into a broad-based cone on the floured surface of the table. She began flattening the cone with a narrow rolling pin, rolling it out into an ever-widening circle. When the dough reached from one side of the table to the other and was almost as thin as a linen sheet, she took a long wooden stick like a pointed sword, shoved it under the lip of the bread, flipped the dough around the blade and rolled it up. She then dashed with it to an old-fashioned wall oven, which glowed pink inside from the flames of a birch-log fire. Inserting the stick, she unfurled the dough on the floor of the oven and stood by, wiping the flour from her hands while it baked. Within a few minutes the bread was done, and she rushed it, a limp, warm hide dangling down over the stick, to another woman, who instantly grabbed it away, spread it flat and began briskly dusting it off with a whisk broom, raising a tiny cloud of ashes around it.

I watched this process repeated six or seven times, and each time it would culminate in the same neat way, with the bread being dusted off and then folded up like a tablecloth before being hung on a rack to cool and dry out. My fascination, in turn, was fascinating to the women, and one of them when it came time for a break jokingly asked if the gentleman from America would also like to see the way she made coffee.

To their way of thinking, they were doing nothing unusual. But to mine, they were performing a ritual centuries old—laying in a winter's supply of bread. I found this all the more amazing because there was really no need for them to do so. They were a rich family, as witness their new house, and they could have bought similar bread at the baker's. What drove them to make their own? Pride, possibly—theirs was after all the thinnest bread in the valley. Or perhaps it was their way of staying in touch with the past.

What was the bread like? A piece buttered and rolled up like a tortilla had about all the give of a well-starched napkin, and tasted sourish. But of course I was eating it fresh; I should have waited until it had become brittle and then, as is done in winter, broken off a flake at a time to chew.

In addition to the isolation of Scandinavia and the isolation of Scandinavians from each other, something much more elemental has been at work to determine the character of the food and cooking, and this is climate, especially winter. Even today winter continues to be the one inescapable fact of life in the North. The season comes early and lasts long, and, worst of all at least from a contemporary standpoint, it is dark—drearily so. For

Dragging their nets in one of Finland's more than 60,000 lakes, three fishermen create a scene (*opposite*) that is as characteristically Scandinavian as it is timeless. Out of this lake, called Kallavesi, comes the *muikku*, a tiny relative of the salmon, cherished by the Finns for its meat and its tiny beads of light pink roe.

15

centuries, the thinking of the people was shaped by it, and the greater part of their energy during the short, hectic growing season was devoted to making sure that they would live through the winter. If many of the foods of the area have a salty or smoky taste, or are pickled or dried, it is largely because of winter. The preservation of foods was the only kind of life insurance, all important to survival.

The Vikings very early learned to smoke, dry and salt their meats and fish. And in acquiring the means to tide themselves over the barren winter, they also found the wherewithal for their extensive journeys by sea. They took supplies of nonperishable foods with them, in particular dried cod, which was not only an excellent source of protein but could be traded abroad. On one of their boats, a funeral bark dug up virtually intact outside Oslo, Norway, cutting boards were found, scarred by the many whacks of a knife used to chop dried fish and meat into pot-sized chunks. How odd, in a way, to think that it was Scandinavian cooking that arrived on American shores first, via Leif Ericson and his followers (just as it is odd, perhaps, to realize that the Scandinavians introduced the cast-iron stove to the Colonies in the 18th Century and that from this "Norse stove" sprang the American cooking stove).

But knowing how to preserve food was no guarantee that there would be enough of it on hand when needed. During lean years, the Vikings had

to make do with lichens, bark and seaweed. In fact, it was the threat of hunger that drove them to undertake many of their perilous voyages. When suitable land was found, as in Iceland, they dared embark with horses, cows, sheep and chickens in boats that seemed barely big enough to accommodate men. How hard their existence must have been (and how limited their cooking) is suggested by their vision of heaven, a place where they would feast perpetually on boiled pork—supplied by the boar Saerimne, which could be consumed one day, only to reappear whole the next, as fat and meaty as ever.

The conditions of life in Scandinavia continued uncertain well into the 19th Century, one of the reasons that so many people emigrated to the United States. The great irony was that with the arrival of spring near-famine could almost overnight turn into a glut. Cows, so weak from their impoverished winter rations of shredded bark and straw that they often had to be carried out to pasture, would soon calve and their milk once again begin to flow. Salmon would rush upstream into nets and weirs, and lakes freed of their ice cover would vibrate with spawning fish.

During late summer, herring would surge down the coasts under lightning-scarred night skies in such numbers that it was said that the fish "suffocate one another and there is no fisherman's seine strong enough to lift this tumultuous burden." The Lofoten Islanders of northern Norway talked

17

of cod so plentiful that boats would be capsized by the weight of the filled nets. In autumn barley, oats and rye would glitter in granaries that had been empty all summer long; to this day a Finnish hostess can perform no more gracious act than to bake for her company black bread made from newly harvested rye. And with the first cold stab of winter, the rarest of foods—fresh meat—would suddenly lie raw and steaming on the butchering block. The little of it that could be spared would be made right away into soups and stews, while the rest would be smoked, salted and dried—with no part of the slaughtered animal wasted, neither the innards nor the blood.

Largely because they were available in such numbers and lent themselves so readily to preserving, cod and herring became two of Scandinavia's most important foods and biggest exports. The fact that dried and salted cod withstood heat and humidity without becoming moldy brought it popularity in countries of Southern Europe, and today it is still a staple in Italy, Spain and Portugal. Eventually cod won a reputation as the beefsteak of the sea, a standard victual on board every ship, and it had much to do with extending European influence into tropical latitudes and fostering Spain's presence in the New World.

Salt herring had as big a role as cod to play in Europe's destiny. By the 12th Century, it was a staple of the European diet, and it is easy to understand why. Two of these fatty fish furnish roughly 600 calories and two and

a half ounces of protein; this is just about all the protein a person needs in a day. Salt herring saved many an inhabitant of a beleaguered city from starvation, fed many an army on the march and in camp. Indirectly it helped start some of Europe's greatest navies. More than one sailor learned the rudiments of seamanship in a herring boat.

But even with this most plentiful of foods the Scandinavians had a somewhat fragile relationship. The herring, appearing offshore one year in shoals a half dozen miles long and wide, the next year could vanish almost completely. Explanations of the phenomenon varied as much as the runs. As early as the 10th Century a historian called Snorro attributed a magnificent herring run and a fine harvest to a beneficent reign. But when the herring stopped running, the blame was laid on "magic, bad men having sunk a copper horse in the sea." In 1549 the government of Denmark (which then ruled Norway) was sufficiently worried about the possibility of a decrease in the catch to issue an edict: "Since there is danger that God may withdraw his blessing on account of the great sins and vices of inhabitants of the coasts, our tax gatherers, each one in his own district, shall see to it that the people in the fishing stations lead good and Christian lives; that there is preaching every Sunday, and people exhorted to lead a Godly life, so that God may be moved by the prayers of good Christians to extend his blessing to us also in the future."

Racked row on row, cod dry slowly in the cold, pure air of a fishing village in Norway's rocky Lofoten Islands, north of the Arctic Circle. Known at this stage as *stokkfisk*, these cod may then be turned into *lutefisk*, a dish prepared by soaking the fish in a lye solution before cooking.

So venerated was the herring that it was looked upon as a bearer of divine messages. In 1587 anxiety spread through the realm when two herring fished from the North Sea off the coast of Norway flopped over to reveal Gothic letters on their sides. The Danish king interpreted the letters as foretelling his death, but three wise men intervened and read the message differently: "You will not fish for herring so well in the future as other nations." This turned out to be true, but since that interpretation was no less gloomy than the first, other learned men took up the task of trying to figure out the fish-borne prophecy. One scholar published a work that argued that the herring's message spelled the doom of Europe.

Even when the herring were abundant, there was always the hazard that there would not be enough salt available to preserve the catch. The Baltic's waters are too sweet to yield salt in any appreciable amount, and although the salinity of the North Sea is higher, a pale and unreliable sun prevented the Scandinavians from utilizing with much success the evaporation method employed by the French and the Spaniards. When dune grass was burned along Denmark's west coast to extract the salt from the grass, a method followed by the Dutch, the destruction of the plants enabled the sand to spread, overwhelming gardens and farms. The Scandinavians had no alternative but to import their salt, and in this the Germans saw an opportunity. The merchants of Lübeck began exchanging it for goods and wound up by moving en masse into Scandinavian ports, eventually taking over the lucrative herring trade. The imposing Gothic ruins of the Hanseatic League city of Visby on the island of Götland, Sweden, attest to the power and wealth the German Hansas thus obtained for themselves.

A taste for salt

Because of its rarity, salt was long an expensive commodity in Scandinavia, a commodity to the rich, but a source of envy to the poor. When the price of salt dropped, those who could suddenly afford the condiment scrambled to buy it and tended to use it with such zeal in preserving their foods that they gave themselves violent thirsts.

The specter of starvation that once drove fishermen and farmers to salt their fish and meats and hoard them against winter no longer motivates Scandinavian housewives, but the desire for salted food lingers and is expressed in multitudinous ways. In Finland, where body salts are likely to be sweated out in the heat of the sauna, there is actually a condition sometimes called "salt hunger." In Sweden the *smörgåsbord* would be a barren thing without its array of salty fish. And in both Sweden and Denmark, many a housewife will still buy meat or poultry with the intention of pickling it—not, as of old, to store, but to eat right off. Cooks in either country will submerge a goose or duck in brine. Sometimes a bit of saltpeter will be added as a preservative and coloring agent. The bird is then left to soak for a couple of days. This helps to break down the muscle tissue and gives the meat its most marked characteristic, a tender smoothness. A goose so treated is called "burst" by both the Danes and Swedes.

In Denmark the cook will boil a goose in clear, fresh water with a little thyme, and serve it in moist, thick slices with sharp mustard, dark sour rye bread and yellow pea soup containing leeks, carrots, parsnips, onions, celery root and potatoes—and it will be washed down with fiery gulps of ice-cold aquavit and foaming beer. In Sweden a "burst" goose will be boiled and served hot with a crisply frozen whipped-cream sauce, in which there is a sting of horse-radish.

The Danes often use duck as a less expensive substitute for goose. After pickling, it can also be cooked with celery root, carrots and the green blades of a leek. The duck is served cut into pieces, with separately boiled leeks and carrots, green peas, spinach, parsley potatoes, melted butter and—to spark and tie all these various flavors together—the frozen horse-radish whipped-cream sauce.

When salt was in short supply or too expensive to buy, people had to resort to other methods of preserving perishable food, some of them very odd indeed. Often they stored meat and butter in whey; the Vikings did this and the Icelanders still do when preparing one of their national dishes—singed sheep's head. On other occasions, in a primitive attempt at refrigeration, they buried fish in the ground or left it hidden in clefts in the rocks. Inevitably the fish would ferment and whole villages would stink of it—but the inhabitants came to consider such fermented fish a delicacy. One type survives in Sweden; it is *surströmming*, sour Baltic herring, surely one of the world's strangest dishes and a potent expression of the saying that one man's meat is another man's poison.

Caught in the months of May and June, the fish are immersed for a day in brine and then decapitated and cleaned. Next they are stacked in barrels, trundled out into the summer sun and left there for 24 hours to get the fermenting process started. An inch or two of space is left at the top of each barrel so that any gas formed during the fermentation can accumulate without causing an explosion.

Put into a cool storage room, the herring ferment at a slower rate. As they do, their aroma grows progressively stronger, and only the most acute nose can determine the precise point at which they are ready for canning. Among those who like *surströmming* best, and its fans are many, there is the belief that the contents of a can left for a year at a temperature of 68° F. actually improve; the can will have begun to swell, and at its puffiest must be opened gingerly, like a bottle of champagne.

Ripe *surströmming* is eaten with paper-thin hard bread and boiled potatoes, usually an almond-shaped variety that comes from the north. It has a sharp, cutting taste. Milk is sometimes drunk with it, but beer and aquavit more often accompany the dish. Some Swedes down it without a second thought to its smell; others, in order to partake of it at all, first have to rinse it in purifying soda water.

Sales of *surströmming* are on the increase in Sweden, but its future as an export item is, predictably, dim. Although 800 cans of it used to be exported annually to Hollywood when a Swedish movie colony could still be found there, U.S. customs officials have since come to view it with suspicion, despite its proven nontoxicity. Moreover, the product does not always travel well. Only recently a Swede found this out. Thinking to amaze an important New York client and the assembled board of directors with so bizarre a food, he produced the swollen can he had carried all the way from Sweden in his luggage and dramatically laid it on the table. At that moment, the can exploded.

If fermentation sounds like an exotic way to preserve food, bear in mind that the same process also yields wine, cheese, anchovies, olives, sour cream, yoghurt and buttermilk. Without the blessing of fermentation, the Scandinavians would never have been able to turn the greater part of their spring and summer milk supplies into storable dairy products. Nor would they have become the important cheese and butter makers they are today. Denmark has even managed in the past decade to present to the world a great new cheese— the rich, soft Crèma Dania.

Some milk had to be kept on hand to drink, and inevitably it soured. A virtue was made of this, and in Viking times, as later, it was considered fit food to offer company. One of the sagas tells of a man called Bard who served his guests bread and butter and "large bowls filled with curds." As they were very thirsty, they swallowed the curds in large draughts; "then Bard had buttermilk brought in, and they drank it."

What those curds may have been is not certain. Perhaps they were nothing more than *skyr*, or curdled milk, which used to be a common food of Scandinavia. Today *skyr* is found under that name only in Iceland, and there it is eaten fresh, as a kind of yoghurt. In the old days in Norway and Sweden, milk was kept for months on end to make another product called *syr*. *Syr* was sampled by a man at the end of the last century who described it as resembling milk "freshly drawn from the cow," but tasting like "vinegar mixed with something bitterer than aloes." And indeed it did serve on occasion as a substitute for vinegar.

In Norway, farm wives used to make a drink known as *tette* milk, so-named because the *tette*, a meadow plant with a blue flower, was basic to its preparation. A few of the leaves would be put at the bottom of a bowl and boiled milk poured over them. Allowed to sit in a warm place, the milk would thicken; then the leaves would be removed and some of the milk would be spooned as a culture into fresh supplies kept in casks and barrels. Such apparently was the power of *tette* leaves as a preservative that spring milk so treated could still be drunk in winter. By then it would have changed considerably in character and taste, and great care had to be taken not to stir it, as the whey would separate. A little would be dipped carefully out of the barrel and poured into bowls, to which sour cream might be added, probably to make it more palatable.

In the kind of storage economy that dominated Scandinavian households until this century, nothing edible could be wasted. And thus even the whey resulting from the manufacture of cheese and butter was boiled down, a process that took hours to complete, since whey is little more than water. The brown paste so obtained was then put in molds, allowed to set, and eaten as a kind of cheese. The famous goat cheese of Norway is made in this manner. Occasionally leftover whey was drunk, and according to old Norwegian farmers who used to quaff it in the fields, no more thirst-quenching drink could be found in summertime.

The taste for tart dairy products remains strong among the Scandinavians. In any of the countries it is not unusual to see a bowl of milk sitting on a window ledge or at the back of a cupboard, like an offering to the household gods. When it has become good and thick, sugar is sprinkled on top (in Denmark, crumbs of sour rye are added), and the whole is spooned up greedily. Although the Danes display this predilection for sour or thick milk

—*tykmaelk* as they call it—they had to wait for the United States Army in Germany to introduce them to sour cream. Having started out by manufacturing it exclusively for GI consumption, they soon woke up to its multiple possibilities in cooking, and are now busily promoting it at home—thus finally catching up with the Norwegians, Swedes and Finns, who for centuries have known what a good thing it is.

So far I have been speaking about Scandinavian food in general terms. Now is the time to say that there is no such thing as "Scandinavian food"—no such thing, that is, if Denmark, Norway, Sweden, Finland and Iceland are all thought of as sharing one big cauldron from which all dishes come out tasting pretty much the same. Just as there are noticeable differences in temperament between Dane and Swede, near neighbors across a narrow sound, so there are differences in their approaches to eating. And even when the ingredients are the same, the results are not.

Cuisines that vary with the terrain

Much of this has to do with the countries themselves, the kinds of places they are. Denmark is a green and rolling land; its foods are those of field and pasture, rich and fat. Norway is all mountains; in such a perpendicular landscape, farming is difficult and people learned long ago to supplement their meager diet with fish from the sea. Finland, squeezed between the Soviet Union and Sweden, stretches northward, a phalanx of forest, and its foods are those that grow in humus, in shadowed nooks, in beds of moss, or that swim in any of the innumerable clear lakes. Sweden exhibits features of the other Scandinavian countries, and its cooking is accordingly varied. And Iceland, a treeless, lava-scored island, has a national cuisine as spare as its landscape—strong, but almost untranslatable into foreign terms.

Much of the best cooking of the Northern countries—Denmark, Norway, Sweden and Finland—recommends itself to the American kitchen; almost all of it can be duplicated with American products, or for that matter, with Scandinavian products, now abundantly available in specialty shops in cities throughout the country. Not having grown up with such cooking, non-Scandinavians are actually at something of an advantage: they can pick and choose among the recipes, without worrying about rigid rules that say such and such goes with such and such and nothing else. The *smörgåsbord* alone —ceremoniously staged in Sweden in four acts on a table large enough to float the feast across the Atlantic—could yield, in any of its parts, dozens of dishes for different kinds of dining, from backyard picnicking on a hot summer's evening to a buffet supper, warm or cold.

But something else recommends the cooking of these countries: its ingenuousness. In our own family's zeal to amaze our friends with the brilliance of our performance in the kitchen, I know that there have been times when we overreached ourselves and found ourselves too bone-weary at table to enjoy our own cooking. While Danish roast loin of pork stuffed with apples and prunes and served with red cabbage, sugar-browned potatoes *(pages 51, 190, 191)* and a big glass of beer on a snowy evening may not sound as elegant as *pigeon à la maître Jacques*, it is far easier to prepare and its sustenance is of a sort to make guests smile, bringing awareness of the weather outside, the warmth inside—and within.

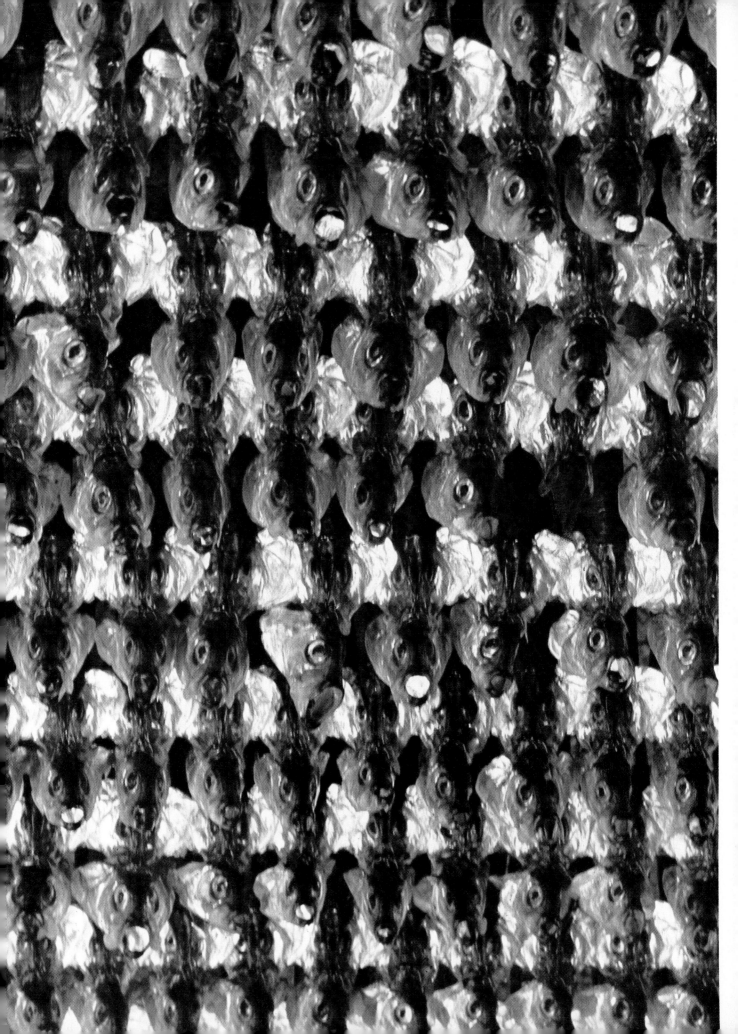

A Baltic Alchemy: Changing Silver into Gold

One of the finest seafood treats of Scandinavia is smoked Baltic herring, and nowhere is it quite so delicious as on the Danish island of Bornholm. Here the herring are caught, cleaned and smoked on the same day, and then shipped by fast boat to Copenhagen, often arriving still warm, with juices and flavor intact. It is their tender fragility, however, that is the "Bornholmers'" greatest drawback, for they do not travel well and must be sampled in Denmark or not at all.

In the photograph on the opposite page, they are shown cleaned and racked, ready for the smokehouse. At left, they have emerged from a haze of alder smoke, transformed from silver into gold. And above, filleted, they rest on a slice of buttered Danish rye, garnished with radishes, snipped chives and a raw egg yolk.

To serve 8 to 10

1 cup finely chopped herring (salt,
  matjes, pickled, Bismarck)
½ pound finely chopped cooked
  tongue or veal (optional)
½ cup diced cold boiled
  potatoes
3 cups finely chopped cold beets,
  freshly cooked or canned
½ cup finely chopped apple, cored
  and peeled
⅓ cup finely chopped onion
½ cup finely chopped dill pickle
4 tablespoons finely chopped fresh
  dill
2 tablespoons white wine vinegar
Salt
Freshly ground black pepper

DRESSING

3 chilled hard-cooked eggs
1 tablespoon prepared mustard
2 tablespoons white wine vinegar
¼ cup vegetable oil
2 to 4 tablespoons heavy cream

SAUCE

3 tablespoons beet juice
½ teaspoon lemon juice
1 cup sour cream

Sillsallad
HERRING SALAD WITH SOUR - CREAM SAUCE

In a large mixing bowl, combine the finely chopped herring, optional meat, potatoes, beets, apple, onion and pickle. Mix three tablespoons of the dill with the vinegar, and add salt and pepper to taste. Pour over the salad ingredients and toss gently with a wooden spoon.

DRESSING: Remove the yolks from the hard-cooked eggs. Mince the whites and set them aside. Force the yolks through a sieve into a small bowl with the back of a large spoon, then mash them to a paste with the tablespoon of prepared mustard. Gradually beat in the vinegar and oil, then the cream, a tablespoon at a time, until the sauce has the consistency of heavy cream. Pour over the salad, mix lightly but thoroughly, cover, and chill for at least 2 hours.

Just before serving, transfer the salad to a large serving bowl or platter and sprinkle it with the minced egg whites and the remaining chopped dill.

SAUCE: Stir the beet and lemon juice into the sour cream until it is smooth and well blended. Pass this sauce separately.

To prepare *gravlax* in the Swedish manner, place dill
sprigs and a mixture of salt, sugar and white
peppercorns on the lower half of a section of boned
salmon *(below)*. Replace the top half *(opposite)* before marinating.

Gravlax
SALMON MARINATED IN DILL

To serve 8 to 10

Ask the fish dealer to cut the salmon in half lengthwise and to remove the backbone and the small bones as well.

Place half of the fish, skin side down, in a deep glass, enamel or stainless-steel baking dish or casserole. Wash and then shake dry the bunch of dill, and place it on the fish. (If the dill is of the hothouse variety and not very pungent, chop the herb coarsely to release its flavor and sprinkle it over the fish instead.) In a separate bowl, combine the salt, sugar and crushed peppercorns. Sprinkle this mixture evenly over the dill. Top with the other half of the fish, skin side up. Cover the fish with aluminum foil and on it set a heavy platter slightly larger than the salmon. Pile the platter with 3 or 4 cans of food; these make convenient weights that are easy to distribute evenly. Refrigerate for 48 hours (or up to 3 days). Turn the fish over every 12 hours, basting it with the liquid marinade that accumulates, and separating the halves a little to baste the salmon inside. Replace the platter and weights each time.

When the *gravlax* is finished, remove the fish from its marinade, scrape away the dill and seasonings, and pat it dry with paper towels. Place the separated halves skin side down on a carving board and slice the salmon halves thinly on the diagonal, detaching each slice from the skin.

Gravlax is served as part of a *smörgåsbord* or as an appetizer, and is accompanied by mustard sauce *(Recipe Booklet)*. When *gravlax* is presented as a main course, it is garnished with lemon wedges as well as the mustard sauce and served with toast and perhaps a cucumber salad *(page 48)*.

Ingredients

- 3 to 3½ pounds fresh salmon, center cut, cleaned and scaled
- 1 large bunch dill
- ¼ cup coarse (kosher) salt, or if unavailable, substitute regular salt
- ¼ cup sugar
- 2 tablespoons white peppercorns (or substitute black), crushed

II

The Danes' National Pastime

There is a saying so often repeated in Scandinavia that it must be true—or true at least in part. It runs like this: the Danes live to eat, the Norwegians eat to live, and the Swedes eat to drink. Whatever the truth of the rest of the aphorism, one part is indisputable: the Danes *do* like to eat. The one and only time I ever saw their King he had been eating. It was his birthday. A throng of parents and children had gathered in the courtyard of his palace and were cheering him out onto his balcony. He eventually emerged through its French doors, a tall man with big ears and a big smile, and he was carrying something—a white table napkin. He proceeded to wave it in mock surrender, to the delight of all the people below. But when the high-pitched cheering began to die down, the King saw his opportunity: he went quickly back inside to resume his dining, and his subjects scattered, presumably to begin theirs.

It is easy to form the impression that the Danes like to eat. Not that they are all fat. But a short walk through their capital, Copenhagen, will reveal on every side such tempting displays of food that to the hungry eye the baroque belfries and steeples of the city will begin to look like giant dinner bells—and the ringing of their chimes will begin to sound like a call to table, which of course it often is to the Danes.

Practically every block in the heart of town shelters a restaurant, a sandwich shop, a café or a bakery. Behind the plate-glass windows, Danish pastries rise in tiers to counter level—flaky buttery twirls, crescents, envelopes, trickled with melted sugar, dabbed with custard or jam and sprinkled with slivered almonds. I defy the iron-willed to pause for more than a minute in front of such an array of calories and not obey the compulsion to go inside and have just one small piece with a rectifying cup of coffee. Close by in the sandwich shops, *smørrebrød* (literally, buttered bread) artfully constructed from slices and tidbits of colorful and tasty food, crowd teak trays, and in their lettuce-leaf frills and cress garnishes resemble nothing so much as corsages. And outdoors, all the way from the town hall square to the Kings New Square and beyond, there are fruit stands and sausage wagons, strategically placed, like relief stations in a war zone, dispensing curbside nourishment to the famished in a hurry.

A small, hospitable nation

Why do the Danes live to eat? What motivates some of them to pause as often as five or six times a day for food? What makes a remark like this one—"It was a good funeral, but there were no red beets to go with the roast"—seem so funny to us and so much a reflection of Danish life? Why are life's landmarks—christenings, first communions, engagements, weddings—ticked off in festive meals, and why, 30 years afterward, are the guests likely to remember what the dessert was? I think it all has to do with Denmark's being a small country. Lacking the wild natural surroundings of their northern neighbors in which to climb and hike, the Danes have made eating their national pastime, both their sport and their recreation. I think eating is also for them a way of forgetting, of smoothing down the rough edges of reality—and even of loving and being loved. A jesting Dane has said that half the population wants to be taken care of and the other half wants someone to take care of. What better place for the mutually needy to meet than at table? It is probably not for nothing that the Danes hold the reputation of being the friendliest and most generous of the five peoples of the North, always prepared to extend an invitation to dinner or accept one.

On our first day in Copenhagen, my wife, Liet, and I found ourselves dining in the house of complete strangers, seated with them at table, delicious food in front of us, and beer and aquavit and kindness flowing all around us. It had happened unexpectedly, and in New York, from where we had just come, the event would have seemed a miracle, but it was not out of character in Denmark.

A man I had gone to see at the foreign ministry—whose first official act on my behalf was to invite me to share his lunch of open-face sandwiches at his desk—insisted that Liet and I come that very evening to his place for a Danish meal. He telephoned his wife, and then he looked at me sadly; she was running for Parliament, you see, and she had a meeting that night and would be flying off to Jutland day after next, but could we come on Sunday?

Before I had a chance to convince this kind Dane that we did not want to impose upon him and his family, he had called up his mother. Could we go to dinner there tonight instead? If we arrived a little late, say, at seven o'clock, that would give our hostess enough time to make her preparations for dinner, and of course she and her husband would be delighted to have us as their guests.

How was the mother ever going to meet the challenge of unexpected company? We pondered this as our new friend from the foreign ministry drove us toward his parents' home on the outskirts of town. The answer: nobly. Her table glittered with silver and candlelight. Fresh flowers stood in the shadows. Our hostess was a beautiful and charming woman, amazingly relaxed but nevertheless obviously eager to have us enjoy ourselves as much as she seemed to be enjoying herself, the mark of a true Danish hostess. Her husband, a merry man who looked like Santa Claus without a beard, began the toasting. If Liet and I had felt any anxiety about coming, it now dissolved, and soon we mellowed into the mood of the evening, ready to go on knowing these pleasant people forever because, it seemed, we had always known them.

Considering the haste with which the meal had been put together, the second course, like the first—steaming bowls of oxtail soup—was very good indeed. It consisted of tender pork in a rich sauce, buttered potatoes and mountains of the savory mushrooms in which Denmark abounds. Then we had not one but two desserts: a fresh fruit salad—into which had gone the last of the blackberries from the garden, cold and plump from the slow nurturing of the dwindling days—and the son's favorite cake, granted a day old, but only the better for it in Danish eyes because the whipped cream that cushioned its yellow layers had had a chance to seep into them.

The dinner was a triumph of what the Danes call *hygge,* a word that connotes a sense of well-being, of visceral and mental comfort when the world has somehow been reduced to dining-room size and the curtains have been drawn against the night. It is an atmosphere that all Danish hostesses try to create for their guests, an extra something to go with the food and to which food itself contributes. More candles must be burned per capita, more flowers bought in the pursuit of this hospitable aura in Denmark than in any other country in the world. Perhaps a truer picture would be given of the Danes if it were said of them that they like less to eat than to dine. One of their sayings puts the matter this way: "First flowers on the table; then food."

A miracle of agricultural planning

The Danes are the happy beneficiaries of a man-made agricultural miracle. Without the Norwegians' mountains to assault, the Finns' forests to fell or the Swedes' underground resources, they turned a century ago to the challenge inherent in their land. The soil was embarrassingly poor for a country with agricultural pretensions—thin and sandy in most places, boggy or overgrown with heath. But by using imagination, they turned a handicap into an asset. While other countries of Europe were clamping down tariffs on imports of cheap American grain, the Danes let it flood in. Their idea was to feed it to livestock and then export meat, poultry and dairy products to Great Britain and other nearby markets. This helped free them of the burden of growing grain themselves, and they devoted the land they otherwise would have needed for grain to raising high-output crops. As their agricultural productivity soared and the numbers of their animals increased, they found in stable manure an unexpected bonus—the means by which to increase the fertility of their soil.

Continued on page 34

Two Copenhagen matrons peering through a coffee-shop window contemplate a decision dear to their hearts—what kind of cake they should buy for their midmorning coffeebreak. The display—ordinary by Danish standards and therefore suggestive of Denmark's bounty—includes at least 20 different kinds of buttery baked delicacies, from creamcakes and tarts to flaky Danish pastries, seen enthroned on the highest trays. During an average day this shop, which stands not far from Copenhagen's Raadhuspladsen, or Town Hall Square, sells 600 pieces of Danish pastry alone to its sweet-toothed customers.

33

Denmark's green and tended land today yields a bounty that the countries farther to the north might well envy, and probably do. The Danish diet is the richest in Scandinavia. Few, for example, are the fancy dishes that the Danes do not in some way pamper with the butter and cream endlessly supplied by their shiny black-and-white and red cows. They put cream into soups, salads, sauces and desserts. They leave it out of their coffee, for fear of growing fat. I once ate pigeons cloaked in a silky cream sauce into which a tablespoon of currant jelly had been stirred for good measure. And, as if that were not enough, the accompanying salad consisted of tart shreds of apple folded into unsweetened whipped cream—a substitute for mayonnaise and, considering its fluffy lightness, not a bad one. The dessert was *romfromage,* a cloud of whipped cream, frothed egg and sugar, brought down to earth with a saturation of dark rum and an overlay of liquored cherries.

With food a big business in Denmark, the government could be expected to keep an eye on quality, and this it does zealously. Eggs are stamped with individual numbers that enable dealers to see for themselves that they have received an absolutely fresh consignment from the packer. Cheese is cultured from tested milk and cream under close supervision in dairies so glistening white that on a sunny day sunglasses seem in order. Ice cream from the same source is what ice cream should be—frozen cream. And pork comes from pink pigs that spend all of their short, happy lives lolling around in heated, well-lighted barns, with the best of everything on hand, including their mamas, the prolific sows that grow as large as couches.

The pleasant duty of eating

So well does the Danish government do its job of maintaining high standards of quality that it might even be accused of putting temptation in the way of the people: it is everyone's patriotic duty to eat—and to eat Danish. The Ministry of Agriculture has gone so far as to set up an organization called Ekkodanmark, housing it in a modern, sharp-edged building in Copenhagen. Ekkodanmark's sole duty is to promote Danish food. To its headquarters Danish housewives (and interested tourists) can come to watch cooking demonstrations (given twice an hour) and they can take away with them recipes prepared under the watchful eyes of two of Denmark's most charming and most talented women, Mrs. Gudrun Winkel and Mrs. Gerda Andersen, who are firmly convinced that preparing dishes with love is as essential to flavor as any of the ingredients.

All this makes for good eating and good cooking, but it does not mean that Denmark is a cook's utopia. As in other countries of the North, climate has imposed its restrictions, and even in this day of frozen foods and mass markets the taste for green vegetables and leafy salads remains undeveloped. At the same time, the climate has provided a kind of poetry. Each spring everyone looks forward to the first strawberries, the first new potatoes, the tiny shrimp no bigger than a fingernail. These are greeted as eagerly and as wonderingly as the unfolding buds of beech trees in earliest spring, when people leave the cozy seclusion of their homes to go out in crowds and admire the faint green leaves emerging to veil the silver-gray branches—and to do one of the things that they like best, which is to visit a favorite inn

Small, snug Lykkegaard (Happy Farm) is a prolific producer of a variety of crops as well as milk and beef cattle.

for lunch and sit down outdoors to a sun-dappled meal of the open-face sandwiches that Danes call *smørrebrød*.

At its most basic, Danish food is hearty fare, served in quantity, often temptingly arranged with an eye to color on platters from which everyone helps himself. It is not spicy food, except where foreign influences have come to prevail. In dishes requiring an assertive note, some onion will do the trick, or chopped parsley or scissored chives. And if a contrast seems in order, horse-radish, mustard, pickled beets or cucumbers, or a sweet-sour cucumber garnish called *asier* can be counted on.

Making much out of little

Meat and potatoes are the staple of the Danish diet—excluding *smørre-brød*, which is eaten for lunch by everybody from nine months to 90 years and which can range from plain to elaborate in construction and in taste, and can consist, as has been said, of everything between heaven and earth. Fish, though always available and always first-rate, is not nearly as popular in this seagirt kingdom as might be supposed. It is generally served only once a week as an entrée. But Danes do not overlook their plaice, a relative of the flounder (fried gently in butter so that only the outside becomes crisp while the inside remains moist and sweet, *page 53*), or their oysters, delicately pure in flavor and carrying about them a slap of the nearby sea.

Denmark's favorite meat is pork. It might even be contended that the country's national beast is the pig, svelte from years of controlled breeding and solid all the way through. But the Danes still go on tinkering with it. Already they have managed to reduce the weight of the pig's head by a couple of pounds, to flatten out its arched back, and to shift its center of gravity from the front to the rear. The 11.5 million pigs annually produced in Denmark outnumber the 4.8 million Danes, and pork in the form of hams, loins, slabs of bacon and other pink cuts continues to be one of the country's key export items. What can't be sold abroad the Danes are perfectly willing to eat themselves. They have numerous ways of preparing pork, all of them good. But it would be hard to find more delicious versions, I think, than the dish they roast with the scored rind left on so that a golden crackling forms that locks in the juices, or the one they stuff with a combination of tart apples and prunes *(page 51)*.

Despite the abundance of pigs and cows, meat continues to be an expensive item in most Danish household budgets because so much is exported. In Denmark, as throughout Scandinavia, meat is bought in relatively small quantities and eked out in various ways. Stews and pan dishes are popular, but everyone's favorite meat-stretcher is *frikadeller (page 52)*. It can be made according to several recipes, with various kinds of meat, but I like it best when both pork and veal are used. Ground and then reground, the meat is mixed with chopped onions, flour or bread crumbs, eggs, and milk or (preferably) soda water for a lightening effect. It is then shaped into cakes and fried in butter and oil until almost crusty on both sides. The relatively mild taste of *frikadeller* requires that something fairly sharp be eaten with it, like pickled beets *(page 48)* or *asier*. Yet, for all its simplicity *frikadeller* is a dish that provokes strong reactions among its many partisans, one housekeeper believing that only she guards the secret for making it the

To preserve a tie to the land they love so deeply, many city-dwelling Danes rent garden plots and huts from municipal governments. Kristen Olsen, a retired roof thatcher, pays $40 a year for the right to raise potatoes, carrots, lettuce and strawberries on this little patch in the outskirts of Roskilde. He is shown serving coffee to his neighbors, the Harald Jensens.

right way, while another will look down her nose at *frikadeller* made *that* way.

Minced pork and veal find other uses. A lid will be cut off a fat cabbage, the head hollowed out and the meat stuffed down inside the vegetable. Reassembled, the cabbage will be tied up in cheesecloth and then simmered slowly, finally to be served well cooked with melted butter. Or the *frikadeller* mixture—forcemeat, as it is sometimes called—will be molded around a cauliflower, the whole wrapped up in cheesecloth and simmered. Or again, forcemeat may be molded into teaspoon-sized dumplings and dropped into bubbling broth.

Both beef and veal can be good in Denmark, but because the farmer used to wait until the cow had grown old and gone dry before slaughtering it, the memory of toughness lingers—which is perhaps why *hakkebøf* continues to enjoy high esteem. *Hakkebøf* translates as hacked beef, though it might better be called chopped meat—or perhaps even hamburger. Made into patties and sautéed, it is served with thick brown sauce and golden onions.

Danish poultry is also of a high order. But, like the cow, until quite recently the chicken was valued more as a producer than as a one-shot candidate for the roasting pan, no matter how highly regarded its meat may have been. This notion has been discarded, and mass breeding of plump-breasted hens has turned what was once one of the most expensive birds a Dane could buy into the cheapest. Fortunately, the old reverence that enshrined the chicken on the Sunday dinner table persists, and many a Dane can think of no finer way to cook chicken than to stuff it with parsley and a big lump of butter, and then stew it in an iron casserole *(Recipe Booklet)*. Just before serving, heavy cream is swirled into the parsley-spiced drippings and this flavorsome golden sauce is then poured over the chicken.

What vegetables, besides potatoes, do Danes eat with all this meat? Leeks, kale, carrots, beets, celery root and cabbage have all along had an outsized importance in Danish cooking because they keep through the winter and are consequently available year round. In the hands of a Danish housewife, kale is reduced from crinkly toughness to appetizing tenderness by being first boiled, then chopped fine and served with a cream sauce *(Recipe Booklet)*. Kale prepared this way makes an excellent accompaniment to an old Danish favorite, cured loin of pork (which is now exported from Denmark), and it goes equally well with ham. The same cook will take cabbage and serve it braised, pickled, or flavored with caraway seeds. And she will

Twelve famous Danish cheeses are pictured here. From left to right in the top row: Tybo, a northwest Jutland cheese, with caraway seeds imbedded in it, mellow and nutty tasting; Danbo, firm and bland; Danish Brie. Second row: Havarti, semifirm and slightly acid; Danish Camembert; Christian IX, a salute to a turn-of-the-century king, refreshing and slightly acid. Third row: Danish St. Paulin; Crèma Dania, a major addition to the world's best cheeses; Danish Blue; and Danish Port-Salut. Bottom row: Danish Swiss, smooth and nutty; and Tybo again, this time without caraway seeds.

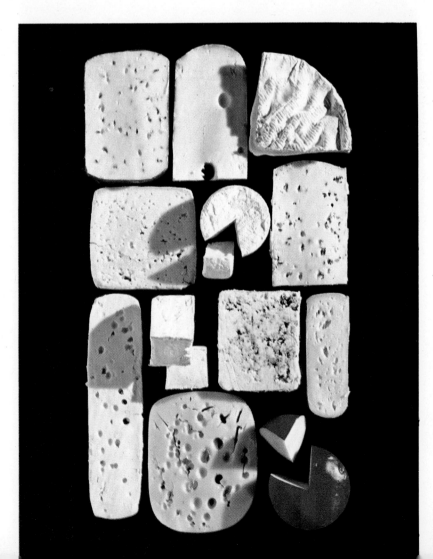

know just what to do to turn the red variety of the vegetable into a festive dish—by adding a sliced sour apple and a little currant juice. Together, they contribute a piquancy far more subtle than could vinegar alone—the traditional seasoning for the vegetable. Red cabbage thus prepared is served with roast pork, goose or duck *(page 190)*.

Economy in years past prompted the Danish housewife to make use of animal parts that might have gone politely ignored elsewhere, and dishes made with them persevere, including *blodbudding*—blood pudding. Giblet ragoût and giblet soup are old standbys. Beef heart, stuffed with parsley and butter, simmered in bouillon and served in cream-thickened sauce with currant jelly is another, and it can be a good dish, slightly rusty in flavor. Mock turtle—a euphemism for calf's head—is still another and is one of the most elaborate dishes in the Danish cuisine. It requires hours of work, but by the time the cut-up meat and tongue are added to a Madeira-flavored, mahogany-colored stock, the effort begins to seem worthwhile. When tiny dumplings and white and yellow wedges of hard-cooked eggs are set to floating on top, it pays off. *Forloren skildpadde*—as mock turtle is called—is served in soup plates, and Danes love it.

While many other people might not care for mock turtle, few could resist Danish liver paste *(page 53)*. Made of pork or calf's liver, to which some anchovy is added, this famous Danish *postej* is firmer than a French pâté and perhaps less refined, but it is excellent when mounded up on a

In Assens, Denmark, the milkman still makes his rounds with a horse-drawn cart, announcing his approach with a tinkling bell. Despite scenes as charmingly old-fashioned as this, the Danish dairy industry is one of the world's most modern, and the country's 1.4 million hard-working cows produce more than one billion gallons of milk a year.

slice of dark Danish rye and garnished with strips of sweet-sour cucumber and little cubes of topaz-colored meat jelly.

Liver paste is an essential part of a Danish institution, the *kolde bord*— the cold table. The *kolde bord* has a great deal in common with the Swedish *smörgåsbord* but gives its national character away in its salads and in specialties such as *rullepølse*, a spiced and larded meat roll made of veal, beef or lamb. At the cold table will be found everything needed for making do-it-yourself *smørrebrød*, including herring and Danish cheese, which is another whole story in itself.

A modified cold table used to be the regular Sunday brunch of the Danish family I lived with as a student in Copenhagen, and recalling its bounty to this day sets my mouth to watering. The same people who during the week thought nothing at breakfast of downing uncooked, dusty oatmeal, splashed lightly with thin milk and sugar, would suddenly become gourmets, needling their tongues with tiny radishes, searching among the assembled plates for just the right piece of smoked eel or a little curl of smoked salmon to put on their buttered bread. And many an explosive sigh would follow on each new thing tasted, and bellies would be rubbed and patted all around until the table had been swept clean and the time had come for a digestive nap.

A dessert could hardly have been expected to follow the cold table. But desserts do rank high in Danish esteem. Pancakes wrapped around

From tiny Denmark's cornucopia of agricultural plenty pours a staggering and almost miraculous amount of food each year: 11.5 million pigs, 176,000 tons of creamy butter, 52 million chickens, 1.5 billion eggs. This mass production has not gotten in the way of high quality. The jaunty egg standing on end in the foreground of the picture at the far right bears a coded number, indicating that it was delivered to the plant by the farmer no more than 48 hours before being packed for market.

vanilla ice cream, lemon mousse and cream rings filled with diced pine-apple or peaches are all favorites. There are marvelous fruit puddings, and the best of these is *rødgrød med fløde,* an impossible combination of words that only Danes can pronounce, letting it slide from their lips as smoothly as cream from a spoon. The phrase means red gruel with cream, but it is actually a pudding, a mellifluous blend of thickened raspberry and currant juices, into which large puddles of sweet cream are poured (a Danish variation, using berries easily available in America, is on page 55).

The Danish apple cake is not a cake at all, but layers of applesauce and sugared and buttered bread crumbs, often topped—as might be expect-ed—with an ocean of whipped cream on which tablespoons of raspberry jam may float. Sometimes crushed macaroons are added. One variation on the apple cake has the prettiest name of all the Danish desserts: veiled country lass. It is made with rye bread crumbs, applesauce and grated chocolate, and covered with a veil of whipped cream *(Recipe Booklet).*

Although a fruit dessert—or just plain fruit with cheese—is often the cul-mination of a Danish evening meal, serving it is not necessarily an indica-tion that the eating is over. After a few hours have gone by, giving every-one a chance to find a little room in his stomach, cakes, pastries and cookies invariably make their appearance with coffee—and these are so good and so varied that they deserve a chapter to themselves, which they receive later on in this book. Is there any wonder that in Denmark

people who have been out to dinner are almost always asked afterward by their friends not whether they had a good time or heard interesting talk, but what it was they had to eat?

If the typical Danish housewife is a good cook (and she is), it is probably because her mother before her was a good cook, which means, of course, that her mother's recipe file will be in her head. And this will often make her stubbornly traditional in outlook, to the annoyance of those who would like to introduce new foods and even new ways. I recall a farm wife's romance with a coal stove. Although she had fixed up her kitchen with all the modern appliances she possibly could have needed, including a washing machine and an electric mangle, she refused to cook on gas. Having learned from her mother to cook food on a coal stove, she was not going to abandon the iron monster that stood foursquare and ugly in front of her, using a great deal of her working area. She knew its temperament as well as she knew her husband's, and she pointed to the places where dishes could be kept warm for the children coming in from the fields, or where a soup could be left so that it would not boil over.

In this day of culinary change and the rapid development of a supermarket culture, perhaps such stubbornness is to be admired. At least it guarantees that many of the best old dishes will survive another generation or two. But the Danish cook has a basis for her pride: not only is her cooking good, but behind her there stands a long history of good eating, of taking care with food.

Actually the Danish cuisine is a blend of two traditions—the courtly and the rustic. The first lends color to dining, the second assures that nonsense will not dominate the table. The courtly tradition can be traced back through the few cookbooks that were published for the benefit of the aristocrats, patricians and, eventually, the middle class in past centuries. The first of these in Danish came out in 1616, and surprisingly it seems to have been a rather dour volume, considering its sparkling audience. The author—who some Danes would like to think was a German—lamented man's fall from grace and looked upon cooking as a punishment for sin. According to him, the great flood had washed perfect flavor from food, and man thereafter was forced to toil to replace it. Even so, cooking in Denmark seemed already to have taken some extravagant and inconsequential turns—with meat pies, for example, that contained live birds and baby hares slipped in under the crust, presumably at the last minute, to scamper forth at serving time and amuse the astonished guests with their antics among the dinner plates.

Loans from the French

But all this soon changed, to the lasting benefit of the Danes. Chefs came from France to demonstrate that man could be restored to a state of grace through the balm of French cooking. Like missionaries, they proselytized in palace and manor-house kitchens, and soon their recipes and techniques began to find their way into humbler homes. Denmark owes a much greater debt to France than it may realize.

In the late 18th Century a cook in a castle on the island of Fyn took it upon himself to spread the light still further by publishing a cookbook "for the honest housewife." Although the recipes were the most heavily French-influenced of any to that time, some took odd turns. But then those were strange days and ways. That new American delicacy, the potato, had not yet done heavy duty as a staple and was being served as a dessert, hot and salted, in a napkin.

During the 19th Century a Madame Mangor appeared on the scene. Although she was a Dane, she gave away her cooking prejudice by choosing to call herself Madame rather than Fru, Danish for "Mrs." A woman of refinement, she would urge her readers to take a silver dish and go down into the cellar and get some apples to put in it; but she had her hardheaded side as well, and her recipes, despite their occasional extravagances, helped set a standard for Danish cooking and hospitality that continues to be met today. Her book must have been a good one: it went through some 40 editions.

Madame Mangor advised her readers to use three "home-grown spices" in the preparation of food. The first was punctuality—"having definite and firmly adhered-to mealtimes." The second: "a snow-white cloth and a well-laid table." And the third requisite was the most important of all: "the housewife's gentle, friendly face, which like the sun radiates over everything and chases away the small clouds of dissatisfaction or displeasure concerning one thing or another which may be floating in the household sky and occasionally gather into a rainstorm." All three spices continue to be used by Danish housewifes.

Nostalgia from memories of common foods

The other tradition in Danish cooking, the rustic, derives from the time not so long ago when the greater part of the population lived in rural districts. For the Danes, the land did not then provide nearly the number of rich pleasures it does now, and the food of the common man, by all standards, was homely to a fault. Some of the basic dishes live on to this day, little changed, and they can send Danes into fits of nostalgia. Among them are rice porridge with a butter hole in it, salt-pork gravy with boiled potatoes (a favorite of the late King Christian X) and øllebrød, a thick brown soup made of sweet beer and stale rye crusts.

Perhaps in the rural Denmark of old there lies yet another clue to why Danes revere food as much as they do. Life on the farms was a round of hardships in a flat, windy countryside, where rain and winter were twin glooms. Mealtimes came to provide the only relief in what would otherwise have been a dull day.

Breakfast almost invariably included herring in one form or another, the salty variety being put to soak the night before to assure that it would not be "soaked in beer afterwards"—an allusion to the thirst it could create. With the herring, sour milk and bread were eaten. Next came øllebrød, the beer-bread soup, into which milk was often poured to produce lumpy curds. Thus sufficiently fortified, everyone went about the chores until the time came, halfway through the morning, to halt work for a tidbid—some cheese or meat on bread, a beer and perhaps even a snaps —a shot of aquavit.

At noon the third meal of the day was put on the table. Although porridge of some kind usually dominated it, there could also be cabbage or buttermilk soup *(page 55),* yellow peas, potatoes, gravy, boiled dried cod. Pancakes might constitute a special treat, or the little doughnut puffs called *aebleskiver,* made in the dimples of a round copper pan and turned with a knitting needle. But no matter how heavy this meal may have been, nobody could be expected to get through the afternoon's labor without a coffee break and a little snack to tide him over until the evening meal. Supper was usually porridge—perhaps barley boiled with buttermilk, cooked slowly and watched over during the day by the grandmother of the household. And just before bedtime, to settle things down, there was often herb tea to drink.

Blessings for the guests

Food commanded respect in Denmark as it did throughout Scandinavia. If any fell on the floor, it was picked up, dusted off and eaten. To this day a Dane, in company, never fails to say at the end of a home-cooked meal, *"Tak for mad"*—"thanks for the food". And the wife, the mother, the hostess, beaming, will always reply, *"Velbekomme,"* which can be translated as "if you please," but is really much more in the nature of a blessing: "May it become you well."

In the farm household, the farmer's wife had the official title of *Madmor*—food mother. And she was just that, someone on whom everyone could depend, and yet, for all her importance in the scheme of things, she was denied the right to sit down. While the men sat at a long table (made deliberately narrow so that the soup and porridge trails left by their dripping spoons on the way from common bowl to mouth would be short), the women stood. Often the farm wife was so busy serving her family and the hired men that her children found themselves wondering when, if ever, she ate. Even the nursemaid could seem a little better off in their eyes; she was obliged, while standing, to give only every other spoonful of her porridge to the baby she held on her arm.

But hard and bare as this life was for all, there seems to have been spirit in it at mealtimes, and conversation, especially during the lengthening spring evenings when the talking and reminiscing could go on deep into the twilight. And then there was the bowl, the communal bowl from which everyone ate. Woe to the man who took more than his share, like poor old Jens, who, legend records, dipped his spoon so close to the butter hole in the middle of the porridge that he carried far more than his share of this melted gold to his lips. Perhaps his crime would have gone undetected had not someone peered into his milk mug and seen the incriminating coins of butter floating on top of it. Reprimanded, Jens had an excuse ready—his lips were so chapped that he had needed the butter to soothe the hurt.

The common bowl has long since vanished from Danish tables, but the almost tribal feeling of community remains. In the last analysis it may well be this that prompts a Danish housewife to buy all those flowers and candles, to take such care with the food, and for her guests to join together at the end of a meal and thank her for it.

The Danish Sandwich—
a Many-splendored Thing

Smørrebrød means buttered bread, but anyone who has eaten it knows that it is also a whole lot more. *Smørrebrød* is, among other things, the Danish lunch, daily devoured by hundreds of thousands of Danes. Even calling it a sandwich does it injustice, for it is more—and less. It consists of only a single slice of bread, and a thin slice at that. Moreover, it is generally eaten with knife and fork. What really sets *smørrebrød* apart, however, is what goes on top of the bread, and in Danish this is called *paalaeg*—literally, "something laid on." The *paalaeg* can be leftovers from the previous evening's warm meal, slices of fine meat, bits of lobsters or crab, sautéed fish fillets, rich salads. *Paalaeg* can also be, at its homeliest, a couple of apple slices with currant jelly, or slices of cold boiled potato or crisp cucumber. According to taste, these toppings may be laid on thickly or thinly—or toweringly, as at Oskar Davidsen's Restaurant in Copenhagen where the extravagant sandwich menu is four feet and 178 entries long. Basically all that matters as far as the *paalaeg* is concerned is that the ingredients complement each other and that the tidbits themselves be arranged attractively on the bread.

There is nothing difficult about assembling Danish open-face sandwiches. Most Danish women construct them in a couple of minutes. They are careful, however, to use the right bread; not any piece will do. The preferred type of bread is sour rye, dark, moist, tight in texture, only an eighth of an inch or so thick. It is always buttered evenly and thickly, since the butter acts as a juiceproof seal. Oddly, the sour rye flavor in the finished sandwich does not call attention to itself, but rather acts as a sort of catalyst to the other flavors. White bread with a hard crust is usually employed for *smørrebrød* only when the topping is to be shrimp, lobster, smoked salmon or sometimes cheese.

Smørrebrød is so much a part of daily life in Denmark that shops selling it abound everywhere, and the white-garbed women who make the sandwiches seem to be as essential a part of the national labor force as the farmers and fishermen. They are skilled laborers, too, having undergone three years of apprenticeship to qualify as what Danes call "cold virgins," a pun reflecting that upon the completion of their training they are young girls who will work with cold foods. They can rapidly and unerringly spread a slice of bread with exactly five grams of butter—no more, no less—without weighing it out beforehand.

Smørrebrød is a Danish invention, but how it got invented is not known. A theory holds that it evolved in the old days when rounds of bread were used instead of plates. Soaked with meat juices, they would be eaten as the main course or with the addition of honey, as a dessert. Often such bread would be given to the serfs or the poor. *Smørrebrød* is known to have become popular among upper-class Danes too as early as the 18th Century. Today everybody from the Danish King on down loves his *smørrebrød*.

Listed below—and shown on the next two pages—are 12 of the dozens of Danish sandwiches that can be made from easily available ingredients.

1 Pickled herring with onion rings, lettuce and a sliver of tomato, on rye bread.
2 Sliced roast pork *(page 51)*, garnished with pork crackling, prunes and a curl of orange, on rye bread.
3 Sliced hard-cooked eggs and tomatoes sprinkled with chives, on lettuce-covered rye bread.
4 Tiny Danish shrimp on a bed of lettuce, topped with a slice of lemon, on white bread.
5 Liver paste *(page 53)* and sautéed mushroom slices, a strip of bacon and a leaf of lettuce, on rye bread.
6 Sliced *frikadeller (page 52)*, topped with pickled beets and a cucumber slice, on rye bread.
7 Curry salad *(page 48)* on lettuce, with chopped egg whites and yolks and a cucumber twist, on rye bread.
8 Smoked salmon and scrambled eggs sprinkled with chives, on white bread.
9 Roast beef, a gherkin and mustard pickles, on rye bread.
10 Salami rounds and onion rings with a sprig of parsley, on rye bread.
11 Sliced boiled new potatoes with bacon, cocktail sausages, tomato slivers and sprinkles of chopped parsley, on rye bread.
12 Danish Blue cheese with a raw egg yolk encircled by an onion ring, on white bread.

Sandwiches by the Dozen

All of these open-face sandwiches were made from products that are available in the United States, including Danish sour rye bread. Where such rye cannot be found, a dark pumpernickel makes a good substitute.

Karrysalat
CURRIED MACARONI AND HERRING SALAD

To serve 6 to 8

1 small (4-inch) cucumber, peeled and halved lengthwise
⅛ teaspoon salt
½ cup uncooked elbow macaroni
1 pickled or *matjes* herring (2 fillets)
2 raw mushrooms, thinly sliced
2 tablespoons white vinegar
1 tablespoon olive oil
1 teaspoon salt
⅛ teaspoon white pepper

DRESSING
½ cup mayonnaise
1 cup sour cream
2½ teaspoons curry powder

Scrape out and discard the seeds from the halved cucumber with a teaspoon and dice the halves into ½-inch cubes. Place these cubes in a small bowl and sprinkle with salt to draw out their excess moisture. Let the cubes stand 15 minutes, then drain and pat them dry with paper towels.

Cook the macaroni in rapidly boiling salted water for 20 minutes, following the directions on the package. Meanwhile, wash the herring fillets in cold water, pat them dry with paper towels, and cut them into 1½-inch lengths. Drain the cooked macaroni in a colander, run cold water over it to cool it, then spread the macaroni out on paper towels to rid it of any excess moisture.

Place the cut-up herring in a salad bowl along with the cucumber, macaroni and sliced raw mushrooms. In a separate bowl, use a small wire whisk to beat together the vinegar, olive oil, salt and pepper. Pour this mixture over the ingredients in the salad bowl. Mix together thoroughly but gently. Refrigerate the salad for 1 to 2 hours before serving.

DRESSING: For a richer dressing, preferred by the Danes, whip the mayonnaise, sour cream and curry powder together in a small bowl and add to the salad just before serving.

Syltede Rødbeder
PICKLED BEETS

Makes 2 cups

½ cup white vinegar
½ cup water
½ cup sugar
1 teaspoon salt
⅛ teaspoon freshly ground black pepper
2 cups thinly sliced freshly cooked or canned beets

In a stainless-steel or enameled 1½- to 2-quart saucepan, combine the vinegar, water, sugar, salt and pepper, bring to a boil and boil briskly for 2 minutes. Meanwhile, place the sliced beets in a deep glass, stainless-steel or enamel bowl. Pour the hot marinade over the beets and let them cool uncovered to room temperature. Cover the bowl with plastic wrap and refrigerate for at least 12 hours, stirring every few hours to keep the slices moist.

Agurkesalat
PICKLED CUCUMBER SALAD

To serve 4

2 large (8-inch) or 3 medium (6-inch) cucumbers
1 tablespoon salt
¾ cup white vinegar
1 tablespoon sugar
1 teaspoon salt
¼ teaspoon white pepper
2 tablespoons chopped fresh dill

Scrub the wax coating (if any) off the cucumbers and dry them. Score the cucumbers lengthwise with a fork and cut them in the thinnest possible slices; ideally, the slices should be almost translucent. Arrange them in a thin layer in a shallow china or glass dish and sprinkle with salt. Place 2 or 3 china plates on top of the cucumbers (to press out excess water and bitterness) and let them rest at room temperature for a couple of hours.

Remove the plates, drain the cucumbers of all their liquid, and spread them out on paper towels. Gently pat the cucumbers dry with paper towels and return them to their dish. In a small bowl, beat together the vinegar, sugar, salt and pepper. Pour over the cucumbers and strew them with the chopped dill. Chill for 2 or 3 hours and just before serving, drain away nearly all of the liquid. Serve as a salad, as a garnish on different *smørrebrød* (*pages 46-47*), or with meat and poultry.

Flaeskeaeggekage
BACON AND EGG CAKE

Cut the long strips of bacon in half crosswise and fry them over moderate heat in a heavy 10- to 12-inch skillet. Do not let them get too crisp. Drain the strips on paper towels and set them on an ovenproof platter or baking dish and keep warm in a 200° oven. Remove all but a tablespoon of the clear bacon fat from the skillet.

In a mixing bowl, beat the flour and salt into the eggs only long enough to combine them, and then slowly beat in the milk. Warm the fat in the skillet over moderate heat and pour in the egg mixture. Turn the heat down to low and without stirring let the eggs set into a firm custard. Since this will take about 20 minutes, an asbestos pad placed under the skillet will help to prevent the bottom of the egg cake from burning. Arrange the bacon slices and chives over the top of the finished cake. Serve directly from the pan, as a first course, brunch or late-supper dish.

To serve 4

½ pound bacon, preferably Danish
6 eggs, lightly beaten
1 tablespoon flour
½ teaspoon salt
½ cup milk
3 tablespoons chives, finely cut

Egg cake, a traditional Danish favorite, is cooked slowly on top of the stove until it has set to a custardlike consistency. It is served with a topping of crisp bacon and chopped chives.

Pierce a loin of pork with a long, sharp tool—here, a steel knife sharpener.

Fill the tunnel you have made in the loin with prunes and apples.

Pack in the fruit tightly with a blunt, round tool, such as a wooden-spoon handle. Each slice of the roasted loin (*right*) has its own built-in decorative core of prunes and apples.

Mørbrad med Svedsker og Aebler

PORK LOIN STUFFED WITH PRUNES AND APPLES

Place the prunes in a saucepan, cover with cold water, and bring to a boil. Remove from the heat and let the prunes soak in the water for 30 minutes. Then drain, pat dry with paper towels, and set aside. Sprinkle the cubed apple with lemon juice to prevent discoloring. With a strong, sharp knife, make a pocket in the pork by cutting a deep slit down the length of the loin, going to within 1/2 inch of the two ends and to within 1 inch of the other side. Season the pocket lightly with salt and pepper and stuff it with the prunes and apples, sewing up the opening with strong kitchen thread. Tie the loin at 1-inch intervals to keep its shape while cooking.

Preheat the oven to 350°. In a casserole equipped with a cover and just large enough to hold the loin of pork comfortably, melt the butter and oil over moderate heat. When the foam subsides, add the loin, turning it from time to time with 2 wooden spoons. It should take about 20 minutes to brown the loin evenly on all sides. With a bulb baster or large spoon, remove all the fat from the pan. Pour in the wine, stir in the heavy cream, whisking briskly, and bring to a simmer on top of the stove. Cover the pan and cook in the center of the oven for 1 1/2 hours, or until the meat shows no resistance when pierced with the tip of a sharp knife.

Remove the loin from the pan and let it rest on a heated platter while you finish the sauce. Skim the fat from the liquid in the pan and bring the liquid to a boil. When it has reduced to about 1 cup, stir in the red currant jelly, reduce the heat and, stirring constantly, simmer briefly until the sauce is smooth. Taste for seasoning and pour into a heated sauceboat. Cut away the strings from the loin, then carve the meat into 1-inch slices. Each slice of meat will surround a portion of the stuffing. Pass the sauce separately.

NOTE: An alternative method of stuffing the loin is somewhat more demanding but presents a more symmetrical appearance when the meat is sliced. Ask your butcher to tie the loin securely at 1-inch intervals. With a sharp knife make a hole in each end of the loin. Force a long skewer or steel knife sharpener through the length of the loin, turning it to make a tunnel at least 1/2 inch in diameter. Then, with your fingers, insert the apples and the prunes alternately into the tunnel. Push them through from both sides using a round instrument; the long handle of a wooden spoon would be ideal. Complete the preparation of the meat as above.

To serve 6 to 8

4 1/2- to 5-pound boned loin of pork, center cut
12 medium-sized pitted prunes
1 large tart apple, peeled, cored and cut into 1-inch cubes
1 teaspoon lemon juice
Salt
Freshly ground black pepper
3 tablespoons butter
3 tablespoons vegetable oil
3/4 cup dry white wine
3/4 cup heavy cream
1 tablespoon red currant jelly

Flaeskesteg med Svaer

ROAST FRESH HAM WITH CRACKLING

Preheat the oven to 300°. Using a sharp, heavy knife, cut deeply through the rind and fat until you reach the meat, making the incisions 1/2 inch apart lengthwise and crosswise. Rub salt and pepper liberally into these gashes. Insert a meat thermometer into the thickest part of the ham and place it on a rack set in a shallow roasting pan just large enough to hold the meat comfortably. Roast slowly 4 to 4 1/2 hours, or until the meat thermometer reads 180°. Do not baste the meat. When roasted, the meat should be moist and tender, and the rind (or crackling) very crisp. Let the roast rest outside the oven for 10 to 15 minutes for easier carving. A little of the crackling should be included in each serving of meat.

To serve 8 to 10

1/2 fresh ham (butt or shank) weighing about 6 pounds or 6 pounds shoulder of pork with the rind on
Coarse salt or substitute regular salt
Freshly ground black pepper

As Danish as Dannebrog, the Danish flag, are *frikadeller*, ground veal and pork patties fried in butter and served as a dinner dish.

Frikadeller
DANISH MEAT PATTIES

Makes 8 to 10 patties

½ pound boneless veal
½ pound boneless pork
1 medium onion, coarsely chopped or
    grated (½ cup)
3 tablespoons flour
1½ cups club soda
1 egg, well beaten
1 teaspoon salt
¼ teaspoon pepper
4 tablespoons butter
2 tablespoons vegetable oil

Put the veal, pork and chopped onion twice through the finest blade of a meat grinder, or have the butcher grind the meats together and then grate in the onion yourself.

In a large mixing bowl, vigorously beat the flour into the ground meat mixture with a wooden spoon, or use an electric mixer equipped with a pastry arm or paddle. Gradually beat in the club soda, a few tablespoons at a time, and continue to beat until the meat is light and fluffy. Now thoroughly beat in the egg, salt and pepper. Cover the bowl with aluminum foil or plastic wrap and refrigerate for 1 hour; this will make the meat mixture firmer and easier to handle.

Shape the mixture into oblongs about 4 inches long, 2 inches wide and 1 inch thick. Melt the butter and oil over high heat in a heavy 10- to 12-inch skillet. When the foam subsides, lower the heat to moderate and add the meat patties, 4 or 5 at a time, taking care not to crowd them. Cook about 6 to 8 minutes on each side, turning the patties with a wide spatula or with two wooden spoons. When they are a rich mahogany brown, remove them from the pan and set them aside on a heated platter. Continue with the remaining patties. Because *frikadeller* contain pork, they should never be served rare. To be certain that they are cooked through, puncture one with the tip of a small, sharp knife. The juices should run clear and should show no tinge of pink.

Frikadeller are traditionally accompanied by boiled potatoes and pickled beets *(page 48)*, cucumber salad *(page 48)* or red cabbage *(page 190)*.

Leverpostej
LIVER PASTE

To serve 12 to 16

Melt the butter in a saucepan, remove from the heat, and stir in the flour. Add the milk and cream and bring to a boil, beating constantly with a whisk until the sauce is smooth and thick. Let it simmer for a minute, then set aside to cool. Cut the liver into chunks. Roughly chop the pork fat and mix both with the onion and anchovies. Divide the mixture into thirds. Purée each batch in an electric blender set at high speed, adding enough sauce to keep the mixture from clogging the blender. Transfer each completed batch to a large bowl and beat in any remaining cream sauce. (To make by hand, put the liver, pork fat, onion and anchovies through the finest blade of a meat grinder twice, then combine with the cream sauce, beating them together thoroughly.) Beat the eggs with the salt, pepper, allspice and cloves and mix thoroughly into the liver mixture. The blender mixture will be considerably more fluid than the one made by hand.

Preheat the oven to 350°. Line a 1-quart loaf pan or mold with the strips of pork fat. Arrange the strips lengthwise or crosswise; they should overlap slightly and cover the bottom and sides of the pan. If long enough, let them hang over the sides; otherwise, save enough strips to cover the top. Spoon the liver mixture into the loaf pan and fold the overhanging strips (or extra strips) of fat over the top. Cover with a double sheet of aluminum foil, sealing the edges tightly, and place in a large baking pan. Pour into the baking pan enough boiling water to reach at least halfway up the side of the loaf pan and bake in the center of the oven for 2 hours. Remove from the oven and lift off the foil. When cool, re-cover with foil and chill thoroughly. Liver paste may be served in ½-inch-thick slices as a first course, as a luncheon dish or on bread as *smørrebrød (pages 46-47)*.

2 tablespoons butter
2 tablespoons flour
1 cup milk
1 cup heavy cream
1 pound fresh pork liver
¾ pound fresh pork fat
1 onion, coarsely chopped (½ cup)
3 flat anchovy fillets, drained
2 eggs
1½ teaspoons salt
¾ teaspoon white pepper
½ teaspoon ground allspice
¼ teaspoon ground cloves
¾ pound fresh pork fat, sliced into long, ⅛-inch-thick strips or sheets

Stegt Rødspaette
SAUTÉED FLOUNDER WITH SHRIMP

To serve 4

Plaice is the fish that Danes usually prepare in this manner, but flounder is an excellent American substitute. Danish shrimp are the 1-inch variety similar to U.S. West Coast shrimp. Choose the smallest fresh shrimp available.

Rinse the fish in cold water and dry with paper towels. Salt lightly, dip in flour and shake off any excess. Spread the bread crumbs on wax paper. In a mixing bowl, beat the eggs together with the 2 tablespoons of water, then dip each fillet into the egg mixture and coat each side thoroughly with the bread crumbs. Let them rest for at least 10 minutes before cooking. Heat 2 tablespoons of butter and 2 tablespoons of oil in a heavy 10- to 12-inch skillet over moderate heat. When the foam subsides, sauté the fillets for 3 to 4 minutes on each side, turning them with a spatula. When golden brown, transfer the fillets to a heated platter. In a separate pan, melt 2 tablespoons of butter over moderate heat. Add the shrimp and toss them in the butter for 2 to 3 minutes until well coated. Place a line of the shrimp down the center of each fillet. Melt the remaining butter over low heat until it turns a rich, nutty brown, pour over the fish fillets, and garnish with lemon wedges. If you prefer, serve with a parsley sauce *(Recipe Booklet)* in place of the shrimp and brown butter.

4 fillets of flounder, ½ pound each
Salt
Flour
½ cup dried bread crumbs
2 eggs
2 tablespoons water
8 tablespoons (1 quarter-pound stick) butter
2 tablespoons vegetable oil
½ pound small cooked shrimp, peeled and deveined
Lemon wedges

This raspberry pudding is a dessert with the unpronounceable name (save to the Danes themselves) of *rødgrød med fløde*.

Rødgrød med Fløde
RED FRUIT PUDDING WITH CREAM

To serve 6

Remove any hulls from the fresh berries, then wash the berries quickly in a sieve, drain and spread them out on paper towels, and pat them dry. After cutting the larger berries into quarters, place in the container of an electric blender. Blend at high speed for 2 or 3 minutes until they are puréed. If you are using frozen berries, defrost them thoroughly, then purée them in the blender—juices and all.

To make *rødgrød* by hand, rub the contents of the packages or the fresh berries through a fine sieve that is set over a large mixing bowl. Place the berry purée (which should measure about 2⅓ cups) in a 1- to 1½-quart enameled or stainless-steel saucepan and stir in the sugar. Bring to a boil, stirring constantly. Mix the 2 tablespoons of arrowroot and the cold water to a smooth paste, and stir it into the pan. Let the mixture come to a simmer to thicken the jelly (do not let it boil), then remove the pan from the heat.

Pour into individual dessert bowls or a large serving bowl. Chill for at least 2 hours. Before serving the *rødgrød,* decorate the top with a few slivers of almonds and pass a pitcher of light cream separately.

1½ pounds of fresh raspberries or strawberries, or a combination of the two (or substitute 2 ten-ounce packages of frozen berries)
2 tablespoons sugar
2 tablespoons arrowroot powder
¼ cup cold water
Slivered almonds
½ cup light cream

Havregrynskage
OAT CAKES

To make 12

Melt the butter in a heavy 10- to 12-inch skillet over moderate heat and stir in the sugar with a wooden spoon. Let them bubble together for 20 seconds, taking care not to let the butter burn. Add the oatmeal and, stirring occasionally, cook for 5 to 10 minutes, or until the oatmeal is golden brown. Remove from heat and stir in the white corn syrup.

Rinse custard cups or the small cups (approximately 2½ inches in diameter) of a muffin tin with cold water and shake out the excess moisture. Pack the bottom and sides of the cups or muffin pans firmly with the oatmeal mixture, dividing it equally. Refrigerate for at least three hours. Loosen the cakes from their containers by running a knife around the edges; gently slide them out and serve with cold buttermilk soup *(below)*. (In Denmark the cakes are sometimes split and served with the soup poured over them.)

8 tablespoons (1 quarter-pound stick) unsalted butter
¼ cup sugar
2 cups instant oatmeal
¼ cup white corn syrup

Kaernemaelkskoldskaal
COLD BUTTERMILK SOUP

To serve 6 to 8

The flavor of commercial buttermilk varies enormously from dairy to dairy. Natural fresh buttermilk, if available, would be ideal for this unusual summer luncheon or dessert soup, but cultured buttermilk of good flavor will do almost as well.

With an electric beater or a wire whisk, beat the egg yolks in a large bowl. Gradually add the sugar, beating until the eggs fall back into the bowl in a lazy ribbon when the beater is lifted. Add the grated lemon rind and juice and the optional vanilla. Slowly beat in the buttermilk, continuing to beat until the soup is smooth. Serve in chilled bowls and float a spoonful of unsweetened whipped cream on the surface of each serving if you like. Buttermilk soup is traditionally served with oat cakes *(above)*.

3 egg yolks
½ cup sugar
½ teaspoon grated lemon rind
1 teaspoon lemon juice
1 teaspoon vanilla (optional)
1 quart buttermilk
¼ cup whipped heavy cream (optional)

III

Norway's Elemental Foods

Haying in the rain,
Norwegians dressed for harsh
weather work with tractor and
rakes on a steep slope near the
village of Voss on Lake
Vangsvatnet in western
Norway. From such difficult
terrain come the vigorous-
tasting, healthy foods that
give Norwegian cooking
its hearty character.

Mountainous Norway is Scandinavia laid bare, a harsh, strong place—the antithesis of Denmark. Here food can strike sparks in the mouth, a feeling more than once brought home to me during my eating in the country. Consider this meal, cooked for my wife and me by a resident of Oslo who knows a great deal about Norwegian food. It was rustic poetry from beginning to end, and it showed a refreshing disregard of rules. For one thing we ate the meal more or less backwards, the meat having cooked too fast; for another, it was served in the kitchen. That had its compensations, however, for the setting was appropriately simple, and the blue kitchen was immensely cozy, with green, fat-leaved begonias in full pink bloom on the window sill.

I was glad the order of the meal had been reversed. The cool Norwegian air had unleashed inside me a growling appetite, and here was meat of a strength and character to quell it—salt-cured mutton chops, hamlike in color and pungent in flavor, steamed on a bed of peeled birch twigs. Each chop still had the entire rib attached, a convenient, foot-long handle that enabled us to raise the bones to our mouths and nibble the crisp, salty tidbits clinging all along their length. With the *pinnekjøtt* (as this old peasant dish from the western part of the country is called) we had mashed rutabagas, whose bitter earthiness I found myself liking for the first time. We drank a delicious, mellow aquavit and a brown beer with a tan head, made by the Hansa brewery inside a mountain in Bergen.

We were pleasantly relaxed when the second course (which should have been the first) of cold shrimp, rosy-red in a bowl, served whole as they also are in Sweden, made its appearance. Next came the crustaceans known as *langoustes*, pale and prickly, like skinny, undersized lobsters. Both the shrimp and the *langoustes*, we were told, had been caught that day and cooked on board the ship that brought them to Oslo. There was no question about their freshness; the proof lay in their sweet sea taste.

For dessert we were served Arctic cloudberries, stirred with cream. Although an orange-yellow in color, they looked like plump blackberries. They seemed to have a taste about them of the mountain moor on which they had grown—a flavor, perhaps, of moss. After the fruit dessert, there was a Norwegian apple brandy, bright red, not golden like French Calvados and hardly as subtle in flavor, but possessing a compensatory robustness. To round out the meal—and to make sure it would end on a strong note— our host brought forth a great brick of rust-colored goat cheese. Spread on fragile chips of paper-thin flat bread, it had an earthy tang, coupled with a sandy sweetness.

Perhaps it was our acceptance of his food that prompted our Norwegian host to leave the table again and to return this time with one of the infrequently encountered foods of Norway—a brown, mold-splotched cheese that Norwegians normally do not offer to foreigners. It is called *gammelost*. *Gammel* means old and *ost* means cheese; the old does not refer to the cheese's age, but to the ancient method of preparing it from sour rather than fresh milk. I took one small bite. Its sharp flavor and strong aroma were enough to jounce the brain and startle the heart.

This remarkable meal seems to me to have expressed one of the things that is most attractive about Norwegian food—namely, its straightforwardness. But what else distinguishes the cooking of the country? How does it differ from the Danish or the Swedish? There are similarities, of course, as there would have to be in a country that for 400 years was a part of Denmark, and today shares a long border with Sweden.

Still, the differences are outstanding, and they have to do with the kind of place Norway is. I have always felt that living there might be a little like living in an American national park, with mountains all around and the sky arched thin and blue overhead. In Norway even cities have their open feeling, their touches of nature: in Oslo a giant fjord comes to berth at the foot of city hall and it is possible to ski half an hour from the heart of town. In a fresh country like this, where air can sting the nostrils and fill the lungs with exhilaration, appetites are bound to be large, and eating is dedicated to making sound bodies surge up around sound minds. The day gets off to a healthy start with a big breakfast, and the Norwegians, more than most Scandinavians, have the stamina to eat herring bright and early in the morning. A sleepy-eyed foreigner coming down to breakfast for the first time in a hotel or ski lodge may well think that he has instead stumbled on a *smörgåsbord*. In addition to the herring and other salted and pickled fish arrayed on the table from which everyone helps himself, there will be several kinds of bread, as well as pastries, cheeses, hot and cold cereals, soft-boiled and fried eggs, bacon and potatoes, fruit, fruit juice, milk, buttermilk, sour milk, coffee and tea, and a whole lot more.

This hearty kind of breakfast is a virtual necessity for Norwegians. Avid sportsmen, they get to work as early as 8:30, eat a rushed lunch at their desks and leave by 4 p.m.—all in order to have the rest of the day free to go hiking, sailing or skiing. The wish to get the whole family outdoors as soon as possible, to make the most of the sun and air, has placed a priority on convenience, and has helped to give Norwegian cooking a pragmatic base. Thus a soup or a fish chowder may qualify as a meal in itself, one that can be easily prepared and eaten. To be sure, such a soup or chowder will be built on a solid stock base, enriched and thickened with egg yolks and ladled from an enormous tureen into bowls of broad circumference. Cauliflower—white and fine in Norway—is cooked and blended into a creamy soup. Spinach, caraway sprouts or even spring nettles (picked before the sting has developed) are all but melted in thickened broth to make soups of sturdy character, with slices of hard-cooked eggs floated on top for color contrast and additional nourishment (page 78). And the desserts that follow are of a heftiness to guarantee that no one will be hungry for hours afterward: pancakes into which blueberries were tumbled, or waffles crisp and patterned from the hot press of a decorated iron.

Norway differs from Denmark and Sweden not only in how its people eat, but in what they eat. Fish—fresh fish—figures much more in the daily diet. Mutton and lamb crop up so often in meat dishes that one begins to feel that sheep are exclusively Norwegian animals. Stews help meet the national need for substantial, easily prepared food. Although the Norwegians share the Danish liking for pork, they serve it with their own version of sauerkraut, which is not laid away in crocks like the German variety but consumed as soon as it is made, tart with vinegar and sown with caraway seeds. As for specific ingredients, sour cream is one that immediately separates Norway's cooking from Denmark's. The housewife uses it with almost the same abandon that her Danish counterpart does sweet or whipped cream. She dissolves it in her soups and sauces, combines it with salt-cured meats and cold cuts, dresses lettuce with it and potato salad as well, makes a supreme porridge from it, cooks fish in it, spoons it into her waffle batter (page 85), heaps it on crumbled flat bread in a bowl and eats the cream-covered flat bread as a snack. The rich, fresh taste that sour cream gives her cooking seems to charge up food, to complement the mountain scenery.

Freshness and purity that can be tasted

Actually the Norwegian housewife is at something of an advantage when it comes to cooking. The native-grown materials at her disposal may be more limited in kind and number than those available in Denmark and Sweden, but they are of a freshness and purity that can be tasted. Her fish comes from cold, clean, mineral-laden water; her fruits and vegetables mature in cold, clean air, unsmirched by factory exhaust and other pollutants. I think of even the Norwegian earth as clean, protected by mounds of grass and moss, rinsed by rain and dried in the sun—a sun that, as everybody knows, can shine around the clock in highest summer. A Norwegian apple surrounds itself with its own perfume. Thyme tingles on the tongue. Cabbage swells with goodness. And the curious thing is this—the farther north fruits and vegetables grow, the tastier they become, blessed by the ever-shining summer sun into round, full growth, yet never tricked into spending themselves on mere show at the cost of flavor. The cool weather gentles and tempers everything, while the high-walled fjords act as natural hothouses, absorbing heat by day, emitting it by night.

But there is something else that gives Norwegian food its distinctive character. This is mountains. Denmark has a hill that the Danes like to call a mountain, and the Swedes have their Alps, which are really a continuation of the Norwegian ranges. But neither country is in any sense of the word rock-bound, and Norway is. From the southern coast to the Arctic North the mountains jostle each other in a crush of stone and forest. In this perpendicular landscape waterfalls leap from incredible heights to the ground or skip from precipice to precipice into dark fjords; glaciers—one almost as big as New York City—ride over buried peaks. And where mountains meet shoulder to shoulder there are no real valleys, just rock-filled creases. Awesome certainly, and beautiful—but hardly a terrain for agriculture. Here farms take seesaw slants, and clapboard houses and barns seem in imminent danger of sliding downslope; even in the limited area where the land lies fairly flat, enormous boulders must be wrestled from the earth before the soil will lie open to the plow. Of the 125,000 square miles of the country, little more than 5,000 are arable, and but 3,700 are actually cultivated.

Today this is not nearly the handicap it used to be: Norway must still import most of its cereal grains and some of its fruits, but it has become self-sufficient in the production of meat, vegetables and dairy products. In the past the picture was otherwise. Every farm had to function as an independent unit; it was imperative that the *stabbur,* a wooden storehouse built on stilts, contain at least a year's supply of food. A traveler in the North a century ago reported being shown the inside of one of these on a prosperous farm, and there to his amazement he saw rows of hams coated with mildew. Some of the hams were older than the owner, no longer a young man—but all were still edible.

With hunger a constant threat, people learned to eat what was put before them, whether they liked it or not. There was a joke about how a person could swallow so much porridge over a lifetime that he could come to look like it. Shaped as it was by necessity, Norwegian cooking had little chance to develop frills. The author of a housekeeping manual of the 18th Century looked upon cooking more as technology than art, and he lumped it together with such other requisites for survival as brewing, spinning, weaving, churning, cheese-making, salting and distilling.

But while the mountain environment imposed its limitations on the Norwegian kitchen, it also made for a curious kind of variety. Something as simple as flat bread could be baked from entirely different recipes by farm wives living only a few miles apart, but with a mountain or two in between. Villages today still have their own recipes for *lefser,* a thin, saucer-shaped holiday bread made of potatoes cooked on an ungreased griddle, and generally eaten buttered, sugared and folded up like a pocket handkerchief. And the ways of people living at one end of the country (the longest in Europe) can still seem strange to those living at the other end, or even to the people in the middle. The Northerner's predilection for reindeer marrowbones (which would make an ax to crack them open seem a necessary utensil on the dining table) or a powerful drink concocted from seagull eggs and aquavit can be as puzzling to a Southerner as to any other outsider. But then the Northerner might find strange the fuss the Osloan makes over the mussels he obtains by sailing out into the fjord in summer to where the water is purest, so that he may scrape them from the rocks to be steamed in white wine. And certainly almost all Norwegians find it difficult to understand how any of their number could eat octopus, as do some black-eyed descendants of Spaniards who three centuries ago came to the stony Lofoten Islands to work in the cod trade and stayed, passing on to their heirs this remnant of their native diet.

The hardships attending their lives have never prevented Norwegians from enjoying food. From Viking times onward there have been feasts here to boggle the imagination and roil the digestion. On August 24, 1648, for example, a gala was held in Oslo to honor the new king, Frederick III. Since Christian IV had died only a few months before, the decorations were black, and even the almond paste was draped in black taffeta. Close to 1,000 guests attended and they had to be seated in three different buildings since the palace was not big enough to contain them all. For weeks in advance the countryside around the capital had been scoured for eggs, birds, pigs and sheep, and the fjord and inlets all but emptied of their fish. From England, Germany, France and Holland came spirits, candy and barrels of pâté. There were nine courses of several dishes each, and the wine galloped from pitchers: 1,647 glasses were smashed against the wall in toasts. And when the time came for the party to break up, the guests tore off the wallpaper. The bill for the entire celebration totaled 4,000 riksdaler; in those days three riksdaler could buy a cow.

Royal feasts and peasant weddings

Only eight years later another feast to rival this one was held in the same city, with no expense spared—and no dampening of spirits at this party either. Instead of nine courses there were 12, and two French chefs and five Norwegian cooks labored long and hard to prepare 1,387 chickens and 78 whole oxen. Once again the guests were lofted by drink into exuberance, and despite all precautions taken to curtail damages, they smashed windows and tore down draperies.

These were of course royal feasts, paid for out of the treasury and therefore lavish; but even the poor peasantry could lay on parties that had everyone reminiscing about them for years afterward. The greatest social occasion of all was a wedding, and no wedding could be considered a success unless it went on for at least three days and the guests had eaten and drunk as much as they possibly could by the time it was over.

In eastern Norway, the groom came to the bride's home the day before the wedding. He brought the guests with him, and the guests their maidservants. While the families of both the bride and the groom supplied food and drink, it was also the custom for the guests to contribute to the party's success with offerings of their own—anything from home-distilled spirits to flat bread and butter. The festivities started right away, to be interrupted only by sleep and the wedding itself the next day. The merriment was continuous; even the processional to the church could be a noisy affair, with horns and fiddles and salvos fired from blunderbusses. After the ceremony, the wedding feast proper took place. It began with a toast to the newlyweds, drunk in a gulp without a drop remaining. The eating, however, got off to a slow start, since good manners commanded that everyone feign a lack of appetite. When the meal was at last over and all bellies were full, the bride

Continued on page 72

A Norwegian Country Wedding: 17 Cakes for 160 Guests

Getting married in Norway can involve the efforts of an entire community —as it did in the marriage of Martha Nordheim and Terje Auganes, two spirited young Norwegians living in the village of Voss who wanted their wedding to be an old-fashioned and traditional one. Luckily they could count on both their families and their many friends to help make it so. The bride and groom themselves had raised the two pigs that would be needed to feed their 160 guests, while the bride's father had seen to it that the hams were properly cured and smoked in his storehouse. The beer was made by a local man with more than 50 years' experience practicing the brewer's art. Friends and relatives of both the bride and the groom pitched in to bake no fewer than 17 cakes for the festivities. The day before the wedding the women of the bride's family decorated these cakes with whipped cream and pears, plums and morello cherries, all products from the farm of the groom's family. A neighbor of Martha's family was entrusted with the important job of overseeing the preparation and baking of the *brudlaupskling*, the traditional local wedding cake *(opposite)*.

The bride's mother makes *rømmegrøt*, a thick sour-cream porridge that is an indispensable part of a rural wedding feast in Norway.

A wedding cake of bread—a specialty of the Voss area—harks back to the days when white flour was a rare commodity on Norwegian farms and anything made of it was admired and enjoyed. Thus the woman arranging the dough *(opposite)* will still follow the ancestral pattern by covering the unbaked flat bread with a mixture of flour and water to ensure its absolute whiteness when it cooks on the iron griddle to her right. In the final stages *(left)*, the water-softened bread is smeared with butter and a mixture of cheese, heavy cream and syrup. It is then folded over and carefully cut into small, square cakes.

63

A Hungry Stroll to Church and Then, over the Mountains to Home

When so many people are involved in the preparations for a wedding, perhaps it is only natural that they should also *be* the wedding. Thus all the guests at Martha's and Terje's *bryllup* dressed for the occasion in regional costumes. Arranged in strict hierarchical order, with the fathers, fiddlers and master of ceremonies out front and the bachelors closing up the rear, the entire wedding party *(opposite)* paraded through Voss.

Immediately after the brief Lutheran service in the 13th Century stone church *(below)*, which two of Martha's aunts had decorated the day before with birch boughs, flowers and candles, the guests walked to the local hotel for the first of that day's three big meals. The main course consisted of home-cured ham, smoked pork and lamb sausages, Norwegian sauerkraut with caraway seeds stirred into it, cauliflower, sweet peas and carrots. After nearly three hours of dining and rounds of hearty toasting, the guests —or at least those who found themselves up to it—proceeded in a stately column over the mountains behind Voss to Martha's parents' farm *(overleaf)* for the next round of activities. The wearier ones were taken there by bus.

Opposite: Wearing an antique crown borrowed from a friend, the bride walks to church on her fiancé's arm. The children are her niece and nephew, and the man behind the little girl is the master of ceremonies, who must see that all goes as planned. The fiddler—one of a pair—is playing a nine-stringed regional instrument. Its twangs are the sound of Norwegian peasant gaiety. *Below:* the ceremony in the church.

In slow-moving procession, the wedding participants file over the hills to feast again at the bride's home.

With husbandly pride, the groom offers his bride her first sip of the beer brewed especially for their wedding festivities.

The Norwegian Recipe for Living Happily Ever After

After a night of dancing, drinking and general merrymaking, the guests gathered around the tables at 3 a.m. for a final treat. It consisted of sobering portions of pea soup, sour-cream porridge and a concoction called *dravle,* made of curds and whey sweetened with syrup, seen in the bowl in the right foreground above. These dishes were accompanied by slices of salt-cured meats served on small plates. The festivities at the farm had begun with an old-fashioned *skoal,* drunk from a boat-shaped communal bowl. The vessel made its round of the family members and the guests before reaching the bride and groom, who are shown taking their turn on the two preceding pages. The bowl was filled many times over with beer, and before long people began to dance to the regional fiddles. At 11 p.m. everybody had coffee and sampled all the cakes, including one made entirely of almond paste and bearing the couple's initials *(opposite).* Then the party continued to roar on through the night, until the early-morning soup break.

Only a little less decorative than the tinkling, bejeweled crown worn by the bride *(opposite, right foreground)* are the cakes being served at the 11 p.m. snack. The one just in front of the bride is made of marzipan. The cake beside it consists almost entirely of whipped cream. In the wooden bowl in the center of the table are slices of *brudlaupskling,* the traditional wedding cake. The groom, in left foreground, is serving the bride a slice of creamcake. The bride's parents, Ingeborg and David Nordheim, are seated to the left of the groom. Mrs. Nordheim's headdress contrasts with the starched white caps worn by women from the neighboring area.

and the toastmaster had the first dance. She whirled from partner to partner thereafter, and the dancing went on all night, with wilting energies revived from time to time by soup.

At country weddings the dish most anticipated by the guests was the porridge—a very special one known as *rømmegrøt*. It was made by boiling sour cream in an iron pot, stirring in a little flour until the butter fat separated. Then the liquid butter was scooped off, and hot milk and a little more flour were added to the sour cream, which was then cooked until the porridge thickened. Now the dish was ready: poured into a wooden bowl, the *rømmegrøt* would be dusted over with cinnamon and crunchy sugar and some of the liquid butter would be ladled on top. Borne into the room by the bride to the accompaniment of a fiddle, the porridge received the place of honor on the table, and often it would be the first meal that the bride served her new husband. *Rømmegrøt* is still eaten today at farm weddings, after haying and at harvesttime, and on Midsummer Eve. It is considered the national dish of Norway and is really quite good, especially when black or red currant juice is drunk with it to cut its richness. Regrettably, it cannot be duplicated in the United States; the U.S.'s commercial sour cream differs from the product used in Norway.

Other national dishes of Norway include a whole category of delicious salt-cured meats called *spekemat*, and these are indelibly associated with the country's past and completely a product of its mountainous environment and climate. But only in the past 30 years or so have these specialties come into their own; now that it is no longer necessary that they be stashed away in the storehouse, and kept there as reserves against the mountain winters, they can be appreciated for the delicacies they really are.

One of the most prized meats in the *spekemat* category is *fenalår*, dried, salted and smoked mutton, ruddy brown in color, with a dark, strong Norwegian flavor. It is made by a complicated method. An 8- to 10-pound leg of mutton is well rubbed with salt, sugar and saltpeter (to redden the meat), immersed in brine to which sugar has been added, and left to soak for five to eight days. After this it is smoked, securely wrapped in gauze and hung for about a month in a drafty place, often the back of a barn. During the drying and maturing process, which may go on for as long as four months, the meat shrinks by half in weight, but the flavor, rather than dissipating along with the moisture, concentrates inside. When the time comes to eat *fenalår*, great chips are whittled from the bone and consumed with flat bread and freshly churned butter or sour cream.

Ham is cured in much the same manner to produce *spekeskinke*, a kind of Nordic prosciutto. Traditionally laid away in November, it is ready in June. According to an old belief, *spekeskinke* can be eaten when the cuckoo lets out its first cry of the spring. In any event, the readiness of *spekeskinke* is an occasion for joy. It is sliced extremely thin and may be served with butter-steamed new potatoes *(page 81)* and young carrots and peas—the latter not much bigger than a capital O and cooked in the pod. Or it may be accompanied by steamed spinach or scrambled eggs, flecked with bright green slivers of chive. When all but reduced to bone, the ham performs a last vital function as the base for a round, full pea soup.

Sheep and goats, well adapted to Norway's terrain and a diet of scrub, continue to play an important role in food production. Goat cheese retains its popularity, and those who love it best are still willing to hunt up the occasional farm where it may yet be made by hand. Lamb and mutton find their way into a range of Norwegian dishes. One of the most vigorous of the stews is *får i kål*, made only of mutton and crisp cabbage, which can grow to a diameter of a foot or more in the cool climate. In its most classic version this hearty dish is seasoned with nothing more than salt and black pepper *(Recipe Booklet)*. A variation on it called *puss pass* contains carrots and potatoes as well as cabbage. Mutton is also the basis of a famous Norwegian soup, *betasuppe,* which has been described as a cross between a Scotch broth and a French *pot-au-feu,* and mutton is the key ingredient in a larded, spiced and pressed meat roll known as *fårerull.*

Norwegians traditionally have supplemented their meat supplies with game from the mountains. The only undomesticated reindeer in Scandinavia are to be found here, oddly enough running wild in central Norway, and not in the far North, as might be expected. Elk, hare, ptarmigan, grouse, woodcock and various water fowl are all hunted in season. Of these it is probably the tiny ptarmigan with its dark, plump breast meat that ranks highest in the national esteem; the bird is browned in butter, then simmered and lovingly basted in a big pan on top of the stove. The mountain flavor of all this Norwegian game calls for something wild to be eaten with it. This need is met by dark red lingonberries, lightly sugared and sometimes whipped into a pink foam, or an orange-colored preserve, made from the fruit of the rowan, or European mountain ash, a tree I had thought of as having ornamental value only. One of the things that make Norwegian game delicious in addition is the sauce regularly served with it, a rich, smooth, light-brown one with a deep flavor. It is made of sour or sweet cream and melted goat cheese, and such is its versatility that it will complement meat as strong as venison *(page 79)* or as delicate as veal *(page 83).*

From Norway's clear mountain streams and rivers come trout and salmon of fighting spirit, firmness and heft: 50-pounders are caught every year, and American and English sportsmen have been known to pay as much as $435 for the right to lease one of the best pools for only one day and keep only one fish. In Norway salmon is prepared with great reverence. The natural flavor of the fish is respected by simply simmering it whole, and serving it either warm with parsley butter or cold with horse-radish butter *(page 81)* and almost always with a crisp cucumber salad. But it may also be grilled, lightly smoked or even cured, as it also is in Sweden, with dill, sugar, salt and pepper. The Norwegians add a few shakes of Cognac to provide their own touch.

Trout also commands respectful treatment. Out of long experience the fisherman knows that it is best not to wash it but to dry it well and even swab the inside with a paper towel; this prevents the flesh from turning soft during the cooking. Perhaps the simplest and most delicious way the Norwegians have of preparing trout is to sauté it in butter and make a sauce from the pan drippings and sour cream *(page 78).* The oddest is to let the trout ferment. The Norwegians lay it down in layers in crocks or kegs with coarse salt and sugar in between and put a weight on top. This is usually done in late August when the trout are fattest; by early winter they are ready. During the intervening period the tissue breaks down, and the flesh becomes of such buttery consistency that it can be—and in fact is—spread on flat bread. Bright pink in color, fermented trout *(rakørret)* smells like raw petroleum and tastes like strong cheese.

While the mountains have gone a long way toward supplying the Norwegian table with many of its finest delicacies, the sea dominates it. The Norwegians call the sea the blue meadow, and for centuries they have been tapping its resources. All sorts of fish—shoals of herring and cod, waves of haddock, mackerel, halibut, coalfish, salmon—come annually to Norway's coasts to feed and spawn in waters rich with plankton and minerals. Today four fifths of the population—some three million people—live within a dozen miles of salt water. Not surprisingly, in some coastal areas fish is eaten as often as five or six times a week.

Norwegians are as proud of the high quality and absolute freshness of their fish as Americans are of their beef. They can even buy their fish alive. I have watched housewives in Bergen prowling around cement tanks filled with cold, bubbling salt water in which cod and other species swam. When one found a cod to her liking, she would point to it, and the fishmonger would go after it with his net, bring it flopping to a table and kill it. I saw more than one woman rush off with her fish wrapped in paper, the point being to get it home to the kitchen as quickly as possible, out of the paper and into the pot before the slightest bit of goodness evaporated from the flesh. The Norwegians have an expression to describe the quality of such cod—*blodfersk,* blood-fresh.

But even when fish is bought iced, its freshness can be smelled. The paradox here is that it will hardly smell at all, having so recently been killed; this can seem a miracle in Bergen's open-air fish market where the strongest odor is likely to be the hunger-making one of salt water lapping at, and rocking, the white-hulled boats in the harbor. But freshness can also be seen: a walk through the market will reveal on every side fish of sparkling hues—rainbow-tinted mackerel, bluish herring, red-spotted plaice, snowy halibut. About the only jarring sight is whale meat, a dark reddish-purple.

Fish with the sweet sea's flavor

What seems odd is that the Norwegians with their plethora of fish do not have a great many different ways of preparing it, and instead of employing numberless sauces to complement it, they use few—horse-radish cream and mustard sauce being the only two with any real sharpness. I was puzzled by this until I realized that when fish *that* fresh is available, there is no need to do much more than cook it. The sweet sea flavor is all that counts. And in Norway no impediments are put in its way.

Take cod, gastronomically and historically the most Norwegian of fish. It is almost always boiled. And the only seasoning added to the water is salt, although occasionally the cod liver will be cut up and put in or, as in the southern part of the country, a few strands of seaweed will be added. This may seem an all too timid approach, but the Norwegians are in fact audacious about it. They do not use a little water; they use a lot. And they use so much salt that the solution is really a brine. When the water has come to a furious boil, they drop in the finger-thick slices of cod, a few at a time, wait for a second boil, and then remove the pot from the fire. They let the cod sit three to seven minutes in the water—until the bone loosens from the meat—before scooping the pieces on to an oven-hot platter. When this method was first explained to me, I thought it had been devised with a single purpose in mind—to cook the goodness out of the fish. But when the cod was laid before me in a white, horseshoe-shaped piece, I found it firm to the fork and juicy in the mouth. All the flavor was intact.

Cod thus prepared is often served with melted butter or an egg and butter sauce *(page 83)*, parsley-sprinkled boiled potatoes, and, in violation of the old caveat, with red Bordeaux instead of white wine. The Danes, who also have quantities of good fresh cod at their disposal, generally boil the fish whole, and in addition to splashing each portion with melted butter, they often sprinkle it with chopped hard-boiled egg, grate horse-radish on top, and trickle mustard sauce alongside.

From long association with the cod, the Norwegians have learned not only how to cook it well, but how to eat it in its entirety. They claim that the best part of all is the head—the meat on the back of the neck and around the jaws. The dimple of flesh on top of the skull is much appreciated by them. The inch-long tongue is also considered a delicacy, and wherever cod are caught in quantity, the tongues will be amassed and sold. They may be boiled or sautéed and served with lightly browned butter; sometimes they are combined with other morsels of seafood in fish salads or in a colorful aspic called *kabaret*. Yet another delicacy is the pink roe, which is boiled, sliced and used as a garnish to the fish itself, or when floured and sautéed in butter, as a topping for sandwiches. Even the liver is savored; when not boiled with the fish, it will be cooked in only a little salted water to which, at the last moment, both vinegar and pepper are added. Curiously, it does not taste like cod-liver oil.

Fine as their fresh cod are, Norwegians also persist in eating the dried variety. The habit is at least a thousand years old, and the method of drying and cooking the cod has changed little in all that time. The fish are decapitated and cleaned as soon as they are landed, tied by their tails in pairs and hung from wooden racks in the open air. In the cold, crisp Arctic wind, they slowly yield up their moisture, and in six to 12 weeks they gradually become as stiff and hard as paddles. With their water content down by 84 per cent, they will not grow moldy and can be stored like cordwood for long periods—theoretically as many as 20 years. Such dried fish is known as *tørrfisk* or *stokkfisk;* when it is salted as well and spread out on cliffs to dry it is called *klippfisk*.

The dish made most often from dried cod is *lutefisk*. In the past the housewife used to have to soak the fish herself to soften it. This could take as long as two weeks and involved giving the cod a prolonged bath in a lye solution made from birch ashes (*lutefisk* actually means lye fish). Nowadays the housewife can buy *lutefisk* frozen or in slippery, springy chunks; all she need do is boil it. A test of its quality is to add the salt at the last moment: if the *lutefisk* quivers, it is top rate.

The amazing thing is that the fish should retain any nutritive value at all after undergoing such rough treatment, but it does. In addition to being an excellent source of protein, *lutefisk* has the modern advantage of being non-fattening—except of course when bathed in a butter or cream sauce as it often is today.

Unfortunately, *lutefisk* has almost no flavor. My wife and I sat down to a

In Bergen's fish market the shopper has the option of buying his fish live. Professor Knut Faegri, a botanist and cook, is seen grabbing the tail of the particular coalfish he selected to make the soup that is a specialty of the city.

After boiling the coalfish with celery leaves, Professor Faegri pours the fish stock through cheesecloth to clarify it. He will then combine it with cooked diced parsnips, celeriac and carrots, and a little veal stock.

Thickened with sour cream and egg yolks, Bergen fish soup is served with fish dumplings.

traditional *lutefisk* dinner in one of Oslo's best restaurants, where the fish had been cooked especially for us. We had the boiled potatoes and stewed yellow peas that always go with it, and we poured melted pork fat over it, the way we were supposed to. I do not know what I had been expecting, but the fish was a pale, trembly thing, squeaky to eat, and no amount of pepper or mustard sauce could conceal the fact that underneath there was a void. The other customers leaned across their plates to watch us try it: I suppose they found us as much a curiosity for ordering such humble food in such posh surroundings as we did *lutefisk*. It was with relief that we turned back to fresh fish.

One variety of popularity and distinction in Norway is mackerel. Best in the spring when its flesh is fattest, it is prepared in several ways—among others, sautéed and stuffed with parsley, or garnished with parsley that in turn has been deep-fried. As a cheap substitute for expensive salmon, it is sometimes cured, and it is often smoked. Filleted, marinated in olive oil with onion and lemon juice and grilled, it takes on a whole new character; hot from the flame, it is spread with tomato butter that melts down into a pink gold *(page 81)*. After a mackerel dinner, a dessert often served in Norway is rhubarb compote *(page 84)*, a relic of the time when so-called fruit soups could begin or end a meal.

No description of Norwegian fish cookery would be complete without reference to a dish that is eaten once a week in most households: fish pudding. In spite of its unromantic name, fish pudding is a delicate concoction. Prepared from haddock or cod (ground several times), cream, cornstarch, salt and pepper, it is shaped into a loaf and steamed in the oven *(page 82)*. White in color, it can be set off by a pink shrimp sauce *(page 83)* that will also help to enhance its flavor.

But the dish I like best remains fish soup *(page 79)*, a specialty of Bergen and little known outside the country, although it deserves to be. It is made of winter vegetables, sour cream and egg yolks, and it exists in several versions, most recipes for it being family secrets. I had it for the first time at the home of a botany professor and his wife in Bergen, and they took pride in their version. Early in the day they had gone in search of the right fish for the stock—a young coalfish, a relative of the cod. In addition, they had carefully shopped for firm vegetables—parsley root, celeriac, carrots and parsnips. At home they simmered the coalfish, head, tail, fins and all. And when they had obtained the stock from it, they threw the meat away. ("Fish that has been used as a base for stock," said the professor, "is proper food for cats only.") The root vegetables were diced and cooked together in a little stock until almost done, but not quite, a residual crispness being an essential part of their character in the soup. When the stock, vegetables, sour cream and egg yolks had all been combined, my hosts added a tiny bit of veal stock, some salt, and a little sugar to "round off and soften the soup." And that was all: no herbs, no spices, no sherry.

The velvet soup came to the table in a white tureen, sprinkled with chopped parsley and tiny fish dumplings of such whipped consistency that they floated on top. I found the soup so good, so without a fishy taste, that I had another bowl. But what I admired most about it was the way it expressed all that I had come to recognize as finest in Norwegian cooking— honesty, flavor and satisfaction.

Spinatsuppe
SPINACH SOUP

To serve 4 to 6

2 pounds fresh spinach, or 2 packages
　frozen chopped spinach
2 quarts chicken stock, fresh or canned
3 tablespoons butter
2 tablespoons flour
1 teaspoon salt
¼ teaspoon white pepper
⅛ teaspoon nutmeg
2 hard-cooked eggs, sliced

Wash the fresh spinach thoroughly under cold running water to remove any sand. Drain the spinach by shaking it vigorously by hand or in a lettuce basket, then chop it coarsely. If frozen spinach is used, thoroughly defrost and drain it.

Bring the 2 quarts of chicken stock to a boil in a 3- to 4-quart saucepan and add the fresh or frozen chopped spinach. Simmer uncovered about 6 to 8 minutes, then pour the entire contents of the pan into a sieve set over a large bowl. Press down hard on the spinach with the back of a wooden spoon to extract all of its juices. Set the liquid aside in the bowl and chop the cooked spinach very fine.

Melt the 3 tablespoons of butter in the saucepan. When the foam subsides, remove the pan from the heat and stir in the flour. With a wire whisk, beat the hot stock into this white *roux* a little at a time. Return the saucepan to the heat and, stirring it constantly, bring it to a boil. Then add the spinach. Season the soup with salt, pepper and nutmeg. Half cover the pan and simmer the soup over low heat about 5 minutes longer. Stir occasionally.

Garnish each serving of soup with a few slices of hard-cooked egg. On festive occasions, such as Easter, *spinatsuppe* is often served with a stuffed egg half floating in each soup bowl. To make these, remove the yolks from 2 or 3 hard-cooked eggs (depending on how many people you plan to serve) and mash them to a paste with about 1 to 2 teaspoons of softened butter. Roll the mixture into little balls and nestle 2 or 3 into each halved egg white.

Risted Laks med Kremsaus
FRIED TROUT IN SOUR CREAM SAUCE

To serve 4

4 fresh or frozen trout, about ½
　pound each, cleaned but with head
　and tail left on
Salt
½ cup flour
4 tablespoons butter
2 tablespoons vegetable oil
1 cup sour cream
½ teaspoon lemon juice
1 tablespoon finely chopped fresh
　parsley

If you are using frozen trout, defrost them completely before cooking. Wash the fish under cold running water, pat them dry inside and out with paper towels, and sprinkle a little salt into the cavities. Spread the ½ cup of flour over wax paper, roll the fish around in the flour, and then shake off any excess flour.

In a heavy 10- to 12-inch skillet, heat 2 tablespoons of the butter and 2 tablespoons of oil. When the foam subsides, lower the heat to moderate and fry the trout, 2 at a time, for about 5 minutes on each side, turning them carefully with a large spatula. When all the trout have been browned, keep them warm on a heatproof platter in a 200° oven while you quickly make the sauce.

Pour off all the fat from the skillet and replace it with 2 tablespoons of fresh butter. Stir over low heat, scraping up the brown pan drippings with a wooden spoon. Add the sour cream and continue stirring for about 3 minutes, without letting the cream boil. Stir in the lemon juice and pour the sauce over the hot fish. Garnish the platter with the chopped parsley and serve at once.

Dyrestek

ROAST VENISON (OR REINDEER) WITH GOAT-CHEESE SAUCE

Preheat the oven to 475°. Tie the roast up neatly at ½-inch intervals with kitchen cord so that it will hold its shape while cooking. With a pastry brush, spread the softened butter evenly over the meat. Place the roast on a rack in a shallow open roasting pan and sear it in the hot oven for about 20 minutes. When the surface of the meat is quite brown, reduce the heat to 375° and sprinkle the roast generously with salt and a few grindings of pepper. Pour the stock into the pan and cook the roast, uncovered, for 1¼ hours. With a large spoon or bulb baster, baste the meat with the pan juices every half hour or so. The interior meat, when finished, should be slightly rare, or about 150° on a meat thermometer. Remove the roast to a heated platter, cover it loosely with foil and let it rest in the turned-off oven while you make the sauce.

Skim and discard the fat from the pan juices. Measure the remaining liquid and either reduce to 1 cup by boiling it rapidly or add enough water to make up 1 cup. In a small, heavy saucepan, heat 1 tablespoon of butter and stir in 1 tablespoon of flour. Stirring continuously with a wooden spoon, cook this *roux* for 6 to 8 minutes over low heat until it is a nut-brown color. Be careful not to let it burn or it will give the sauce a bitter flavor. Now, with a wire whisk, beat the pan juices into the *roux*. Next whisk in the jelly and the cheese. Beat until they dissolve and the sauce is absolutely smooth, then stir in the sour cream. Do not allow the sauce to boil. Taste for seasoning, remove the strings from the roast, and carve the meat in thin slices. Pass the sauce separately.

Bergens Fiskesuppe

BERGEN FISH SOUP

To prepare the fish stock, which will be the base of the soup, combine the ingredients listed under that heading *(right)* in a 4- to 6-quart saucepan, casserole or soup kettle. Bring to a boil, partially cover the pan, turn the heat low and simmer for 30 to 40 minutes. Strain the stock through a fine sieve into a large bowl, pressing down hard on the vegetables and fish trimmings with the back of a spoon to extract their juices before discarding them. Wash the pan and return the strained stock to it. Reduce the stock to about 6 cups by boiling it rapidly, uncovered, for about 20 minutes. Re-strain through a fine sieve or through a double thickness of cheesecloth lining a regular sieve.

Again return the stock to the pot. Add the finely chopped carrots, parsnips and fish. As soon as the soup reaches the boil, lower the heat and simmer uncovered for about 10 minutes. Add the leeks and simmer 2 or 3 minutes longer. Remove from the heat, lift out the fish with a slotted spoon and set aside on a platter. In a small bowl, beat the egg yolks with a wire whisk; then beat in about ½ cup of the hot soup, 1 tablespoon at a time. Pour this back into the soup in a thin stream, beating continuously with a wire whisk. With a fork separate the fish into flakes and add it to the soup. Season with salt and pepper and reheat, but do not let the soup boil.

To serve, ladle the soup into individual bowls and sprinkle with chopped parsley. If you like, garnish each serving with 1 tablespoon of sour cream.

To serve 6 to 8

3½ pounds boneless haunch of
  venison or reindeer
3 tablespoons butter, softened
Salt
Freshly ground black pepper
1⅓ cups beef stock
1 tablespoon butter
1 tablespoon flour
2 teaspoons red currant jelly
½ ounce brown Norwegian goat
  cheese (Gjetöst), finely diced
½ cup sour cream

To serve 6

FISH STOCK
¼ cup coarsely chopped parsnips
½ cup coarsely chopped carrots
1 large yellow onion, coarsely chopped
  (¾ cup)
1 potato, peeled and chopped (1 cup)
1 teaspoon salt
6 whole black peppercorns
1 tablespoon chopped parsley stems
1 bay leaf
3 stalks of celery with leaves or celeriac
  tops
2 pounds of fish trimmings (heads,
  bones, etc.) washed
4 quarts cold water

SOUP
½ cup finely chopped carrots
¼ cup finely chopped parsnips
1 pound boneless halibut, cod or
  haddock, in one piece
½ cup finely sliced leeks, white parts
  only
2 egg yolks
Salt
Freshly ground black pepper
3 tablespoons finely chopped parsley
6 tablespoons sour cream (optional)

Stekt Marinert Makrell
GRILLED MARINATED MACKEREL

Have the fish dealer remove the backbones of the mackerel without cutting them in half. Preheat the broiler. In a shallow baking dish large enough to hold the fish laid out flat in one layer, combine the oil, lemon juice, salt, a few grindings of black pepper and the chopped onion. Place the mackerel in this marinade, flesh side down, for 15 minutes, then turn them over for another 15 minutes. Brush the broiler grill with 1 tablespoon of the butter and oil and place the fish on it, skin side down. Grill them on only one side, about 3 inches from the heat, basting them from time to time with the remaining butter and oil. In 10 to 12 minutes they should have turned a light golden color and their flesh should flake easily when prodded with a fork. Serve at once, accompanied by butter-steamed new potatoes and tomato or horse-radish butter *(below)*.

To serve 2

2 tablespoons olive oil
1 tablespoon lemon juice
½ teaspoon salt
Freshly ground black pepper
2 teaspoons finely chopped onion
2 mackerel, 1 pound each
3 tablespoons combined melted butter and vegetable oil

Tomatsmør
TOMATO BUTTER

Cream the butter with an electric mixer set at medium speed or by beating it against the side of a bowl with a wooden spoon. When it is light and fluffy, beat in the tomato paste, salt and sugar. Transfer to a serving bowl and chill until ready to serve. Serve cold, with hot grilled or fried fish.

To make ½ cup

8 tablespoons (1 quarter-pound stick) unsalted butter
2 tablespoons tomato paste
½ teaspoon salt
¼ teaspoon sugar

Pepperrotsmør
HORSE-RADISH BUTTER

Cream the butter with an electric mixer set at medium speed or by beating it against the side of a bowl with a wooden spoon until it is light and fluffy. If you are using prepared horse-radish, drain it and squeeze it dry in a kitchen towel or double thickness of cheesecloth. Now beat the horse-radish and the salt into the creamed butter. Transfer the horse-radish butter to a small serving dish and chill until you are ready to use it. Serve cold, with hot grilled or fried fish.

To make ½ cup

8 tablespoons (1 quarter-pound stick) unsalted butter
2 tablespoons freshly grated horse-radish root or 2 tablespoons bottled prepared horse-radish
¼ teaspoon salt

Smørdampete Nypoteter
BUTTER-STEAMED NEW POTATOES

Scrub the potatoes under cold running water; then pat them thoroughly dry with paper towels. Melt the ¼ pound of butter in a heavy, 6-quart casserole equipped with a cover. Add the potatoes and sprinkle them with salt and pepper. Then coat them thoroughly with the melted butter by rolling them about in the casserole. To ensure the success of this dish, the cover must fit the casserole tightly; if you have doubts, cover the casserole with a double thickness of aluminum foil, and pinch down the edges to seal it before putting on the lid. Cook over low heat (an asbestos pad under the pan ensures against scorching) for 30 to 45 minutes, depending on the size of the potatoes. Shake the casserole from time to time to prevent the potatoes from sticking. When the potatoes can be easily pierced with the tip of a sharp knife, they are done. Arrange them on a heated serving plate, sprinkle them with the chopped dill, and serve at once.

To serve 4 to 6

20 to 24 tiny new potatoes (about 1 inch in diameter)
8 tablespoons (1 quarter-pound stick) unsalted butter
1 teaspoon salt
⅛ teaspoon white pepper
3 tablespoons finely chopped fresh dill

Grilled mackerel is served with tomato butter, aquavit and beer to make it "swim" again.

To make 1 pudding or 60 fish balls

1 tablespoon soft butter
2 tablespoons dry bread crumbs
1½ pounds cod or haddock, skinned
    and boned
½ cup light cream and
    1 cup heavy cream combined
2 teaspoons salt
1½ tablespoons cornstarch

Fiskepudding eller Fiskefarse
NORWEGIAN FISH PUDDING OR FISH BALLS

To make an authentic Norwegian fish pudding—white, delicate and spongy in consistency—you should begin with absolutely fresh white fish. The pudding is served weekly in Norwegian homes, usually hot, with melted butter or a shrimp sauce (opposite). Cold and sliced, it is also excellent as part of an open-face sandwich.

With a pastry brush or paper towel, spread the bottom and sides of a 1½-quart loaf pan or mold with 1 tablespoon of soft butter and sprinkle the mold with the 2 tablespoons of dry bread crumbs. Tip the mold from side to side to be sure that the crumbs are evenly distributed, then turn the mold over and knock it gently against a table or other hard surface to tap out any excess crumbs.

Cut the fish into small pieces and place a few pieces at a time in the jar of an electric blender, along with a couple of tablespoons of the combined light and heavy cream to facilitate the puréeing. Blend at high speed, turning the machine off after the first few seconds to scrape down the sides of the jar with a rubber spatula. Continue to blend, one batch at a time, until all of the fish is a smooth purée. As you proceed, use as much of the cream as you need, to form a smooth purée.

Place the puréed fish in a large mixing bowl, beat in the 2 teaspoons of salt and the 1½ tablespoons of cornstarch, and slowly add any of the cream that was not used in the blender, beating vigorously until the mixture is very light and fluffy. Pour it into the prepared mold and then bang the mold sharply on the table to settle the pudding and eliminate any air pockets. Smooth the top with a rubber spatula.

Preheat the oven to 350°. Butter one side of a sheet of aluminum foil and seal it tightly around the top of the mold, buttered side down. Place the mold in a baking pan and pour into the pan enough boiling water to come ¾ of the way up the sides of the mold. Set the pan in the middle of the oven for 1 to 1¼ hours, regulating the heat if necessary so that the water simmers but does not boil; if it boils, the pudding will have holes. When the top of the pudding is firm to the touch and a toothpick or skewer inserted in the middle comes out clean, the pudding is done.

Remove the mold from the oven and let the fish pudding rest at room temperature for 5 minutes, so that it can be more easily removed from the mold. Pour off all of the excess liquid in the mold. Then run a sharp knife around the inside of the mold, place a heated platter on top of it and, holding the mold and plate together, quickly invert the two to remove the pudding from the mold. Clear the plate of any liquid with paper towels and serve the *fiskepudding* while still hot.

TO MAKE FISH BALLS, prepare the fish in the blender as described above. Chill the puréed fish in the mixing bowl for about 30 minutes, then roll about 1 tablespoon of the fish in your hands at a time, to make 1-inch balls. Refrigerate them, covered with wax paper, until you are ready to cook them. Poach these *fiskefarse* by dropping them into 3 or 4 inches of barely simmering salted water for 2 or 3 minutes, or until they are firm to the touch. Scoop them out with a slotted spoon, drain them thoroughly and serve as part of a fish soup *(page 79)*.

Rekesaus
SHRIMP SAUCE

In a 1½- to 2-quart enameled or stainless-steel saucepan, melt the butter over moderate heat. Remove from the heat and stir in the flour. Pour in the milk and cream all at once and, stirring constantly with a wire whisk, place over low heat and cook until the sauce is smooth and thick. Season with salt, pepper and lemon juice, then add the chopped cooked shrimp and cook another 1 or 2 minutes, until the shrimp are heated through. Stir in the dill and serve with hot fish pudding *(opposite)* or boiled fish. Cooked cauliflower, served with this sauce, is a very popular luncheon dish.

To make about 2 cups

4 tablespoons butter
4 tablespoons flour
2 cups milk
¼ cup heavy cream
1½ teaspoons salt
¼ teaspoon white pepper
1½ tablespoons lemon juice
1 to 2 pounds medium shrimp, cooked and finely chopped
2 tablespoons finely chopped fresh dill

Kalvefilet med Sur Fløte
SAUTÉED VEAL SCALLOPS IN SOUR-CREAM SAUCE

Heat 1 tablespoon of butter and 1 tablespoon of oil in a heavy 10- to 12-inch skillet over moderate heat. When the foam subsides, add the onions and cook for 3 to 5 minutes, or until they are transparent. With a rubber spatula, scrape them out of the pan into a small bowl and set them aside. Add the remaining butter and oil to the skillet and when the foam subsides, add the veal scallops. Fry them over moderate heat until they are a light golden brown—4 to 5 minutes on each side. Remove them to a heated platter and keep them warm in a 220° oven while you make the sauce.

Pour off all but a thin film of fat from the skillet and add the cooked onions to the pan. Cook over high heat, stirring constantly, for 2 to 5 minutes. Then lower the heat and stir in the sour cream and cheese a little at a time. Continue stirring until the cheese has melted and the sauce is smooth; do not allow it to come to a boil. Taste for seasoning and return the veal to the skillet. Baste the meat with the sauce and let it simmer uncovered for 1 or 2 minutes. Serve immediately.

To serve 2 to 4

3 tablespoons unsalted butter
3 tablespoons vegetable oil
¼ cup finely chopped onion
4 large veal scallops, sliced ⅜ inch thick and pounded to a thickness of ¼ inch
Salt
Freshly ground black pepper
1 cup sour cream
½ cup shredded Gjetöst (Norwegian goat cheese)

Torsk med Eggesaus
POACHED CODFISH STEAKS WITH EGG SAUCE

If you don't have a long, narrow fish poacher, an enamel roasting pan 5 inches deep will do just as well. Fill the pan with water to a depth of 4 inches and add ½ cup of salt. Bring to a boil (over 2 burners, if necessary), reduce the heat slightly and gently slide the cod slices into the water with a spatula. Lower the heat until the water is bubbling slightly and simmer the fish for about 5 minutes. Be careful not to overcook or the fish will disintegrate. Remove the slices with a slotted spatula and drain them on a linen napkin or dish towel. Arrange the cod attractively on a heated platter and serve with egg sauce *(below)*.

EGG SAUCE: Melt the butter in a 1- to 1½-quart enameled or stainless-steel saucepan. Remove from the heat, beat in ¼ cup of the stock in which you poached the fish and stir in the chopped egg, tomato, parsley and chives. Add salt and pepper to taste. Heat almost to the boiling point, pour into a sauceboat, and serve with the cod. If you prefer, you can simply pour melted butter over the cod and garnish it with lemon slices and parsley. In Norway, this dish is often accompanied by raw diced carrots, sprinkled with lemon juice, and new potatoes *(page 81)*.

To serve 4 to 6

½ cup salt
6 fresh codfish steaks, sliced ¾ inch thick

EGG SAUCE
¼ pound butter
¼ cup hot fish stock *(from above)*
2 hard-cooked eggs, finely chopped
1 medium tomato, peeled, seeded and chopped
1 tablespoon finely chopped fresh parsley
1 tablespoon finely chopped chives
Salt
Freshly ground black pepper

ALTERNATE GARNISH
8 tablespoons (1 quarter-pound stick) butter, melted
1 lemon, thinly sliced
Parsley sprigs

To serve 4

2 pounds cold boiled halibut or cod
    fillet *(page 83)*
4 tablespoons freshly grated
    horse-radish root or 4 tablespoons
    prepared horse-radish
1 pint sour cream
1 teaspoon salt
1/8 teaspoon white pepper
2 tablespoons finely chopped onion
1 teaspoon white vinegar
3 tablespoons finely chopped fresh dill
1 medium head lettuce, preferably
    Boston
2 hard-cooked eggs, sliced
3 tomatoes, peeled and cut in wedges

To serve 6 or 8

2 cups water
3/4 cup sugar
1 1/2 pounds rhubarb, washed, scraped
    and cut into 1/2-inch pieces (about
    4 cups)
1/2 teaspoon vanilla
3 tablespoons cornstarch
1/4 cup cold water

WHIPPED CREAM (optional)
1 cup chilled heavy cream
1/4 cup sugar
1 teaspoon vanilla

To serve 4 to 6

FRUIT POTPOURRI
3/4 cup chopped bananas
3/4 cup halved seedless grapes
1/2 cup chopped walnuts or pecans
1 cup chopped apples or oranges

EGGEDOSIS
5 egg yolks
2 egg whites
5 tablespoons sugar
1 tablespoon brandy or rum

Fiskesalat med Pepperrotsaus
FISH SALAD WITH HORSE-RADISH SAUCE

This salad makes excellent use of leftover boiled fish, but if you intend to use fresh, uncooked fish, prepare it according to the directions for boiled cod (page 83).

If you are using bottled, prepared horse-radish, drain it through a fine sieve, pressing out the excess juice with a wooden spoon, or squeeze the horse-radish dry in a kitchen towel or double thickness of cheesecloth. In a large mixing bowl, combine the horse-radish, sour cream, salt, pepper, onions, vinegar and 2 tablespoons of the chopped dill. Break the fish into 2-inch chunks and carefully fold it into the sour-cream dressing with a rubber spatula. Marinate for at least 30 minutes in the refrigerator, then arrange the fish, sauce and all, on a bed of dried, chilled lettuce leaves. Garnish with the sliced eggs and tomato wedges, and, just before serving, strew the remaining tablespoon of chopped dill over the salad.

Rabarbragrøt
RHUBARB COMPOTE

Dissolve the sugar in the water in a 2-quart enameled or stainless-steel saucepan, and bring to a boil. Drop in the rhubarb, reduce the heat to low and simmer, uncovered, for 20 to 30 minutes, or until the rhubarb shows no resistance when pierced with the tip of a sharp knife. Remove the pan from the heat and stir in the vanilla.

    In a small bowl, mix the cornstarch with the cold water to a smooth paste. Gradually stir it into the stewed rhubarb, and bring it to a boil, stirring constantly. Simmer about 3 to 5 minutes, or until the mixture has thickened. Pour into a serving bowl and chill.

    Although *rabarbragrøt* has a sweet flavor, with a slightly tart edge, many Norwegians prefer it even sweeter—and often garnish it with whipped cream. Make the whipped cream no more than 1 hour before you plan to serve the dessert. Beat the chilled heavy cream in a large chilled bowl with a wire whisk or a hand or electric beater until it begins to thicken. Add the sugar and vanilla and continue to beat until it is just about firm enough to hold its shape. Mask the rhubarb in the bowl with the whipped cream, or squeeze the cream through a pastry tube in decorative swirls.

Himmelsk Lapskaus
FRUIT POTPOURRI WITH BRANDY OR RUM EGG SAUCE

Toss the fruits and nuts together in a serving bowl and chill before serving with *eggedosis*, the rich egg sauce described below. In Norway this sauce is frequently served alone. Although American palates may find it excessively sweet by itself, it is an excellent foil for the tartness of fresh fruits.

    EGGEDOSIS: With an electric mixer set at high speed, whip together the 5 egg yolks, 2 egg whites and sugar. When the mixture has thickened to a custardlike consistency, add the brandy (or rum). To make by hand, whip the yolks and whites to a froth with a wire whisk before gradually beating in the sugar. Continue to beat vigorously until the mixture thickens; then beat in the liquor. Serve immediately in a chilled dish along with the fruit.

Sour-cream waffles in a heart pattern emerge hot and crisp from a modern Norwegian waffle iron—to be eaten with cold lingonberries and fresh butter. In the old days many families owned special irons, made and embossed by the local blacksmith with individual patterns.

Fløtevafler
SOUR-CREAM WAFFLES

Beat the eggs and sugar together for 5 to 10 minutes in an electric mixer or by hand with a wire whisk until it falls back into the bowl in a lazy ribbon when the beater is lifted out. Now, with a rubber spatula, alternately fold in half the flour, cardamom (or ginger), and sour cream, and then the remaining flour. Lightly stir in the melted butter and set the batter aside for 10 minutes. If you use a nonelectric Norwegian waffle iron, heat it, ungreased, until it is so hot that a drop of water sputters when flicked across its surface. Pour about ¾ cup of the batter in the center of the hot iron, close the top and cook over direct heat for 5 minutes on each side. Serve with lingonberry or another tart jam. This batter may be used in any regular American electric waffle iron and cooked according to the instructions for that iron.

Makes 6 waffles

5 eggs
½ cup sugar
1 cup flour, sifted
1 teaspoon ground cardamom
 or ginger
1 cup sour cream
4 tablespoons unsalted butter, melted

IV

Sweden's Groaning Board

"A *smörgåsbord,*" says a happy character in a Swedish novel, "can never be too big." And perhaps because it really cannot be too big, this gigantic feast, this symbol of appetite unleashed—for some to the point of gluttony —has so captured the imagination of non-Scandinavians that it has been imitated throughout the world. Shorn of its accent marks, the word for this gastronomic extravaganza has even come over into English. But away from its homeland, smorgasbord is, all too often, an excuse for offering everybody a little of everything—or, for that matter, anything.

In Sweden, the country of its origin, the *smörgåsbord* (which translates as the preposterously understated phrase "bread and butter table") remains pure in concept—a carefully worked out, carefully arranged feast that is a source of family pride when prepared at home, of national pride when laid out resplendently in a restaurant. It is comprised of many of Sweden's finest delicacies, whose roots stretch deep into the past. And the impression the *smörgåsbord* makes at its most magnificent is of beauty and riches—and therein lies one of its drawbacks. Anyone with a serious intention of eating his way through or around it, as the case may be, will find himself in fairly short order defeated by its parade of dishes. I remember my own misgivings during my first encounter with a homemade *smörgåsbord* in Sweden many years ago. I was naïve enough to think—after putting away several kinds of bread with butter, herring (both pickled and smoked), shrimp, pickles, meatballs, smoked reindeer, boiled potatoes, asparagus soufflé, mushroom soufflé, beer and aquavit—that I had come to the end of the meal. But, no: my plate was whisked away, another was put in its place,

The world's finest *smörgåsbord* is served at Stockholm's Operakällaren Restaurant. The two-tiered table is 25 feet long, and offers more than 60 selections, from salty herring specialties *(foreground)* to hot dishes *(far end)*. The centerpiece is a ceramic aquavit dispenser.

and I was invited to begin the meal proper—pork chops, peas and carrots, pickled tomatoes, applesauce, lingonberry preserves, French bread and red wine, cookies, coffee and (liquor rationing still being in effect at the time) a homemade fruit cordial.

But the home *smörgåsbord* is nothing compared to the restaurant version. I think of the restaurant *smörgåsbord* in terms of fire and ice, and not only because the drink that goes with it is chilled *brännvin*—"burned" wine, another name for aquavit. At one end of the table are the cold dishes, at the other end the hot, and in between is ranged a spectrum of salads, cold cuts and meats. The star performer here is not the smoked salmon, excellent as it may be, or the caviar, a precious heap of black pearls, or the tiny meatballs, beloved by all, but the humble herring. And though the herring may appear a dozen or more times on such a *smörgåsbord*, it will never look, nor will it ever taste, exactly the same way twice. This, I must say, surprised me.

Before going to Scandinavia, I had, like many Americans, thought of the herring as a kind of standard fish, always more or less of the same size, weight, flavor, always marinated in sour cream or pickled, and eaten only as an appetizer. But to my enormous pleasure I have since learned otherwise. I now know facts about the herring as irrelevant as its strange habit of sneezing when caught (a rush of air from its air bladder) or its tendency, during a certain time of year, to float around in the sea, on its head or its tail, in a trance so deep that no amount of light shone into its eyes will snap it awake. But more important I know that you cannot make any general statements about the herring.

A fish of great versatility

The herring exists in several species and its quality fluctuates from place to place and year to year; its excellence also varies according to whether it has spawned or not. Even its size depends to a large extent on the relative salinity and temperature of the water in which it swims. The Icelandic deep-sea herring (of which Sweden is the biggest importer) is always larger than herring caught in Norwegian waters, and the Norwegian herring in turn is larger than the Baltic herring, which the Swedes call *strömming* except when it is smoked and then it is called *böckling*. All the rest they call *sill*. *Sill* is most often salted and must be soaked in water to eliminate the brine before it can be eaten.

To the basic natural variety of the herring, Swedish cooks bring an expertise that makes this fatty fish seem still more versatile, and in this area their supremacy over the Norwegians and Danes (themselves no mean herring fanciers) rests almost entirely on the numerous ways the Swedes have of preparing it for the *smörgåsbord*. They fillet it, slice it, cut it up in tidbits. They marinate it, pickle it. They serve it jellied, fried, layered in casseroles, stewed, baked, wound up like little watch springs on blocks of ice. They ring a hundred tongue-prickling, mouth-watering changes on it through shifting combinations of white and red vinegars, salt and sugar, black and white pepper, powdered mustard, ginger, horse-radish, crushed mustard seed and allspice. And always they succeed in making it look beautiful by serving it with bracelets and chains of red and yellow sliced onion, sprinklings of parsley and chives, garnishes of whole bay leaf and cubes of carrot, gray-green capers and bright green feathers of dill, chopped hard-boiled eggs, billows and furrows of sour cream, scarlet cubes of beet and translucent slices of cucumber.

Considering the staggering numbers of herring dishes alone offered by the *smörgåsbord*, is it any wonder that people arriving at this table for the first time often do so in trepidation? Where to begin? What to eat next? And how to end? Perhaps a *smörgåsbord* can never be too big, but Liet, my wife, and I found ourselves overwhelmed by the one we found at Stockholm's Operakällaren Restaurant, considered by all to be the finest in Sweden. The table was moored, like an enormous pleasure yacht, in the middle of the room, its decks crowded with no less than 60 selections. Luckily the owner, Tore Wretman, a gracious man whose reputation as the authority on the *smörgåsbord* goes unchallenged in Scandinavia, came to our rescue and revealed to us the logic of the meal—the order in which it should be eaten. But first he delivered us a friendly warning: "Make as many visits to the table as you like, but do not overload your plates with too many different foods at the same time—it hardly stimulates the appetite and does not do full justice to the individual delicacies."

Essence of the smörgåsbord

We started with the herring buffet, the salty part of the *smörgåsbord*. Here, at the forward end of the table, the prow, so to speak, were spread at least 20 cold herring dishes, several kinds of crisp breads and an assortment of strong and mild cheeses. We decided to try two of the most traditional specialties first; without these a *smörgåsbord* cannot be called a *smörgåsbord*. I helped myself to the pickled herring, *inlagd sill*, and my wife took the marinated *glasmästarsill*, or glassblower's herring *(page 98)*. This strange name probably arose because the fish is cut up and placed in glass jars with tingling spices, carrots, onions, vinegar and sugar *(see cover)*. My *inlagd sill* had been made from a whole salt herring, sliced diagonally into bite-sized pieces which were then reassembled to look like the whole fish. Over these had been poured a sweet-sour pickle solution containing bay leaf and crumbled allspice, and then a garnish of red onion rings had been laid on top. The effect of both of these dishes on us was electrifying, instantly setting the gastric juices to flowing, and we wondered why herring that appetizing is not available at home. Now we know: the tastiness comes not so much from the fish as from the kind and proportions of the vinegar and the sugar. Swedish white vinegar is more acid than ours, and Swedish cooks do not stint on the sugar. This combination of opposites complements the salty flavor of the herring underneath.

Faced by the expanse of table still awaiting us, we nevertheless went back to the first part. Liet was going to settle for a slice of cheese and a rye crisp to go with it, but then her eye wandered over the *fågelbo*, or bird's nest *(page 99)*, a charmingly eccentric little dish made at the Operakällaren from chopped lettuce (although chopped parsley is often substituted) and onion, pickled beets, capers and finely diced Swedish anchovies (actually sprats or young herring and very salty). The lettuce and various other ingredients had been arranged in concentric rings, like a target. Set into this nest were raw eggs on the half shell. Unable to resist the appearance of the dish, Liet made off with some of the *fågelbo,* including a yolk. The idea was to mix the yolk and other components together, and this she did. (Some Swedes prefer to sauté the mixture quickly.) She found bird's nest sharp and pungent.

Having had the merits of the *strömming,* the Baltic herring, sung to me by various Swedes, I determined to try at least two of the dishes on the *smörgåsbord* made from it. The first consisted of *strömming* baked under a layer of dill-sprinkled sliced tomatoes. In flavor it was not unlike another great Swedish favorite, crayfish; indeed, it is sometimes called poor man's crayfish. My second *strömming* selection had a distinctly novel flavor. Each *strömming* had been split in half and soaked in a rich batter of cream, egg yolks and light, fine flour, then salted, folded together again, dredged in coarse rye flour and sautéed to a golden turn. A herring prepared in this way can be eaten warm, but in this case, while still piping hot, it had been put in a sweet-sour marinade, seasoned with chopped dill and diced onions, and allowed to cool in the refrigerator before being served. The crust had soaked up the marinade, but the fish it sheathed was light and flaky and delicately sweet underneath.

Appetites continuously stimulated

Now was the time for a change of plates and regrets for having to move on without tasting other tempting dishes such as the *kaviartopp,* or caviar mound, the cod roe in dill dressing, the red *löjrom* (roe from a tiny Swedish fresh-water fish served on hard-boiled egg halves with chopped onion), the jellied salmon fins, the herring salad and many others. But stalwart and still hungry (if anything, hungrier), we advanced on the second part of the *smörgåsbord,* the cold buffet, which occupied both sides of the table. Here again the choice seemed limitless: egg dishes of all sorts, smoked and jellied eel, smoked and dill-cured salmon, spareribs, fish salads, roasted veal, pickled cucumbers and beets, liver paste, head cheese, cured ham, jellied pig's feet.

I headed for my favorite, *gravlax*—here a great pink slab of salmon, speckled with broken white peppercorns *(page 27).* And so did Liet. Although we had had *gravlax* several times before, we found that we could not resist an opportunity to have it again; and now that we are adept at making it and its accompanying dill-mustard sauce at home *(Recipe Booklet),* we still have not grown tired of it. And we have learned that *gravlax* can also be delicious when sliced and lightly sautéed.

Moving on down the table, we helped ourselves to Westcoast Salad, a specialty of that fish-blessed area of Sweden. This dish is made from cold boiled lobster or crab, shrimp, mussels, sliced raw mushrooms, tomato wedges and small green peas, over all of which a dressing freshened with chopped dill has been poured. Like the *gravlax,* Westcoast Salad has a gentle character and a clean flavor.

Changing plates once again (there seemed always to be an unobtrusive waiter on hand to carry away the soiled ones), I went back to the *smörgåsbord* to try the jellied veal, a shimmering loaf in which flecks of pink meat lay crowded tightly together. I could taste both the thyme and bay leaf

How to Approach a Smörgåsbord

FIRST STEP: HERRING

In the traditional ritual of the table, the Swedes always begin with herring —perhaps, as here, with six selections. Running clockwise from the bay leaf at the upper left: glassblower's herring; fried, marinated herring; home-cured herring; herring and sour cream; smoked herring; and pickled herring.

SECOND STEP: FISH PLATE

After herring (and a change of plates), other fish dishes are eaten. The selection seen here—one of many possibilities—includes smoked salmon and eel, smoked and fried salmon fins, and poached, jellied salmon with mayonnaise. A cold, vinegar-sharp cucumber salad stimulates the palate.

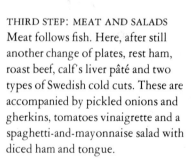

THIRD STEP: MEAT AND SALADS

Meat follows fish. Here, after still another change of plates, rest ham, roast beef, calf's liver pâté and two types of Swedish cold cuts. These are accompanied by pickled onions and gherkins, tomatoes vinaigrette and a spaghetti-and-mayonnaise salad with diced ham and tongue.

FOURTH STEP: HOT DISHES

The final serving comprises such hot dishes as Swedish meatballs (properly prepared without sauce), Jansson's Temptation, deep-fried parsley, herring au gratin, mushroom omelet and a tomato-doused croquette of fowl. Off-camera: a dessert of cheese or fruit salad.

that had gone into the loaf, and I made sure to have with it pickled beets, with which, as I discovered, the veal harmonizes perfectly. I could have gone on and sampled more of the dishes on the cold buffet, but the third part of the *smörgåsbord*, the hot buffet, lay waiting down at the end, and there was no ignoring it.

In Swedish this section is called the *småvarmt*—the small warm. I wonder why, for since there is nothing small about it, Liet and I felt constrained once again to choose wisely, but well. We decided to start with Jansson's Temptation *(Jansson's frestelse)*, an anchovy and julienne potato casserole, baked with cream and onions *(page 100)*. This was a mistake; not because we failed to like this delicious dish but because, as we found out later, we should, according to custom, have eaten it at the start of the *smörgåsbord*, along with the other salty herring dishes. Here was a case of ignorance indeed being bliss.

There are many stories as to how Jansson's Temptation got its name: according to one, the dish is named after Erik Janson, the 19th Century Swedish religious zealot and self-appointed prophet who took his disciples to America and founded a colony called Bishop Hill in Illinois. Although adamantly opposed to the pleasures of the flesh, one day Janson found himself so sorely tempted by this crusty dish that he threw over his principles to eat some—in secret, of course. And as the tale goes, he was caught in the act by a disillusioned follower. The story is a good one but undoubtedly apocryphal—Jansson and Janson are not even spelled the same way—but it does serve to show what the dish can do to a Swede. Its popularity in Sweden is roughly comparable to that of pizza in America, and its briny taste seems to give people a feeling of being in instant communication with the sea. When Mediterranean anchovies are used in place of the salty Swedish variety, the dish is no less rich, only milder. Swedes frequently serve beer and Jansson's Temptation as a kind of *nattmat*, night food, which is offered just before a party breaks up to make sure that the guests go out into the cold and darkness with something warm and strong in their stomachs.

A mistake sensibly compounded

Having made our mistake, each of us compounded it by choosing two stuffed onion rolls, *lökdolmar*, to eat with the onion-flavored Jansson's Temptation. And again we did not mind. These were made from onions that had been parboiled and then pulled apart leaf by leaf; onto the individual leaves a little seasoned ground meat had been spooned and the leaves rolled up around it. Baked in the oven, they were moist and smooth in their succulent wrapping *(page 99)*. This dish is supposed to have originated in the stuffed grape and fig leaves of the Middle East. Legend has it that King Charles XII brought the idea for onion rolls back to Sweden after his release from captivity in Turkey at the beginning of the 18th Century. But in cool Sweden a substitute had to be found for grape leaves, and thus cooks came to use onion and cabbage leaves instead. Whatever the origin, *lökdolmar*, along with stuffed cabbage, are both important dishes in the Swedish cuisine today, and very good ones.

We were now well satisfied, but there could be no turning away from the *smörgåsbord* without sampling a few of the tiny meatballs *(page 98)*. Although Swedes insist to a man that no meatballs are quite so good as mother's, we found these excellent and assumed that they had been made by someone's mother. They were a light, fine blend of ground veal, beef, pork and bread crumbs, seasoned with only a little onion, salt and pepper, and they were free of the unctuous gravy that so often clings to Swedish meatballs presented on the *smörgåsbord* table in the United States. But light and good though they were, we found ourselves incapable of returning to the table for any further helpings. We passed up the dessert of fruit salad and had a cup of coffee.

A restaurant for relaxing

Now we sat back to enjoy ourselves and to watch the activity that surrounded us, secure in the knowledge that no one would come along with the check and hustle us out simply because we had stopped eating. The Operakällaren is a wonderful place to relax—one of those crisp, efficiently run restaurants, all too rare in the world, where time, like food, is recognized as a luxury. Here waiters function almost as unseen presences and the maître d'hôtel whisks around in tails and a high, starched collar so stiff and tight it balloons out his pink, razor-smoothed cheeks. The spacious room in which the *smörgåsbord* sits by day (the *smörgåsbord* is a daytime meal in Sweden) dates from the late 19th Century and could be ironically identified in style perhaps as Late German Renaissance Revival. The walls of the room are paneled in a rich, dark wood; the windows are tall and wide; the brass chandeliers are massive. The floor, which is richly carpeted, has such breadth and sweep that tables can be set far enough apart to keep conversations at one table from mingling with those at the next. While Liet and I rested deep down inside ourselves, we watched with amused contentment as new arrivals flocked to the *smörgåsbord* and made quick, eager dives at it, like so many hungry seagulls.

Hard as I found it to believe, I learned from studies made by Professor Gösta Berg, a cultural historian, that the *smörgåsbord* has had a checkered career in Sweden, that it almost died out a few years ago and that it is not the ancient feast everyone imagines it to be. In its present incarnation, it goes back to the 1880s when food, both in its appearance and proportions, could be as full blown as the decor that surrounded it. And, strangely, one of the things that helped give the *smörgåsbord* its start was canning. This new method of preserving food opened up to the Swedes the possibility of laying a really lavish table, stretched to the limits of credibility with out-of-season fish, roe and liver paste specialties and other ready-prepared delicacies in tins; even today no one is embarrassed when herring is placed on the table in open cans.

Still another impetus to the development of the *smörgåsbord* was the invention of the steam engine and the building of railroads. With large numbers of people traveling long distances, new hotels had to be built to lodge them, new restaurants opened to feed them, and none of these could be considered worthy of the designation "grand" if it did not feature a *smörgåsbord* of majestic proportions.

A charming description of the preparations attendant upon just one such hotel *smörgåsbord* exists in F. N. Piraten's book, *The Goat in the Garden*. The atmosphere is one of tension and expectancy; it is Monday morning in early spring and the doors to the dining room have not yet been opened. The headwaiter, all nervous efficiency, oversees the busboy, a pale 13-year-old whose single ambition is to become a headwaiter, diligently stacking bread "in the northeast and southwest corners of the table." Three girls with trays begin to fill up the empty areas of the table with food. Two hams, one cured and one boiled, are placed at the foot of the imposing aquavit dispenser with its six taps that enable the diner to choose his favorite among the six different flavors contained within it. The headwaiter adjusts the silverware and the aquavit glasses, which are flanked by seven kinds of herring, canned anchovies, sardines, eels and cold fried pork. Platter after platter arrive at the table. Mountains of food build up. Now, with only minutes to go before opening time the headwaiter bends over the table to test the temperature of the aquavit dispenser with the back of his hand. Finding it just the right degree of coolness, he lights the chandelier and compares his watch with the clock on the wall. The *smörgåsbord* has been assembled and the aquavit dispenser, in appearance a cross between a samovar and a milk can, dominates it, like "a church in the middle of the village." Hotel Horn is ready to receive its guests.

Although the *smörgåsbord* as it is known to the world today took shape in the late 19th Century, there had already existed in Sweden a tradition for putting all the food to be eaten at one meal out on the table at one time. People had begun doing this as early as the 16th Century, and by the 18th Century it was the custom in most homes; why, no one seems to know—perhaps for convenience. A couple of English visitors found it an appalling way to serve a meal, and wrote about it individually and at some length. What dismayed them even more than the poor taste displayed in the arrangement of the various dishes on the table was the fact that the food grew cold as a result of the ritual that preceded the meal. Guests were invited to put an edge on their appetites before sitting down to eat by helping themselves to herring, cheese, bread and aquavit from a separate "aquavit table." While one of the Englishmen was willing to lay this all to the cold, damp weather and the need for sustaining fare, the other could find no excuse for it whatsoever and complained that the Swedes' meals were like their compliments, a caricature of the French. What he had in mind is not entirely clear; perhaps he saw the aquavit table as a parody of the French *hors-d'oeuvre variés*.

Revival of a fading tradition

When the big *smörgåsbord* came into existence, it grew out of the aquavit table; in a sense, this table is still there as the cold buffet, the first part of the feast. Anyone who may have wondered why the Swedes often eat cheese or pot cheese, *potkäs*, at the beginning of the *smörgåsbord* rather than at the end now has the answer: custom, especially when it is several centuries old, dies hard. The aquavit table survives in another way: the SOS that appears under the appetizer heading on many Swedish menus is nothing more than the abbreviation for *smör, ost och sill*—butter and bread, cheese and herring. SOS can be considered the *smörgåsbord* in its most scaled-down version. The *smörgåsbord,* for all the veneration in which it was held, nearly disappeared from the Swedish scene a dozen or so years ago. During World War II the government prohibited it, and not until 1949, when the food shortage was over, could it be served in restaurants again. By then, however, the pressures and spiraling costs of postwar living were standing in the way of its full revival. It took too much time and effort to prepare, and many worried about how fattening it could be. It disappeared from one restaurant after another, and, even as a fixture at large family gatherings at home, it was sliding toward extinction. Understandably, Swedes who cared about good food were alarmed, and several determined to do something about it.

Among these was Tore Wretman, the owner of the Operakällaren. A cook as well as a restaurateur, Wretman, who is also caterer to the royal household, was an effective spokesman for Swedish food. One thing he did was to revive interest in the *smörgåsbord* through his radio and television shows; he publicized tradition. Another thing he accomplished was to create a *smörgåsbord* for the Operakällaren, the likes of which had never been seen before, and which now serves as a model for all.

A return to authenticity

When Wretman set out, he faced an unusual task—less a matter of reviving or restoring the *smörgåsbord* than returning it to its traditional Swedish form. Abroad it had been adapted to other tastes and in most cases distorted beyond recognition, and yet the foreign versions were asserting that they were the legitimate heirs to the ancient Swedish tradition. Wretman wanted to make his as authentic as possible, a showcase for his country's cuisine, yet he also wanted to give it a modern look. This meant ridding the *smörgåsbord* of the furbelows—the swans made of ice and the fruit contrived to look like flowers—that had been part of its inheritance from the 1880s. Wretman worked closely with a ceramicist on the design of a set of serving plates that would resist decoration of any sort. The plates they eventually came up with are for the most part sharp-cornered and rimless; they fit closely together on the table, so that, when they are laden with food, they form a colorful mosaic.

That Wretman and the others who went to the rescue of the *smörgåsbord* succeeded in saving it is more than evinced by its return to restaurants. It has also, to some degree, come back to the home, although here the giant meal of the past is indeed a thing of the past. But whereas many housewives were about to abandon the *smörgåsbord* altogether a few years ago, they have since found in its variety many possibilities for convenient yet gracious home entertaining, and what they now do is pick and choose among possible dishes and serve only their favorites. An example of such a modified *smörgåsbord* is shown on pages 96-97, for which there are recipes on pages 98 through 100 and elsewhere in the book; such a *smörgåsbord* should be as easy for an American to prepare as for a Swede, especially since some of the foods used can be bought ready-made. And still another example is the miniature *smörgåsbord* depicted on page 101—small enough to be arranged on a couple of platters, complete enough in its flavors to be quintessentially Swedish.

Smörgåsbord

A tempting *smörgåsbord* that any housewife could prepare for a merry occasion is pictured on the next two pages, roughly arranged in the traditional serving order. Cold dishes are shown on a block of ice, room-temperature dishes on a bare board and piping-hot dishes on a red tablecloth.

ICE-COLD DISHES
1 "Save the Family"—fillets of *matjes* herring surrounded by a ring of sour cream topped with mounds of chopped egg, parsley and sliced radishes.
2 Cucumber salad, to be eaten as a condiment with other food.
3 Chopped chives, a garnish.
4 Herring salad, with sliced eggs.
5 Sour-cream sauce for herring salad (pink because it contains beet juice).

ROOM-TEMPERATURE DISHES
6 "Bird's Nest," or "Eye of the Sun" —chopped parsley, red beets, capers, onions and anchovies encircling a raw egg yolk.
7 Halves of hard-cooked eggs filled with red cod roe and Danish caviar.
8 Mustard sauce for *gravlax.*
9 *Gravlax.*
10 Liver paste.
11 Sliced cucumber, to garnish the liver paste.
12 Swedish cheeses, including a spiced cheese, Fontina and Herrgård, usually eaten to end the meal.
13 An assortment of Scandinavian breads, including two Swedish rye crisps, a Finnish crisp and a Danish rye.

PIPING-HOT DISHES
14 "Jansson's Temptation"—potato strips, onions, anchovies, cream, topped with bread crumbs and baked.
15 Swedish meatballs.
16 Onion rolls stuffed with meatballs.

A Smörgåsbord Sampler

To serve 6 to 8 (about 50 meatballs)

1 tablespoon butter
4 tablespoons finely chopped onion
1 large boiled potato, mashed (1 cup)
3 tablespoons fine dry bread crumbs
1 pound lean ground beef
1/3 cup heavy cream
1 teaspoon salt
1 egg
1 tablespoon finely chopped fresh
    parsley (optional)
2 tablespoons butter
2 tablespoons vegetable oil
1 tablespoon flour
3/4 cup light or heavy cream

To serve 6 to 8

PICKLING LIQUID
3/4 cup white vinegar
1/2 cup water
1/2 cup sugar

2 salted herring, 1 to 1 1/2 pounds
    each, cleaned and scraped, and
    soaked in cold water for 12 hours,
    or substitute 4 canned *matjes*
    herring fillets
1 1/2-inch piece fresh horse-radish root,
    scraped and thinly sliced, or
    substitute 2 tablespoons prepared
    horse-radish, drained and squeezed
    dry in a kitchen towel
1 medium carrot, scraped and thinly
    sliced (3/4 cup)
2 small onions, preferably red,
    peeled and thinly sliced (3/4 cup)
1/4-inch piece scraped ginger root,
    thinly sliced (optional)
2 teaspoons whole allspice
2 teaspoons whole yellow mustard
    seeds
3 small bay leaves

Små Köttbullar
SMALL SWEDISH MEATBALLS

In a small frying pan, melt the tablespoon of butter over moderate heat. When the foam subsides, add the onions and cook for about 5 minutes, until they are soft and translucent but not brown.

In a large bowl, combine the onions, mashed potato, bread crumbs, meat, cream, salt, egg and optional parsley. Knead vigorously with both hands or beat with a wooden spoon until all of the ingredients are well blended and the mixture is smooth and fluffy. Shape into small balls about 1 inch in diameter. Arrange the meatballs in one layer on a baking sheet or a flat tray, cover them with plastic wrap and chill for at least 1 hour before cooking.

Over high heat, melt the 2 tablespoons of butter and 2 tablespoons of oil in a heavy 10- to 12-inch skillet. When the foam subsides, add the meatballs, 8 to 10 at a time. Reduce the heat to moderate and fry the balls on all sides, shaking the pan almost constantly to roll the balls around in the hot fat to help keep their shape. In 8 to 10 minutes the meatballs should be brown outside and show no trace of pink inside when one is broken open with a knife. Add more butter and oil as needed, and transfer each finished batch to a casserole or baking dish and keep warm in a 200° oven.

If the meatballs are to be served as a main course with noodles or potatoes, you may want to make a sauce with the pan juice. Remove from the heat, pour off all but a thin film of fat from the pan, and stir in 1 tablespoon of flour. Quickly stir in 3/4 cup of light or heavy cream, scraping up any browned bits clinging to the pan. Boil the sauce over moderate heat for 2 or 3 minutes, stirring constantly, until it is thick and smooth. Pour over the meatballs and serve.

If the meatballs are to be served as an hors d'oeuvre or as part of a *smörgåsbord,* they should be cooked as above, but formed into smaller balls and served without the sauce.

Glasmästarsill
GLASSBLOWER'S HERRING

Bring the vinegar, water and sugar to a boil in a 1- to 1 1/2-quart enameled or stainless-steel saucepan, stirring constantly until the sugar completely dissolves. Then remove the pan from the heat and let the pickling liquid cool to room temperature.

Meanwhile, wash the herring in cold running water and cut them crosswise into 1-inch pieces. Arrange a thin layer of onions in a 1-quart glass jar (a Mason jar, if possible) equipped with a tightly fitting cover. Top with a few slices of herring, carrots, ginger root and horse-radish, and scatter with allspice, mustard seeds and a bay leaf. Repeat until all of the ingredients have been used, making 3 or 4 layers.

Pour the cool pickling liquid into the jar; it should just cover the contents. Close the jar securely and refrigerate it for 2 or 3 days. Serve as an appetizer, or as part of the *smörgåsbord.*

Lökdolmar
STUFFED ONION ROLLS

Place the peeled onions in a 2- to 3-quart pot, add enough cold water to cover, and bring to a boil over moderate heat. Lower the heat and simmer the onions, uncovered, for 40 minutes. Remove the onions from the pot with a slotted spoon, drain them and let them cool on a platter while you make the meat stuffing *(opposite)*.

Pull off each onion layer separately. They should slide off quite easily. Cut the largest outer layers of the onions in half, but remember to leave them large enough to enclose the stuffing. Discard the inner part of the onions (or use them for some other purpose) if the leaves are too small to stuff. Put a heaping teaspoon of the meat stuffing in the middle of each onion leaf and enclose it by folding over the edges of the leaf. (At this point they may be covered with plastic wrap and refrigerated for up to 2 days before cooking.)

Preheat the oven to 400°. In a shallow 1- to 1½-quart flameproof baking dish, melt 3 tablespoons of butter over low heat. Remove the dish from the heat and place the onion rolls, sealed side down, side by side in the butter, first rolling each in the butter to coat it. Bake 15 minutes, then baste with the butter in the dish, sprinkle with the bread crumbs, and bake another 15 minutes, until the onions are lightly browned and the crumbs crisp. *Lökdolmar* may be served as part of a *smörgåsbord*, or as a main dish.

To serve 4 to 6

½ Swedish meatball recipe *(opposite)*
3 large yellow onions (½ pound each), peeled
3 tablespoons butter
2 tablespoons fresh bread crumbs

Familjens Räddning
"SAVE THE FAMILY" HERRING PLATTER

This dish is composed of bits of food (often leftovers) often on hand in Scandinavian kitchens. It makes a pleasant cold luncheon or late-supper dish, and can also be part of the smörgåsbord.

Arrange the herring fillets side by side on a long chilled platter. With a sharp, heavy knife, make diagonal cuts ½ inch apart through both fillets. Spread the sour cream (or sour cream and mayonnaise) in a circle around the herring fillets. On the border of the platter, arrange alternate mounds of chopped egg white, egg yolk, cucumbers, beets and parsley.

To serve 2

2 fillets of canned *matjes* or pickled herring, drained
½ cup sour cream, or ¼ cup sour cream combined with ¼ cup mayonnaise
2 hard-cooked eggs, the whites and yolks finely chopped separately
1 small cucumber, peeled, halved, seeded and finely chopped or ½ cup pickled cucumbers *(page 48)*
½ cup finely chopped pickled beets, canned or freshly made *(page 48)*
¼ cup finely chopped parsley

Fågelbo
BIRD'S NEST

This dish should be served on individual plates and is called a Bird's Nest *(fågelbo)* or an Eye of the Sun *(solöga)* because the ingredients are arranged around a raw egg yolk. Place 1 egg cup, cookie cutter or small juice glass in the center of each of 4 salad plates to reserve a space for the egg yolks. On each plate make a border around the glass with a thin ring of chopped anchovies, then a ring of chopped onions, one of capers, one of chopped pickled beets and one of chopped fresh parsley. The plates may be prepared ahead of time and refrigerated. Before serving, remove the glass from each plate and replace it with a raw egg yolk. Each person then mixes his own ingredients at the table. This may be served as a first course, as part of a *smörgåsbord*, or as a late-supper snack with beer.

To serve 4

1 two-ounce can of flat anchovy fillets, drained and finely chopped
½ cup finely chopped onions
⅓ cup capers, drained, washed, dried and chopped
½ cup finely chopped pickled beets, canned or freshly made *(page 48)*
½ cup finely chopped parsley
4 raw egg yolks

To serve 4 to 6

7 medium boiling potatoes, peeled and
 cut into strips 2 inches long and
 ¼ inch thick
2½ tablespoons butter
2 tablespoons vegetable oil
2 to 3 large yellow onions, thinly
 sliced (4 cups)
16 flat anchovy fillets, drained
White pepper
2 tablespoons fine dry bread crumbs
2 tablespoons butter, cut into
 ¼-inch bits
½ cup milk
1 cup heavy cream

Jansson's Frestelse
JANSSON'S TEMPTATION

Preheat the oven to 400°. Place the potato strips in cold water to keep them from discoloring. Heat 2 tablespoons of butter and 2 tablespoons of oil in a 10- to 12-inch skillet; when the foam subsides, add the onions and cook 10 minutes, stirring frequently, until they are soft but not brown.

With a pastry brush or paper towel, spread a 1½- to 2-quart soufflé dish or baking dish with the remaining half tablespoon of butter. Drain the potatoes and pat them dry with paper towels. Arrange a layer of potatoes on the bottom of the dish and then alternate layers of onions and anchovies, ending with potatoes. Sprinkle each layer with a little white pepper. Scatter bread crumbs over the top layer of potatoes and dot the crumbs with the bits of butter. In a small saucepan, heat the milk and cream until the mixture barely simmers, then pour it slowly down the sides of the dish. Bake in the center of the oven for 45 minutes, or until the potatoes are tender when pierced with the tip of a sharp knife and the liquid is nearly absorbed.

Makes 6 sandwiches or 24 hors d'oeuvre

½ loaf day-old homemade-type white
 bread, unsliced
10 anchovy fillets, finely chopped
4 tablespoons softened butter
2 tablespoons prepared mustard
4 hard-cooked eggs, finely chopped
¼ cup finely chopped dill, or ¼ cup
 combined dill, parsley and chives
⅛ teaspoon freshly ground black
 pepper
2 tablespoons butter
2 tablespoons vegetable oil

Vårsmörgåsar
SPRING SANDWICHES

Trim the crusts from the loaf of bread and cut it into 12 slices ⅛ inch thick. In a small bowl, mash together the chopped anchovies, butter, mustard, eggs, herbs and pepper. The mixture should be quite smooth. Thickly spread it on 6 slices of bread. Top each slice with another piece of bread, and lightly press them together. At this point, the sandwiches may be wrapped in wax paper and refrigerated for up to 3 days or even frozen (they should be thoroughly defrosted before using).

Over moderate heat, melt the butter and oil in a 10- to 12-inch skillet. When the foam subsides, add the sandwiches, 2 or 3 at a time, and fry for 2 to 3 minutes on each side, until they are crisp and golden brown. Drain on paper towels and serve while hot, either whole as a main luncheon course or a snack, or cut in quarters to accompany cocktails.

To serve 4

3 large boiling potatoes, peeled and
 cut into ⅛-inch-thick slices
1 large onion, thinly sliced
2½ tablespoons butter
2 *matjes* herring fillets, cut in ½-inch
 diagonal slices
Freshly ground black pepper
1 tablespoon fine bread crumbs
⅓ cup light or heavy cream
1 tablespoon butter, cut into tiny bits

Sillgratin
HERRING AND POTATO CASSEROLE

Preheat the oven to 400°. Place the potato slices in a bowl of cold water to prevent them from discoloring. Heat 2 tablespoons of the butter in a small frying pan; when the foam subsides, add the sliced onions and cook them over moderate heat, stirring frequently, for 5 to 8 minutes, or until the onions are soft and transparent but not brown. Set them aside.

Choose a 1- to 1½-quart baking dish attractive enough to bring to the table and, with a pastry brush, spread with the remaining ½ tablespoon of butter. Drain the potatoes and pat them dry with paper towels. Arrange alternate layers of potatoes, herring and onions in the baking dish, seasoning each layer lightly with pepper and ending with a layer of potatoes. Pour in the cream, sprinkle the top layer of potatoes with bread crumbs and dot with the bits of butter. Bring to a boil on top of the stove, then bake for 1 hour, or until the potatoes are tender when pierced with the tip of a sharp knife. Serve from the baking dish.

Moving clockwise around the egg-shaped glass centerpiece (starting at 9 o'clock), a miniature *smörgåsbord* includes: toasted bread circles topped with crab-meat stew; meatballs and tiny onions on toothpicks; cherry tomatoes filled with cream cheese and bacon; sliced cheese topped with cucumber and radish slices, and cucumber slices topped with egg slices and caviar; sautéed spring sandwiches, and beef à la Lindström on bread circles; mushrooms filled with liver paste and topped with crumbled bacon, and boiled-potato slices topped with herring, dill and sour cream. Recipes can be found by consulting the Recipe Index.

V

A Return to Native Cookery

The Swedes are the wealthiest, the most powerful and the most worldly of all the Scandinavians. They build skyscrapers in Stockholm, satellite communities outside. They drive around in expensive cars of Swedish and foreign make, and they travel abroad a great deal. As they grow more and more worldly, they become more and more sophisticated in their tastes. They import all kinds of foodstuffs—artichokes from Spain, green grapes from Southern Europe, blood oranges from Israel, corn-fed beef from America—and what they cannot buy fresh or in season, they now purchase frozen (next to the United States, Sweden is the biggest consumer of frozen foods). Swedes cherish a long and proud tradition of court dining; several of their kings were great gourmets, and a regal influence is evident in some of their most famous dishes, such as royal pot roast *(page 117)* and *kalvfilé Oscar,* which celebrates King Oscar II's love for veal topped with béarnaise sauce, white asparagus and lobster. Of late they have come to know foreign dishes and to experiment with foreign recipes; their recent cookbooks are lavish affairs, veritable compendiums of world cooking. Yet in spite of all these culinary distractions, they have happily not forgotten their own cuisine.

The real Swedish cooking is called *husmanskost,* and it is plain, delicious and charming, a foil to extravagance. In the past this was what people ate every day while reserving the *smörgåsbord* for special occasions; today it is a cherished thing—the remembered cooking of childhood. In a reversal of the Scandinavians' embarrassment over the simplicity of their native dishes, the Swedes have even taken to serving *husmanskost* in some of Stockholm's finest restaurants. The Operakällaren, for one, has found that both Swedes and foreigners relish the style.

The classic *husmanskost* dish is yellow pea soup. During winter most Swedes have it as their regular Thursday night supper, with crisp-edged pancakes and lingonberry preserves for dessert *(page 122)*. This is so strong a custom that a cultural historian with whom I was discussing it felt confident that if he called his home (this being a Thursday) to ask what his wife was making for supper, she would be puzzled by such a silly question and tell him pea soup, of course. He made the call anyway, and then put down the phone and turned to me exasperated. "No pea soup tonight. My boys are home today. They don't want daddy's pea soup." It would seem that in Scandinavia, as elsewhere, even the strongest traditions are subject to the power of individual preferences.

Swedish pea soup is less a soup than it is a porridge or a gruel. It is cooked from dried yellow peas, boiled in water with salt pork and onions, and the skins of the peas are as much a part of its character on the tongue as are the ginger and marjoram that go into it *(page 122)*. How long the Swedes have been eating this *ärter med fläsk* on Thursday nights no one knows. The habit may have begun in the Middle Ages when Sweden was Roman Catholic, and Thursday was often bracketed on the calendar by two meatless days. Putting the salted meat into the pot with the peas not only helped to extend it but made it more palatable.

In touch with a rural past

The loving respect in which this simple soup is held has much to say about the Swedes, who would no more think of changing it or improving it than of leveling the old city in Stockholm to put up a modern development on the site. They may be the most sophisticated of the Scandinavians, but under their urbanity there is a great deal of feeling for country ways. Only 100 years ago 90 per cent of them lived in rural areas; now about 75 per cent live in the city. The Swedes cannot have shaken all the hayseed out of their hair even yet. One sure sign that they have not is the fact that along with their repertoire of more complicated recipes they still make dishes as ancient as salt herring and sour cream; pork sausages fried crisp and served with pickled beets; seaman's beef, a beer-flavored stew; *kalops,* simmered chunks of beef punctuated by allspice and bay *(page 115);* and baked brown beans *(Recipe Booklet)* served with the lean, meaty back bacon often called Canadian bacon in the United States. And though the fruit soups that only a few years ago could precede or follow the main course may now be on their way out, there is one that will never be abandoned—*nyponsoppa*, made from the orange-red seed capsules of the rose, rich in vitamin C and served cold with almonds and clouds of whipped cream. Swedish babies are raised on rose-hip purée. Our baby daughter loved it.

Holding onto these old country foods is one way Swedes have of retaining a connection with the regional past. Salmon pudding—actually a casserole made from salt salmon, sliced raw potatoes and onions with an egg custard on top—marks the table of the city family with its roots in the province of Halland. *Pitepalt,* potato dumplings the size of tennis balls, stuffed with pork, set off the Northerner—and besides, only he will know the right way to eat them. The method is precise: it involves cutting a wedge from the dumpling, removing the core of pork and replacing it with a lump of butter which melts into a subterranean lake. Each small bite of *palt* is then dipped into melted butter.

Many of the old specialties were reserved for festive occasions, and they retain that function today. *Spettekaka,* the towering egg and sugar cake of the southern province of Skåne, continues to be an important feature of the family dinner at holiday time. Such a cake, standing a yard high, takes six to seven dozen eggs and a great deal of confectioners' sugar to make. First the yolks are beaten together with the sugar until almost white and creamy, whereupon a little flour is added and then well-beaten egg whites are folded in. Next this golden batter is fed slowly and arduously onto a rotating cone-shaped spit in front of a low-burning fire. The batter dries layer upon layer in patterns as complex as those of a Jackson Pollock action painting, and the finished cake is an airy marvel to behold. Depending on the season, it can be decorated on top with holly leaves, real flowers or tiny roses made from white, red and green sugar icing. There are several ways of eating *spettekaka:* some people contend that the best way is to start at the bottom—the cake is likely to be chewiest there. But usually window-shaped pieces are gently sawed from the tower with a sharp knife to leave a fragile superstructure. Into this lacework a burning candle may be inserted to send the perfume of the cake through the room and set shadows and lights to dancing on the walls.

Småland, another of Sweden's provinces, has its own festive dessert, a cheesecake that is made with as lavish a hand as *spettekaka*. There are said to be at least 100 different ways of making a good Småland *ostkaka,* but a single recipe is enough to give some idea of its richness. This one calls for a total of 40 cups of milk, four cups of flour, two cups of heavy cream, two and a half cups of sugar, eight eggs and a cup of almonds (with three or four bitter ones thrown in for flavor). After the milk and flour are combined, some rennet is added to the mixture to curdle it and then the whey is strained off. Next, the resulting "cheese" is mixed with the eggs, sugar, ground almonds and cream and baked in a mold. The cake—which is actually more of a pudding—is served cold, often accompanied by cherry compote or strawberry jam.

Importance of an untouched cake

Today, Småland *ostkaka* can be bought ready-made in most shops throughout Sweden, which some people regard as a pity. Ria Wägner, one of the country's TV personalities, recalls the excitement in her parents' home when *ostkaka* was the dessert at parties. Each woman guest would enter the house with a round object—her cake, still in its copper mold and wrapped in a gleaming white damask napkin. The lady would go directly to the kitchen and place her offering on the table with the others. At the end of the meal all of the cakes—often as many as eight—were brought to the dining table, and the donors would expect each to be tasted. The guest of honor would be invited to take the first spoonful, and, if he or she had any manners or sense, would be sure to begin in the middle. Making an *ostkaka* look as little touched as possible the first time around was important because the hole in the middle could be filled with fresh fruit the next day—and the cake be eaten as a "new" dessert.

With the majority of the Swedes now urbanized, the simple *husmanskost* style could be called the country cooking that came to the city to stay. But there is at least one province where it is still going strong: Skåne, the nation's granary and its gastronomic heartland. A tour through Skåne's plump landscape is likely to turn up many of the local specialties, but what these are will depend almost entirely on the season. For example, late summer brings the peas, which are boiled in broth, piled high in a big dish and eaten in the pods which are dipped one by one into egg cups filled with melted butter. But autumn is the best time of all. Goose is eaten then, with everyone looking forward to St. Martin's Eve, November 10, when the bird comes crackling hot from the oven, bursting with apples and prunes. If the dessert is not the fabulous *spettekaka*, it may well be another old-time favorite: apple cake with vanilla sauce *(Recipe Booklet)*, or something lighter, like a fine compote.

Fall is also the season for eel. The natives refer to this time of year as "the time of the eel darkness," and it has a mood all its own. The nights are black and damp, and the eels on their migration back to their ocean breeding grounds southeast of Bermuda in the Sargasso Sea slither into the special traps put out for them around the coast of Skåne and in the waters between Sweden and Denmark. They are taken by the thousands and prepared and eaten in numerous ways—right in the huts where they are smoked (the most fun), at special home dinners or at large banquets. Often an entire meal will be made of them, with the eel soup usually preceding the dessert course.

Veneration of the potato

Even if all these old dishes were still not around to demonstrate how strong a tie the Swede has to the countryside, there would be one item of the daily diet to suggest that the agrarian past is for many of them at least a recent thing—the potato. Many Swedes still eat potatoes at lunch and again at dinner (in contrast to the Danes, Swedes have two warm meals a day), and they do not hold back on them—some put away as many as four or five. "The potato is the frame around the Swedish meal," said one well-fed Stockholmer, throwing out his arms in happy expansion. "We say that without it, eating is not eating." And yet, mindful of calories like many of his countrymen, he confessed that he now forgoes them at lunchtime and sometimes even at dinner.

The Swedes' veneration of the potato is founded in their history. Down through the centuries harvests failed often enough for the Swedes to have known starvation. Not until the potato began to be cultivated on a large scale did the possibility exist—but only the possibility—of there being sufficient food to go around in difficult times. Yet despite its lifesaving role the potato was a long while catching on in Sweden. As early as the middle of the 17th Century, this immigrant vegetable from South America was being grown in a few gardens, but its appeal at that time seems to have derived from its decorative, rather than its food, values.

One of the first to recognize the potato's potential as food was Frederick the Great of Prussia. In the middle of the 18th Century, he not only had seed potatoes distributed to the peasants but compelled each farmer, under the threat of punishment, to plant them. Swedish soldiers who had served in Prussia returned home with praise for this prolific new vegetable, but a prolonged period of plenty stood in the way of its being accepted as anything but food for animals. Then came the famine year of 1771-1772, and the potato, sometimes called the earthpear, made its first appearance on the tables of the poor. "One sees pleasure, yes, sheer joy and health," wrote a Swede of the time, "in the parents and the fat, well-nourished children seated around their earthpear dish." By the 1840s, the Swedes were using such books on potato cookery as *The Potato Friend, an Indispensable Book for Rich and Poor, in Town As Well As in the Country*. The potato had arrived.

Potatoes in glamorous guises

A sure sign of the reverence in which the potato continues to be held in Sweden is the price new potatoes fetch on the market in the spring—anywhere from five to 10 kronor (one to two dollars) per kilo the first week. They are at that time much in demand, and always seem to be in short supply. Anyone with a garden of his own is sure to grow new potatoes. Unearthed when they are plum-sized, they have such tender skins that they are peeled simply by rolling them between the palms of the hands. The rule is not to expose them to air for more than an hour or so. They must be popped into well-salted boiling water with some fresh dill and cooked for 15 minutes or so. Served with really fresh butter and dill, they can taste as good as asparagus—better, the Swedes insist.

Although potatoes go on being boiled, fried and creamed in Sweden, they are now also prepared in ways that make them seem different. And in at least one instance a modicum of American influence can be detected: a potato baked in its jacket will be slit open while steaming hot, buttered inside and filled with as much chilled sour cream as it can hold. Then some pink smoked cod roe will be squeezed onto the sour cream—such roe comes in tubes in Sweden. The effect is not only colorful, but tangy.

If the baked potato Swedish style sounds a little too American to be truly different, there is always the Hasselback potato, peeled and roasted whole, but scored beforehand in such a way that it fans open in the heat of the oven and each rib acquires a crunchy edge *(page 119)*.

Swedes are as fond of French fries as any other people, but some housewives prepare a variation that avoids deep-frying *(page 119)* by using an old method with modern virtues. In this neat trick the potatoes are peeled, cut into wedges, parboiled and then roasted in a lightly buttered baking dish. They come out crisp, mercifully free of the jacket of calorie-rich fat that French fries must wear.

For people who love the crunchiness of pan-fried potatoes, the Swedes have a treat, *rårakor*. They grate up raw potatoes, add a little salt, pepper and chives, and drop this mixture, a couple of tablespoons at a time, onto a hot lightly oiled and buttered frying pan. Spread out into a thin golden lace, the potatoes become deliciously brittle around the edges *(page 119)*.

There is an excitement to Swedish cooking today—as even some of these simple ways with potatoes would suggest. While experimentation with for-

Continued on page 110

Chef Persson grows so fond of the geese he feeds that he stays away for the three days in the fall when they are killed.

Geese and Eels Cooked at an Ancient Village Inn

Like most other countries, Sweden can be divided into gastronomic regions. Easily the most lavishly endowed of these is the southern province of Skåne. At the Skanör Gästgifvaregården, a tavern in the ancient fishing village of Skanör, all the best of this area's splendid cookery may be tasted—like roast goose stuffed with apples and prunes. Here are found, regularly, 15 different kinds of herring dishes, and in the chill days of autumn the chef (*right*) prepares eel in one of the several variations he offers. But because eel is a rich food the inn offers a traditional remedy against indigestion—aquavit in which a branch of wormwood (*opposite*) has been steeped. The bitter herb, in combination with the alcohol, is said to help "cut" the fatty food and rouse the appetite.

Chef Börje Lennart Persson samples his chervil-flavored eel soup. *Opposite:* smoked eels, with shears for clipping off a piece of any desired length; eel baked in a copper pan; and—behind the frosted glasses ready for the aquavit—eel soup and eel baked on straw.

eign recipes grows, people are coming back to native pleasures—finding in *husmanskost* food of distinction. The "country" is being taken out of it and more sophistication is being put into it. Sauces have been freed of their traditional burden of flour, fat has been wiped out of the bottom of the pan and replaced by butter and oil, and the sugar that used to be sprinkled into almost everything as though it were a spice rather than a sweetener is now employed with restraint. What has emerged is some of the finest—and most interesting—cooking of Scandinavia.

Many dishes, like yellow pea soup, remain inviolate; but others are undergoing a face-lifting. There is a sturdy peasant dish from Skåne called *äppel-fläsk*, often made in the old days with fat pork, sour apples and onions, a munchy, greasy thing, fine for farmers who had hard work to do in a cold, damp climate but hardly suited to more modest nutritional needs. Now it has been transformed: the sliced apples and onions are still there, but they have been sautéed in a little butter, and the fat pork has been replaced by a leaner variety resembling Canadian bacon. The combination of apple, onion and bacon is a very good one, and the ease with which the dish is prepared recommends it for a Sunday brunch *(page 116)*.

Still another of the transformed dishes is *pytt i panna (page 114)*. It can be a hash (and in many Swedish homes it still is), but it can be much more than a simple hash, as implied by its name, which means tidbits in a pan. Forgoing yesteryear's boiled potatoes for raw ones cut into neat, tiny cubes and substituting good leftover beef and ham for the indifferent chunks of meat used in the past can make all the difference. Then *pytt i panna* is a true delicacy. The potatoes are fried until crisp, and the chopped onions and diced meat are sautéed together. As they cook they send off an appetite-gripping aroma that can have people sitting on the edges of their chairs in hungry anticipation of the meal to come. Finally all the ingredients are combined and the dish is seasoned with salt, pepper and chopped parsley. Guests are often given their choice of a raw egg yolk—a delicious catalyst to flavor—to mix with the *pytt i panna*, or a fried egg onto which, before the white has set, some parsley is sprinkled with emerald effect.

Tempting innovations

Swedes like meat, and they are innovators here as well. But because a great deal of the meat available to them still leaves much to be desired in tenderness (largely because they are reluctant to pay any more for meat than they are already paying), they often chop it up or buy it in sausage form. Some of their dishes in this line are worth copying. *Biff à la Lindström* may look rather like a hamburger on the outside, but it is something else again inside—a piquant and juicy blend of beef, finely diced beets, chopped onions and capers *(page 125)*. *Färsrulader* follows the old Scandinavian custom of wrapping meat around a filling of some sort, usually bacon and onions or bacon and apple wedges, but in a tempting variation the meat (veal, in this case) is finely minced, mixed with various ingredients to bind it, flattened out and then rolled around a core of thinly sliced leeks *(page 124)*.

Much the most interesting meat the Swedes have at their disposal is reindeer—unfortunately available in the United States in only very small supply. It is a new food, which is odd, the reindeer having lived in Scandinavia for thousands of years. But until recently there was no convenient way of processing the meat in quantity and shipping it from the far North. Now it can be bought frozen almost everywhere, not only in Sweden but in Norway and Finland, where herds are also raised for the market. The meat is delicious, wild in flavor, yet not nearly so strong as might be supposed. The reindeer's diet of lichens, buds, tender leaves and mushrooms may have something to do with this. In fact, mushrooms are the reindeer's favorite food, and it is said that an old animal will actually taste like them, and its fat will have the brownish tinge of the fungi themselves.

Reindeer are migratory animals, and cannot be thought of as exclusively Swedish, Norwegian or Finnish, roaming as they do over the northern boundaries of all three countries. But they can be said to belong to a people, the Lapps, who for more than a thousand years have herded them—and who, in many cases, still live in a storage economy, much as did Scandinavians of old. A Lapp's wealth is still often reckoned by the number of animals he owns, and he is zealous about branding those that belong to him—by notching their ears with his own sign (10,000 such signs are on record in Swedish Lapland alone). In past years the Lapps' dependence upon this animal was complete. It was food, it was clothing, and the bones and antlers were made into tools for handicrafts. From the mares came milk to drink, no more than a cupful a day per animal at the height of the season, but so rich in fat that when butter or cheese was made from it there was hardly any whey or skimmed milk left over.

Intermingling of old and new

In large measure the Lapps' dependence upon the reindeer continues today. For the herders among them, the so-called mountain Lapps, the reindeer is a way of life as they follow along behind the animals through the seasons of the year. In September and again in December and January the slaughter of the young bulls takes place. Although the greater part of the meat is dried and stored, some of it is always eaten fresh and then there is a great feast. The cooking pot bubbles with fresh meat and liver, and the marrow bones stick up out of it. By the time the food is ready, appetites are all but aflame. The meat is eaten by the handful, sloshed down with the rich gravy from the pot. The marrow is crammed into the mouth with the liver and blended there before being swallowed. The Lapps' love for the delicious marrow begins at an early age; mothers use it as a kind of pacifier, popping it into their babies' mouths.

While the Lapps may cling to old ways (salting their coffee and dunking reindeer cheese in it), time is catching up with them, and reindeer herding, among other pursuits, is becoming more and more modern. Some Lapps go to the grazing grounds today in helicopters and airplanes. Behind such change stands the Swedish government. It has opened a breeding station with the goal of producing a superior beast, and it carefully regulates the slaughter of the animals and the processing and shipment of the meat to markets in the south. Reindeer meat is becoming increasingly popular and some Swedes have even adopted the ancient Lapp custom of shaving it frozen into a hot frying pan to frizzle it—one more example of the truth in the Scandinavian saying that the old shall reach the new.

The Lapps and Their Reindeer

Lapps, like the family shown above, travel with their omnipresent reindeer throughout Lapland, a broad belt of land extending across the far north of Scandinavia. Each year these nomads migrate with the reindeer from lowlands to mountains and back. The reindeer diet is based on lichens, a type of plant that flourishes in the lowlands in winter, and on grasses that grow in the uplands in summer. But there is a good deal of argument among scholars as to whether the Lapps drive—or follow—their herds of reindeer from place to place. No one can be quite sure who is boss. At all events Lapps must stay close to reindeer, the basis of life in Lapland. Reindeer provide them with furs, milk, cheese and the meat (*opposite*) that constitutes the greatest part of their diet.

A display of reindeer meat shows the shoulder at the top. In the middle, at far left, is smoked steak with bone, and to the right are reindeer tongue and a square pot of bouillon. At the bottom are the saddle and a plateful of reindeer bones with marrow picks.

Pytt i Panna
SWEDISH HASH

To serve 4 to 6

5 to 6 medium potatoes, peeled and
  diced into ¼-inch pieces (4 cups)
1 pound roast or boiled beef or lamb,
  diced into ¼-inch pieces (2 cups)
½ pound smoked or boiled ham,
  diced into ¼-inch pieces (1 cup)
2 tablespoons butter
2 tablespoons oil
2 medium yellow onions, finely
  chopped (about 1 cup)
1 tablespoon finely chopped parsley
Salt
Freshly ground black pepper
4 to 6 fried eggs or 4 to 6 raw egg yolks

The ingredients in *pytt i panna,* unlike those in most hashes, are cooked separately to retain their individual character. To present this dish in its most attractive and traditional form, it is essential that the potatoes and meat be diced into small pieces as neatly and uniformly as possible. Peel the potatoes and cut them in half lengthwise. Place them flat side down and cut them lengthwise into ¼-inch strips. Then cut these strips crosswise into ¼-inch dice. Drop the resulting dice into cold water to prevent them from discoloring. When ready to use, drain them in a colander, spread them out in a single layer on paper towels, and pat them thoroughly dry with more towels. Similarly cut the meats into ¼-inch dice.

Melt the butter and oil in a heavy 10- to 12-inch skillet over high heat. When the foam subsides, add the potatoes. Lower the heat to moderate and fry the potatoes for about 15 to 20 minutes, turning them about in the pan with a spoon until they are crisp and golden. Remove them from the pan and set them aside to drain on a double thickness of paper towels. Add a little more butter and oil to the pan if necessary, and in it, cook the onions until they are soft and transparent but not brown. Add the diced meats, raise the heat slightly, and fry with the onions about another 10 minutes. Shake the pan often so that the meat cubes brown lightly on all sides. Stir the fried potatoes into the meat and onions and cook briefly to heat the potatoes thoroughly. Then sprinkle the hash with parsley. Add salt and freshly ground black pepper to taste.

Arrange individual servings of the hash on warm plates. Make a depression in each serving with the back of a large spoon and top with a fried egg. Or you may wish to serve the hash in the traditional Swedish way: to do this, place a raw egg yolk in half of an eggshell and nestle the eggshell into each serving. The diners themselves mix the raw yolk into the hot hash.

Fruktsoppa
OLD-FASHIONED FRUIT SOUP

To serve 6 to 8

¾ cup dried apricots
¾ cup dried prunes
6 cups cold water
1 cinnamon stick
2 lemon slices, ¼ inch thick
3 tablespoons quick-cooking tapioca
1 cup sugar
2 tablespoons raisins
1 tablespoon dried currants
1 tart cooking apple, peeled, cored
  and cut into ½-inch-thick slices

Soak the dried apricots and prunes in 6 cups of cold water for 30 minutes. Since the dried fruit expands considerably as it absorbs the soaking liquid, you will need a saucepan (of stainless steel or enamel) with a capacity of at least 3 quarts. Add the cinnamon stick, lemon slices, tapioca and sugar and bring to a boil. Reduce the heat, cover the pan, and simmer for 10 minutes, stirring occasionally with a wooden spoon to prevent the fruits from sticking to the bottom of the pan.

Stir in the raisins, currants and apple slices and simmer an additional 5 minutes, or until the apples are tender and offer no resistance when pierced with the tip of a sharp knife. Pour the contents of the saucepan into a large serving bowl and let them cool to room temperature. Remove the cinnamon stick, cover the bowl with plastic wrap and set the bowl in the refrigerator to chill. Serve the fruit soup in compote dishes or soup bowls as a light year-round dessert.

Pytt i panna—tidbits of potatoes and meats fried in a pan—takes on added vigor when a raw egg yolk is stirred into it.

Kalops

BEEF STEW WITH SOUR CREAM

Preheat the oven to 350°. Heat the butter and oil in a heavy 10- to 12-inch skillet. When the foam subsides, add the meat and brown it well on all sides. Transfer the meat to a 3- to 4-quart casserole equipped with a cover. Add the sliced onion to the skillet (with more butter and oil if necessary) and cook over moderate heat for about 6 minutes, until soft and transparent. Scrape into the casserole, add the flour and toss the ingredients lightly with a wooden spoon to coat them evenly. Add the salt, allspice, pepper and bay leaf. Pour the stock into the skillet and boil it over high heat for 2 or 3 minutes, scraping into the liquid any browned bits of meat and onions clinging to the pan. Pour into the casserole. Bring the casserole to a boil on top of the stove, cover it tightly, then set in the lower third of the oven. Cook, lowering the oven heat if necessary, so that the sauce in the casserole barely simmers. In about 1¼ hours, the meat should be tender when pierced with the tip of a sharp knife. Remove the meat to a deep, heated platter and cover it lightly with foil to keep it warm. With a large spoon, skim the fat from the liquid in the casserole and discard it. With a wire whisk, beat in the sour cream, a tablespoon at a time. Taste for seasoning, reheat if necessary, and pour the sauce over the meat.

To serve 4

2 tablespoons butter
2 tablespoons vegetable oil
2 pounds boneless beef chuck, cut in 1½-inch cubes
1 large onion, thinly sliced
1 tablespoon flour
½ teaspoon salt
¼ teaspoon ground allspice
⅛ teaspoon freshly ground black pepper
1 bay leaf
1¼ cups beef stock, freshly made or canned
2 tablespoons sour cream

Easy to prepare, *äppel-fläsk* combines onions and apples with Canadian bacon.

To serve 4

2 to 4 tablespoons butter
1 pound Canadian bacon
2 large red, tart cooking apples,
 unpeeled, cored and cut in
 ½-inch-thick rings
2 large onions, thinly sliced
Freshly ground black pepper

Äppel-Fläsk
SMOKED BACON WITH ONIONS AND APPLE RINGS

Melt 2 tablespoons of butter in a heavy 10- to 12-inch skillet, and when the foam subsides, add the bacon. Fry 5 to 10 minutes, or until the bacon is lightly browned. Remove from the skillet with a slotted spatula and set aside on paper towels to drain.

Fry the onion slices for 6 to 8 minutes in the fat remaining in the skillet, adding more butter if necessary. When the onions are soft and transparent, add the apple rings and cover the pan. Simmer over low heat for 5 to 10 minutes, shaking the pan gently at intervals to prevent the apples from sticking.

When the apple rings are sufficiently cooked (they should offer little or no resistance when pierced with the tip of a sharp knife), return the drained bacon to the skillet. Cover the pan and simmer an additional 3 to 5 minutes, or until the bacon is heated through. Grind black pepper liberally over the top and serve the *äppel-fläsk* directly from the pan as a luncheon entrée or Sunday night supper.

Dillkött på Lamm

LAMB IN DILL SAUCE

To serve 6 to 8

In a heavy 4- to 6-quart casserole that is equipped with a cover, cover the lamb with 4 to 5 cups of cold water and bring it to a boil, uncovered, over high heat. Lower the heat to moderate and with a large spoon skim off and discard the scum as it rises to the surface. Add the bouquet and the salt and peppercorns to the pot. Partially cover the pot and simmer the lamb very slowly for about 1½ hours, or until the meat is tender when pierced with the tip of a sharp knife. With a slotted spoon, remove the lamb to a deep heated platter or casserole, cover with foil and keep warm in a 200° oven.

To make the sauce, strain the lamb stock from the casserole through a fine sieve into a 1½- to 2-quart shallow saucepan and boil it down rapidly over high heat until it is reduced to 2½ cups. Meanwhile, in another 1-quart saucepan, melt the 2 tablespoons of butter. Remove this pan from the heat, stir in the 2 tablespoons of flour, then add all of the reduced lamb stock at once, stirring it rapidly with a wire whisk. Return the pan to the heat and bring the sauce to a boil, whisking constantly, until it is smooth and thick. Simmer the sauce over low heat for about 5 minutes, stirring frequently. Add the chopped dill, vinegar, sugar, salt and lemon juice. Stir a couple of tablespoons of the hot sauce into the beaten egg yolk, then pour this mixture slowly back into the sauce, beating constantly with a wire whisk. Heat through again, but do not let the sauce boil. Taste for seasoning, add salt and pepper if necessary, and strain the sauce through a fine sieve over the lamb. Garnish the platter with additional sprigs of dill and lemon slices, and serve with buttered boiled new potatoes or rice.

4 pounds breast or shoulder of lamb, cut in 2-inch cubes
4 to 5 cups water
Bouquet of 1 bay leaf, 5 sprigs dill and 5 sprigs parsley, tied together with a string
1 tablespoon salt
4 whole peppercorns, white if possible

DILL SAUCE
2 tablespoons butter
2 tablespoons flour
2½ cups reduced lamb stock (*from above*)
3 tablespoons chopped fresh dill
1 tablespoon white vinegar
2 teaspoons sugar
½ teaspoon salt
½ teaspoon lemon juice
1 egg yolk, lightly beaten
Dill sprigs
Lemon slices

Slottsstek

ROYAL POT ROAST

To serve 6 to 8

Preheat the oven to 350°. In a heavy 5- to 6-quart casserole equipped with a cover, melt the butter and oil over moderate heat. When the foam subsides, add the meat and brown it on all sides; this should take at least 15 minutes. Remove the meat from the pan and set it aside. Add the chopped onions to the casserole and let them cook over moderately high heat for 6 to 8 minutes, stirring occasionally, until they are lightly browned. Remove the pan from the heat and add the flour. Stir gently to dissolve it, and pour in the dark corn syrup, white vinegar and 2 cups of stock. Add the bay leaf, anchovies and bag of peppercorns, replace the meat in the casserole, cover and bring to a boil on top of the stove. Place the casserole in the lower third of the oven, regulating the heat so that the liquid in the casserole barely simmers. The meat should be tender in about 3 hours. To test, pierce it with the tip of a sharp knife; the roast should offer no resistance.

Transfer the pot roast to a heated platter and cover it lightly with foil to keep it warm. Remove the bay leaf and bag of peppercorns from the casserole and discard them. Skim off any surface fat and taste the remaining sauce; add salt and pepper if necessary. If the sauce seems to lack flavor, boil it briskly, uncovered, over high heat for a few minutes to reduce and concentrate it. Pour into a heated sauceboat and serve with the meat. In Sweden *slottsstek* is usually accompanied by red currant jelly or lingonberries, and often with gherkins and boiled potatoes.

2 tablespoons butter
2 tablespoons vegetable oil
4 pounds boneless beef: bottom round, rump, brisket or chuck roast
1 cup finely chopped onions
3 tablespoons flour
1 tablespoon dark corn syrup
2 tablespoons white vinegar
2 cups beef stock, fresh or canned
1 large bay leaf
6 flat anchovy fillets, washed and dried
1 teaspoon whole peppercorns, crushed and tied in cheesecloth
Freshly ground black pepper
Salt

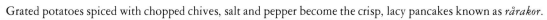

Grated potatoes spiced with chopped chives, salt and pepper become the crisp, lacy pancakes known as *rårakor*.

Rårakor med Gräslök
LACY POTATO PANCAKES WITH CHIVES

Peel the potatoes and grate them coarsely, preferably into tiny slivers, into a large mixing bowl. Do not drain off the potato water that will accumulate in the bowl. Working quickly to prevent the potatoes from turning brown, mix into them the chopped chives, salt and a few grindings of pepper.

Heat the butter and oil in a 10- to 12-inch skillet over high heat until the foam subsides. The pan must be very hot, but not smoking. Using 2 tablespoons of potato mixture for each pancake, fry 3 or 4 at a time, flattening them with a spatula to about 3 inches in diameter. Fry each batch over medium-high heat for 2 or 3 minutes on each side, or until they are crisp and golden. Add more butter and oil, if necessary, after each batch.

To serve 4

4 medium-sized baking potatoes
2 tablespoons chopped fresh chives
2 teaspoons salt
Freshly ground black pepper
2 to 4 tablespoons butter
2 to 4 tablespoons vegetable oil

Brynt Potatis i Ugn
OVEN-BROWNED POTATO WEDGES

Preheat the oven to 450°. Peel the potatoes and cut them in half lengthwise. Stand each half upright on a chopping board and slice it in thirds down its length, making 3 wedge-shaped pieces. Blanch the wedges by cooking them rapidly for 3 minutes in enough unsalted boiling water to cover them. Drain and pat them dry with paper towels.

With a pastry brush or paper towels, butter a baking dish large enough to hold the potatoes side by side in a single layer. Dribble melted butter over the tops and sprinkle them liberally with salt. Roast them in the center of the oven for 15 minutes, turn them, and roast another 15 minutes.

These crisp potato wedges make excellent accompaniments to roasted meats or poultry.

To serve 4 to 6

4 medium-sized baking potatoes
4 tablespoons melted butter
Salt

Hasselbackpotatis
ROASTED POTATOES

Preheat the oven to 425°. Peel the potatoes and drop them into a bowl of cold water to prevent them from discoloring. Place one potato at a time on a wooden spoon large enough to cradle it comfortably, and beginning at about ½ inch from the end, slice down at ⅛-inch intervals. (The deep, curved bowl of the wooden spoon will prevent the knife from slicing completely through the potato.) Drop each semisliced potato back into the cold water.

When you are ready to roast them, drain the potatoes and pat them dry with paper towels. With a pastry brush or paper towels, generously butter a baking dish large enough to hold the potatoes side by side in one layer and arrange them in it cut side up. Baste the potatoes with 1½ tablespoons of the melted butter, sprinkle them liberally with salt, and set them in the center of the oven. After 30 minutes sprinkle a few of the bread crumbs over the surface of each potato, baste with the remaining melted butter and the butter in the pan, and continue to roast another 15 minutes, or until the potatoes are golden brown and show no resistance when pierced with the tip of a sharp knife. If you wish to use the cheese, it should be strewn over the potatoes 5 minutes before they are done.

To serve 6

6 baking potatoes, about 4 inches
   long and 2 inches wide
1 tablespoon soft butter
3 tablespoons melted butter
1 teaspoon salt
2 tablespoons dry bread crumbs
2 tablespoons grated imported
   Parmesan cheese (optional)

To avoid slicing all the way through the potato, place it in a deep spoon.

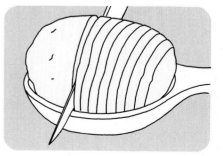

With a rubber spatula, lightly spread the almond topping over the poached apples.

To complete the apple cake, bake it in the center of the oven for about 20 minutes, or until the surface is a golden brown. Serve at room temperature.

To serve 6

2 cups cold water
¼ lemon
4 large tart cooking apples
½ cup sugar
2 teaspoons unsalted butter, softened
¼ pound unsalted butter, softened
⅔ cup sugar
3 egg yolks
½ cup ground blanched almonds
2 teaspoons lemon juice
3 egg whites
Pinch of salt

Fransk Äppelkaka
BAKED APPLE HALVES WITH ALMOND TOPPING

In a 1½- to 2-quart saucepan, combine the cold water, the juice of the lemon quarter and the lemon quarter itself. Halve, peel and core each apple and, as you proceed, drop the halves into the lemon-water to prevent discoloration. Then stir the sugar into the water. Bring it quickly to the boil, stirring occasionally, lower the heat and simmer uncovered for 6 to 8 minutes, or until the apples are tender. Remove them from the pan and drain on a cake rack.

Preheat the oven to 350°. With a pastry brush or paper towel, grease a shallow baking dish (just large enough to hold the apples in one layer) with the 2 teaspoons of soft butter. Place the apple halves in it side by side, cut side down. Cream the ¼ pound of butter by using an electric beater set at medium speed, or by beating it against the sides of a bowl with a wooden spoon until it is smooth. Now beat in the ⅔ cup of sugar, a little at a time, then the egg yolks one by one, and last the almonds and lemon juice. With a balloon whisk or electric beater, beat the egg whites with a pinch of salt in a large mixing bowl (preferably of unlined copper) until they form stiff, unwavering peaks. Mix 2 tablespoons of the stiff egg whites into the creamed sugar-butter-egg mixture, then gently fold the remaining mixture into the egg whites with a rubber spatula, using an under-over rather than a stirring motion. Spread the almond topping lightly over the poached apples and bake in the center of the oven for about 20 minutes, or until the surface is golden. Serve at room temperature.

Hovdessert
MERINGUES WITH CHOCOLATE SAUCE

Makes 18 to 20

MERINGUES: Preheat the oven to 250°. In a large bowl, beat the egg whites and salt with a wire balloon whisk or a rotary or electric beater until the mixture is foamy. Gradually beat in the sugar and continue beating for at least 5 minutes, or until the egg whites are very stiff and form solid, unwavering peaks when the whisk is lifted out of the bowl.

With a pastry brush or paper towels, grease a cookie sheet with the soft butter, sprinkle it with flour and shake the pan to coat it evenly. Now turn the pan over and tap it against a hard surface to knock off any excess flour.

Drop mounds of meringue (about 1 tablespoon) onto the cookie sheet. The mounds should be about 2 inches high and 1 inch wide; their shape and size will not alter in the baking process. Set the cookie sheet in the middle of the oven for 50 minutes. This is actually a drying rather than a true baking process and the meringues should remain as colorless as possible. If they seem to be taking on color, turn the oven down to 200°. They should be dry and crisp, but tender, when they are done. Serve with the following sauce.

CHOCOLATE SAUCE: Bring the sugar and water to a rolling boil in a heavy saucepan and boil briskly for 2 minutes. Remove the pan from the heat and add all of the cocoa, beating rapidly with a wire whisk until the sauce is smooth and satiny. Spoon about 1 tablespoon over each meringue. (Two meringues per person is a customary serving.) This sauce may also be served hot or cold over ice cream, or used as a cold syrup to make chocolate milk or hot cocoa.

MERINGUES
4 egg whites (at room temperature)
Pinch of salt
1 cup superfine sugar
1 tablespoon soft butter
2 tablespoons flour

CHOCOLATE SAUCE
1 cup sugar
¾ cup water
1 cup unsweetened cocoa

Hökarepanna
COACHMAN'S PAN

To serve 4 to 6

Preheat the oven to 350°. Peel the potatoes and slice them ⅛ inch thick; set them aside in a bowl of cold water to prevent discoloration.

Heat the butter and oil in a heavy 10- to 12-inch skillet over moderately high heat. When the foam subsides, add the onions and cook them until they are soft and lightly colored. Remove them to a dish with a slotted spoon. Add more butter and oil to the skillet if necessary, and in it brown the kidneys and pork slices quickly, turning with tongs several times to brown them evenly. Remove the meats from the skillet and slice the kidneys ¼ inch thick. Now deglaze the pan by adding the beer, stock and sugar and boiling them over high heat for 2 or 3 minutes, meanwhile scraping into the liquid any browned bits of onions or meat clinging to the bottom and sides of the pan. Remove the pan from the heat and set aside.

Drain the potatoes and pat them dry with paper towels. Arrange 2 or 3 layers of potatoes, meat and onions alternately in a 3-quart oven-to-table casserole, finishing with a layer of potatoes on top. Season each layer with salt and pepper as you proceed, and place the bay leaf in the center of the top layer. Pour in the deglazing liquid; it should just cover the top layer in the casserole. Add more stock if it does not.

Bring the casserole to a boil on top of the stove and then bake, uncovered, in the center of the oven for about 1 hour and 40 minutes, or until the top potato layer is brown and tender when pierced with the tip of a sharp knife.

Serve directly from the casserole as a one-dish meal.

2 pounds boiling potatoes
2 tablespoons butter
2 tablespoons vegetable oil
3 medium onions, thinly sliced
4 lamb kidneys, or 1 veal or 2 pork kidneys
¾ pound boneless pork loin, in ¼-inch-thick slices
1½ cups beer
1½ cups beef stock, fresh or canned
½ teaspoon sugar
Salt
Freshly ground black pepper
1 bay leaf

To serve 4 to 6

1 pound (2 cups) dried yellow Swedish
    peas or substitute domestic yellow
    split peas
5 cups cold water
2 finely chopped medium onions
1 whole onion, peeled, studded with
    2 cloves
1 pound lean salt pork, in 1 piece
1 teaspoon leaf marjoram or
    ¼ teaspoon powdered marjoram
½ teaspoon thyme
Salt

Ärter med Fläsk

PEA SOUP WITH PORK

Wash the dried peas in cold running water and place them in a 2- to 3-quart saucepan. Cover with 5 cups of cold water and bring to a boil over high heat. Boil briskly for 2 or 3 minutes, then turn off the heat and let the peas soak in the water for an hour.

Skim off any pea husks that may have risen to the surface, add the finely chopped onion, the whole onion, salt pork, marjoram and thyme and again bring to a boil. Immediately lower the heat and simmer with the pot partially covered for about 1¼ hours, or until the peas are quite tender but not all have fallen apart. Remove the whole onion and the salt pork from the soup and cut the pork in slices about ¼ inch thick.

Ärter med fläsk is served piping hot in either of two variations. Place a few slices of pork in individual serving bowls. Season the soup with salt to taste, and ladle it over the pork. Or, if you prefer, serve the soup alone, accompanied by a separate plate of the sliced salt pork and spicy brown mustard.

NOTE: If domestic yellow split peas are used, they need not be soaked for an hour. Wash them carefully, cover them with 4 cups of cold water and proceed with the recipe as above. They will take somewhat less time to cook than the Swedish peas.

To serve 6 to 8

3 eggs
2 cups milk or 1 cup of milk and 1 cup
    of light cream
1 cup flour
6 tablespoons unsalted butter, melted
½ teaspoon salt

Plättar

SWEDISH PANCAKES

This is a famous Swedish dish, customarily served with lingonberries or fruit preserves. In the wintertime, it is part of the traditional Thursday night dinner, following the main dish of pea soup with pork (above).

Beat the eggs together with ½ cup of milk for 2 or 3 minutes with a rotary beater or whisk. Add the flour all at once and beat to a heavy, smooth consistency. Beat in the remaining milk and then the melted butter and salt. Because of the large amount of butter in the batter, the skillet will require little, if any, additional buttering.

If you have the Swedish 5- or 7-section pancake pan, heat it, ungreased, over medium-high heat. When the pan is so hot that a few drops of water flicked on its surface bounce around and evaporate instantly, drop a tablespoon of batter into each depression. The pancakes should bubble almost immediately. After 1 or 2 minutes, when the edges begin to brown, turn the pancakes with a narrow spatula and cook another 1 or 2 minutes to brown the other side.

A heavy cast-iron skillet can be used as successfully as the sectioned pan, but first grease it lightly with a pastry brush or paper towel dipped into a little melted butter (this step need not be repeated). When the skillet is very hot, drop 1 tablespoon of batter into the pan for each pancake; each should form a 3-inch circle. When the edges brown lightly after about 1 minute, turn the pancakes with a spatula and cook another minute or two. In Swedish families, the *plättar* are served "from pan to plate," but if necessary, set each batch of pancakes aside on a platter and keep them warm in a 200° oven while you complete the rest.

The Swedes' Thursday night supper in darkest winter consists of thick yellow pea soup, spiced with marjoram and thyme and eaten—by many—with a good-sized slice of pork fat.

Thursday night's dessert in Sweden is *plättar*—the butter-crisped pancakes that the country's housewives like to serve with the lingonberries that form a natural complement to the dish.

123

Makes 16 roulades (to serve 4 to 6)

2 cups cold water
1 medium boiling potato, peeled and
    quartered
2 tablespoons butter
¼ cup finely chopped onions
1 pound finely ground veal
3 tablespoons fine dry bread crumbs
⅓ cup heavy cream
2 tablespoons water
1½ teaspoons salt
½ teaspoon white pepper
1 egg
2 tablespoons finely chopped parsley
1 tablespoon cornstarch
½ cup paper-thin slices of leeks,
    white part only
8 tablespoons (1 quarter-pound stick)
    butter
¼ cup heavy cream

Färsrulader
STUFFED VEAL ROULADES

In a 1- to 1½-quart saucepan, bring the water to a boil. Add the quartered potato and boil 10 to 15 minutes, or until tender. Drain and mash with a fork. In a small frying pan, melt 2 tablespoons of butter. When the foam subsides, add the chopped onions and cook 7 or 8 minutes, stirring frequently, until they are soft and transparent but not brown. Scrape the onions into a large mixing bowl, and add the mashed potato, ground veal, bread crumbs, cream, water, salt, pepper, egg, parsley and cornstarch. Mix well, then refrigerate at least 1 hour. Brush a large wooden pastry board (or another hard, smooth surface) with water and pat or roll out the mixture to a 16-by-16-inch square about ⅛ inch thick. Your hands or the rolling pin should be moistened with water to prevent the ground-meat mixture from sticking. With a pastry wheel or small, sharp knife, cut the rectangle of meat into 16 squares of 4 by 4 inches each. Put a thin layer of leek slices (about 1½ teaspoons) on each square. Now with the aid of a knife or, better still, an icing spatula, roll up each square, jelly-roll fashion. Ideally, they should now be chilled, but they may, if necessary, be cooked immediately.

Heat 2 tablespoons of butter in a heavy 10- to 12-inch skillet. When the foam subsides, add the roulades, 4 at a time, turning them gently with a spatula so that they brown on all sides. When they are a rich brown, set them

1   Before rolling out the meat, moisten the rolling pin and pastry board with cold water to prevent sticking.

2   After the meat has been rolled flat and cut into squares, sprinkle the whole surface with sliced leeks.

3   Using the flat of a knife or a spatula, roll up each square separately as if you were making a jelly roll.

4   Handled with extreme care, the *färsrulader* will retain their consistency as they are rolled up.

124

aside on a heated platter in a 200° oven. Repeat the process, adding 2 tablespoons of fresh butter for every 4 roulades. Pour the ¼ cup of heavy cream into the empty pan and boil it rapidly for 3 to 5 minutes, until it thickens, meanwhile scraping up the browned bits in the pan with a rubber spatula or a wooden spoon. Taste for seasoning, add salt if needed, and pour over the waiting roulades. If you must, cover the platter with aluminum foil and keep warm in a 200° oven for not more than 15 minutes.

Pikanta Oxrulader
ROULADES OF BEEF STUFFED WITH ANCHOVIES AND ONIONS

To serve 4

2 pounds top round steak
Freshly ground black pepper
4 tablespoons butter
4 tablespoons vegetable oil
1 cup finely chopped onions
2 tablespoons flour
Salt
16 flat anchovy fillets, washed and dried
½ cup water

Ask the butcher to cut the meat in 8 slices, each approximately ⅜ inch thick, 6 inches long and 3 inches wide, and to pound them to ⅛ inch thick, or cut and pound it yourself between 2 pieces of wax paper with a meat pounder or the flat of a cleaver.

Heat 1 tablespoon of the butter with 2 tablespoons of the oil in a small skillet and sauté the chopped onions in it for 5 to 8 minutes, or until they are tender and golden. Remove from the heat and stir in the flour. Now return to low heat and cook for 1 to 2 minutes, stirring constantly. Reserve 2 tablespoons of this *roux* for the sauce. Sprinkle each slice of meat liberally with salt and a few grindings of pepper, and spread the remainder of the *roux* evenly over each slice of meat. Lay 2 anchovy fillets on each slice, roll them up securely and either tie with a loop of cord at each end or fasten with a wooden toothpick inserted through the roll lengthwise.

Heat the remaining 3 tablespoons of butter and 2 tablespoons of oil in a heavy 10- to 12-inch sauté pan over moderate heat. When the foam subsides, add the roulades, 4 at a time. Turn the roulades with kitchen tongs to brown them on all sides. Arrange the browned roulades in a single layer in a 2- to 2½-quart casserole or baking dish equipped with a cover. The preparation of the roulades may be done in advance up to this point.

Preheat the oven to 350.° Deglaze the pan by pouring in the ½ cup of water and boiling for 1 or 2 minutes, stirring to scrape up any bits clinging to the pan. Add the reserved *roux*, stirring briskly until the sauce has thickened. Pour over the roulades, cover and bake for 45 minutes. Serve the *oxrulader* with mashed potatoes and gherkins or relish.

Biff à la Lindström
HAMBURGERS À LA LINDSTRÖM

To serve 4 to 6

1 tablespoon butter
2 tablespoons finely chopped onions
1 pound lean ground beef
4 egg yolks
1 tablespoon capers, drained and finely chopped
1½ teaspoons salt
Freshly ground black pepper
2 teaspoons white vinegar
½ cup heavy cream
¼ cup finely chopped drained beets, freshly cooked or canned
2 tablespoons butter
2 tablespoons vegetable oil
4 to 6 fried eggs (optional)

In a small pan, melt the 1 tablespoon of butter. When the foam subsides, add the onions and cook for 2 or 3 minutes, or until they are soft and transparent but not brown. Scrape into a large bowl, and add the meat, egg yolks, capers, salt, a few grindings of pepper and white vinegar. Mix together and moisten with the heavy cream. Then stir in the drained chopped beets. Shape the mixture into 12 to 14 round patties, about 2 to 3 inches in diameter. In a heavy, large skillet, heat the butter and oil. When the foam subsides, add the patties, 3 or 4 at a time, and cook over moderately high heat for 5 to 6 minutes on each side, or until they are a deep brown. In Sweden, these spicy hamburgers are frequently served with a fried egg set atop each, in which case they are made larger and thicker.

VI

Aquavit: The Water of Life

Aquavit, the popular Scandinavian drink, has many versions. In Norway it comes in 13 varieties, flavored with such ingredients as caraway, anise, star anise, guinea seed, fennel and coriander. The bottle on the cask contains a seagoing aquavit that accidentally traveled from port to port for several years during World War II—and grew better all the time from the aging and constant jostling.

W hy is it that the drink of a country often goes best with the native food? It is as though the two were married. French cooking is never so good as when the result is served with French wine. And the more robust Italian dishes come into their own with a good, strong Italian wine to wash them down. The rich specialties of Denmark, Norway and Sweden—all the smoky, salty things, the pungent cheeses, the cream-laden salads and even the sweet-tasting crabs and lobster—have their complement in aquavit, "the water of life." Tipped quickly out of a glass into the mouth and swallowed, it has been likened to a flaming sword. Jolting but delicious, it makes the brain smile, provides appetite and helps bind miscellaneous flavors together. And drunk as it is with rich, heavy food, it has the further advantage of being an aid to digestion.

Not the least wonderful thing about aquavit is its variety. In the United States, when it is served at all, the brand most often used is the Danish Aalborg Taffel Akvavit—a good one, certainly, strong in its alcoholic content and in its assertion of the herb caraway. But this is only one of nine types available in Denmark alone, to say nothing of the three dozen or so that can be found in Norway and Sweden (in Finland the drink is vodka), ranging in flavor from the all but tasteless through modulations of caraway and other herbs and spices to mouth-surprising infusions of purslane and bitter wormwood. In Denmark people even add a yellow meadow flower called *pericum* to the bottle; undergoing a chemical change, it tints the normally colorless aquavit a light orange.

Like whiskey, aquavit can have different degrees of maturity. Made

127

from potato or grain spirits, water and flavoring agents, it may be consumed young, but when left to age in oak sherry casks, it will not only begin to glow with the golden tint of light bourbon, but even to taste like it. (Although aquavit is normally drunk Arctic-cold from a Y-shaped glass, a really old bottle can be offered at room temperature and consumed gently, a few appreciative sips at a time.)

One of the smoothest aquavits is produced in Norway, and it comes by its mellowness in a most unusual way. It is called Linie Aquavit—*linie* meaning equator. This popular spirit—a little of which slips into the United States each year—actually makes two crossings of the equator in the holds of the Wilhelmsen Line's ships on their passages to and from Australia. Rolling around inside well-seasoned oak casks, and subjected to sharp temperature changes, the aquavit grows ever smoother. When it is finally bottled in Norway, it bears a label that tells the name of the ship on which the aquavit traveled and the dates of the voyage. How this custom got started no one knows, but seamen in sailing ships undoubtedly were quick to notice that their own aquavit improved with the journey.

A well-traveled aquavit

When World War II broke out and Norway fell to the Nazis, a shipment of Linie Aquavit failed to make it home; by the war's end it was the most traveled aquavit of any—and one of the best. The label proudly told the story of its odyssey: "This aquavit has passed the line four times and is thus double line aquavit. It was shipped by M.S. [motorship] *Tudor* from Oslo in December 1939, arrived in Melbourne via Cape Town in February 1940. From there the boat went to Port Said, where the aquavit was stored until November 1941. Here it was bombed. Then it was taken to Suez and went from there on the M.S. *Troja* to Fremantle, December 1941. In February 1942, it was shipped by M.S. *Tijuca* via Cape Town and Freetown to Bristol, where it arrived in May 1942, having happily escaped bombing, German cruisers and U-boat attacks."

The important thing to remember about aquavit is that it is meant to go with food, with the Danish cold table and with the Swedish *smörgåsbord* in particular. It enhances cold dishes like herring and shrimp, and a few hot ones like eel, boiled cod and Danish pea soup. Above all, it is the perfect accompaniment to Scandinavian cheese. Aquavit is chilled, and is mixed with only one other beverage, coffee, and then rarely. This powerful combination of stimulants is called "a little black one" in Denmark ("coffee cuckoo" in Sweden). It is made by placing at the bottom of a cup a 10-øre piece, which is about the size of a dime, and pouring coffee over it until the dark liquid makes the coin disappear from sight. Then, aquavit is added until the mixture is clear enough for the coin to reappear.

The other great beverage of Scandinavia is beer. Either because the Scandinavians have been brewers longer than most other people or because they were among the first to take a scientific approach to brewing, their beers are outstanding, certainly among the world's finest. The pleasant thing about this, from an American viewpoint, is that many of the Scandinavian brands, especially Denmark's Carlsberg and Tuborg, and Norway's Ringnes, are widely available in the United States.

What is sad, perhaps, is that although the volume of Scandinavian beer imported into the United States is high, the choice remains somewhat limited, restricted almost everywhere to a single type labeled "export." In Denmark, by contrast, there seems to be a beer for every mood and need, ranging from the lightest of pilsners to the heaviest of lagers (a word the Danes gave to the English language). The Carlsberg Brewery alone produces at least 12 types, of which four, by any standard, are very strong indeed. One bottle of Easter Brew, a seasonal specialty with an alcoholic content of 7.7 per cent, can set the head to spinning, and the Special Brew is a powerful one (9.1 per cent) no longer sold in Denmark. There is still a market for it in Scotland, however. There, the story goes, the natives take it as a chaser after a noggin of Scotch.

Scandinavians are fond enough of their golden beer for many of them to drink it once or twice every day, usually at lunch or supper (in tiny Denmark alone the daily consumption is three to four million bottles). Like aquavit, it is the natural complement to many Northern foods. It is even drunk, on occasion, with aquavit. Although this combination may sound dangerously like the powerful American drink called a boilermaker, few persons would be reckless enough to drink beer and aquavit together unless they were eating at the same time. And while the strength of the beer drunk with aquavit depends upon personal preference, most people would choose one of the weaker kinds.

The chilled aquavit is taken first; it leaves a delicious flavor in the mouth and cuts a cool trail all the way down the throat until it reaches the stomach, where it glows warmly. Its taste, often reflecting those of the herbs used to flavor it, is an inducement rather than a deterrent to dining; it stimulates the taste buds, and sets the mouth to watering. But since hunger and thirst usually go together where so many salty, spicy things are eaten, beer—dry, effervescent and light, standing in a tall glass next to the emptied aquavit glass—is most welcome.

Any reader who remains unconvinced of the merits of aquavit and beer in combination should try them with Danish *smørrebrød* or the Swedish *smörgåsbord*. Conversion is guaranteed. But again it should be emphasized that the aquavit must be served cold—so cold that the outside of the glass will mist up. A dramatic touch can be added by freezing the aquavit bottle in a block of ice and wrapping the chilled mass in a napkin, as is done in some Scandinavian restaurants. Freezing the bottle into the ice is easy if the height of the refrigerator freezing compartment is greater than that of the bottle. You pour a little water into a wide can and allow it to freeze as a base for the bottle, put the bottle into the can, add water to the brim and return to the freezer. The block of ice with the bottle encased in it can be removed by dipping the can into hot water for a moment.

Drinking with food has definite advantages. In Scandinavia the martini is only beginning to replace the light sherry before dinner, and people still come to the table hungry, delighted by all the trouble to which their hostess has gone (and she will have gone to great trouble) to set a beautiful table and serve a beautiful meal. Even on those rare occasions when a party may begin with two shots in a row, "an aquavit for the aquavit," food is still the solid foundation on which the evening's merriment will build.

One of the pleasantest aspects of drinking and feasting in Scandinavia

Among the many odd drinking vessels devised by the Scandinavians for downing beer, the strangest is this combination of cup and halter. The drinker had to put his head through the carved wreath, then lean back and swallow the contents all at once—without using his hands. This cup, the only one to survive in Finland, where the type originated, was made in 1542 from a single piece of wood.

HOW TO SKOAL WITH STYLE
Swedish film star Max von Sydow engages his drinking partner's gaze.

Tipping his glass backward, von Sydow drains the chilled aquavit in one deceptively cool gulp.

Lowering the glass to the level from which he raised it, von Sydow again meets his companion's eyes.

is the ritual of the *skoal* (a word from Old Norse, originally meaning "bowl," and now "toast" or "health"). The ritual goes back to the Vikings, who used to drain their drinking horns in enormous quaffs. Everyone was obliged to drink the toast at the same time, and, apparently because Viking beer and mead were quite weak, great quantities had to be imbibed before any effect could be felt. That this could be a chore to some is attested by the touching request of a king's bodyguard who in his old age asked the king for special permission not to have to drink as much as everyone else. During the Middle Ages, the ritual of the *skoal* involved passing the drinking vessel—usually a large bowl—from person to person with a blessing and a warm clasp of the hand. And on really formal occasions, each guest had to drop to his knees and uncover his head before drinking. When many healths were drunk, the toasting could go on for hours. During the Renaissance, King Christian IV, who ruled Denmark from 1588 to 1648, simplified matters by providing drinking vessels for all his guests, and with these they were invited to toast each other; presumably from this innovation came the *skoal* as it is known today.

Learning to *skoal* is easy, and it is well worth learning—it adds considerable charm to dining in the Scandinavian manner and assures that an evening will be a success by bringing the guests into visual and verbal contact with each other right off. The ritual varies somewhat in the different parts of Scandinavia. In Sweden, for example, it is a bit more formal, because Swedes follow the custom established by military officers who began the toast by holding their glasses at precisely the level of the third uniform button—but basically it proceeds along simple lines. All that is required is a drink in the hand and a cooperative partner. The proposer of the toast engages the eye of the person being toasted, and *"skoal"* is said. A slight bow of the head, and a twinkle of the eye—and the aquavit is drained in one gulp (if the drink is wine, a sip is taken). Just before the glass is put

Aquavit on the rocks: No matter where consumed, a drink between friends in Scandinavia calls for a convivial *skoal*. Out enjoying the new spring sunshine, Swedish picnickers are toasting each other with cups filled with the drink.

back on the table, the eyes meet again and there is another friendly nod.

At a formal dinner party, the host usually makes a little welcome speech and then offers the first *skoal*. Once this formality is out of the way, guests are free to drink by themselves or to *skoal* each other as often as they wish, with the men taking the lead; but they must not *skoal* the hostess when there are more than six people at the table. This would be bad form, since the hostess must be allowed to maintain her composure, which she would not be able to do if each guest at the table raised a glass in her direction at least once during the evening; the hostess has to drink when she is being toasted. On the other hand, she is expected to *skoal* the guests as a group. At big dinners she can do this by looking at several people during a *skoal* and thus reduce the number of toasts she drinks.

Drinking is rendered even more civilized in Scandinavia by an abundance of good wine. Although Scandinavians produce no grape wines, they are great wine lovers, and have been for at least a thousand years. The Vikings used to trade cod and hides for wine; their modern counterparts buy it outright and in enormous quantities. The Swedes alone purchase seven million dollars' worth from France each year—seven million gallons in all from France, Italy, Spain and other countries. Because they buy wine from France in such vast amounts and pay good cash for it, the Swedes get preferential treatment from the French and can take the pick of the best vintages. And to a large extent, this holds true for the other Scandinavians as well; recently a Frenchman who could not find his favorite Cognac at home discovered it in ample supply in Oslo.

It is the custom at large and formal dinners to serve several wines with a meal, one for each course, sometimes including the dessert. Danes favor Madeira, a brown, sweet wine, and they use it to round off a meal; Swedes, on the other hand, prefer sherry. After dinner, the brandies make their appearance, often together with Scandinavian fruit cordials and liqueurs.

Easily the best of these, with a world reputation today, is the Danish Cherry Heering, prepared from an old recipe and well aged in oak casks.

Although good sense today may mark the drinking habits of most Scandinavians, this was not always the case. The monotony and hardships of life on the farms and the gloomy weather contributed to a severe problem of widespread alcoholism that has been alleviated only within this century through strict legislation, government sales of spirits and high taxes on most beverages. The trouble started sometime in the 15th Century when the technique of distillation became known in the North. At first aquavit was looked upon largely as a medicine, in particular as a remedy against plague, and people did all sorts of strange things with it. They rubbed it on their bodies to ease pain. They applied it to their necks and drank it three mornings in a row to ease sore throats. They stifled coughs with it. In old age, they used it as a panacea for almost any trouble. A few drops in the ear were supposed to revive flagging hearing, and a little of it trickled into the mouth of a dying man was thought to restore speech. Even today aquavit has not entirely lost its medicinal connotations and Scandinavians go on reminding each other how good it is for them.

In time people learned to like their medicine, and soon they not only were drinking aquavit for pleasure, but spooning it from bowls, like soup, into which they sometimes broke bread. In alarm, governments began to raise tariffs on imported spirits and to slap controls on domestic production. In 17th Century Sweden, for example, only clergymen were allowed to make aquavit. This should have curtailed its use—and perhaps would have, if the clergymen had not gotten in the habit of dispensing aquavit as a kind of special and expensive blessing at baptisms, weddings and funerals. Even women who refused to drink it were not above sprinkling it on their handkerchiefs to sniff. As the taste for aquavit became more widely developed, the clergymen took to renting out their stills. In 1683, the governor of Sweden's northernmost province complained to Charles XI about the amount of drinking going on in his jurisdiction, and in 1686 the Crown stepped in to remind the men of the cloth that only they were supposed to make aquavit and, further, that they were to make it only for their own use. But the dam had given way, and as a Swedish historian has put it, "a torrent of liquor burst forth."

Edict after edict was passed to limit aquavit production in first one area of Sweden, then another. At a certain point the members of the third estate became so angry with the aristocrats and the clergy for pushing through legislation prohibiting the sale of aquavit to the peasants that they retaliated by supporting a law that banned coffee-drinking. They had nothing to lose and everything to gain, since coffee-drinking was then restricted to the upper classes.

When King Gustavus III in 1775 thought to improve the situation by making aquavit a state monopoly, he only worsened matters. Now with the profits from the sale of spirits going to the royal treasury, it became everyone's *duty* to drink. Bars were opened up outside churches to lure parishioners on their way home from worship. As the national thirst grew, many a grain crop that should have been eaten as bread was distilled instead—much of it in home stills—and workers were even paid in liquor rather than the traditional milk, potatoes and grain.

Although home-production of aquavit was finally prohibited in the mid-19th Century, and excessive drinking diminished, home-brewing of beer was allowed to continue, and it goes on in Scandinavia to the present day. In Norway it was formerly the custom for everyone to brew his own beer, and at harvesttime farmers often used only the finest of their grain for brewing. They invariably reserved some of the beer for unexpected use, such as a celebration or a funeral, and people would lend some to those caught short when death came and thus make it possible to drink a dead man over into the next world with proper ceremony. To make sure that the beer would be strong, everything from aquavit to black pepper and tobacco was added to it, and if in the end it took the breath away, it was good beer.

I have had home-brewed beer to drink in Norway, and I can report that it is indeed breath-taking. It was passed around at a party in a wide, wooden bowl, with two carved horses' heads for handles, and it gave me a certain fortitude—enough, in fact, to eat a smoked, grilled sheep's head, an ancient specialty of the ski-resort town of Voss.

Looking like a wizard of old, 75-year-old Knut Ullestad of Norway pursues the ancient art of making beer. Here, leaning over a steaming cauldron, he adds juniper boughs to boiling water which will be poured over malt. The juniper acts as a disinfectant.

VII

The Vigorous Diet
of Finland

Crayfish are a late-summer favorite in Finland, where they are cooked with plenty of dill, including the flowers of the herb which Lempi Saarela is tossing into the pot. Coarse salt ground in a mortar, sugar, vinegar and beer complete her recipe.

Finland is the green vigor of a forest. All its modernity, all the dynamic architecture, the glittering frosted glass, the bold ceramics with which it is making its reputation in the world today seem related to nature, to an earth force. So it is with the people themselves—and with their foods. The Finns had need to propitiate the virgin forest, of which they said: "Food and drink you gave our people." And the bear hunters of old used to address the forest as "lovely woman," "gold-glittering gilded hostess," "most bountiful benefactress."

In Finland the forest is everywhere, even in the city. Tapiola, a garden community of 20,000 inhabitants outside Helsinki, stands in a forest; a housewife can walk from the neatest of shopping centers right into the primeval woods. Her house or apartment building will be surrounded by pines, the path leading to it will have on either side boulders covered with shaggy moss and lichens, and here and there—a flash of red in the greenery —will be a berry of some sort.

The forest comes right into Helsinki. It is there in the smell of burning wood, an odor that in winter suggests warmth and the knife-sharp heat of the sauna. It is there in the pines that stand in the parks, a reminder of the wildness that lies beyond the city limits. And it is there in the open-air markets—in the berries, in the mushrooms, in the black, wet loam clinging to freshly dug potatoes.

Surrounded as they are by forest, the Finns still see food as a part of nature, and they enjoy it as a gift. My wife and I were surprised to find so much natural beauty in Helsinki's harborside market—and so much freshness, although it was late autumn. Outdoors we wandered in the mist from stall to stall. Flowers—mostly rusty-red chrysanthemums—blazed up in the cool blue light. Close by stood vats in which lingonberries and cranberries glittered under water. In a wooden tub lay salted mushrooms, and in an adjacent barrel, jade-green pickles. The vegetables and fruits looked polished: tomatoes glowed with a red incandescence; great globular turnips seemed enameled with patches of green, purple and yellow pigment. Radishes had been so thoroughly washed their roots shone white. Fat white cabbages lolled next to gleaming purple ones. Everything—crisp lettuces; long, skinny, dark-green cucumbers; white heads of cauliflower; tiny brussels sprouts; bunches of celery three to four feet long—seemed to have been arranged with an eye for design. And everywhere, much as though it were a floral decoration rather than an herb, sprouted sprigs and plumes of dill.

Down by the fish stands seagulls strutted among shoppers; in the boat basin wild ducks swam back and forth. At quayside were moored small launches from which peasant women in white aprons and black boots sold silvery fish and white-breasted game birds. We entered the enclosed part of the market, a large building containing a huddle of little stands painted a clean white. The smell was of smoke, and it came from hams and slabs of meat, black with carbon outside, pink inside. There for the first time we saw sauna-cured legs of lamb—dried, shriveled joints whose appearance, we were to discover, belies their tender mellowness. On counters stood bottles of ketchup-red pig and cattle blood, to be used in making asphalt-colored pancakes and puddings, and in glass cases we saw meat pies—large rectangles, glazed with egg and decorated with ribbons and diamonds of crust—and all kinds of bread, some loaves so plump, so fat with leaven that they had burst in the baking, leaving jagged crevices in their crusts.

Food for a man's appetite

Wherever we went in the Helsinki market we were impressed by the vitality we encountered. In the days ahead we found that vitality and virility were outstanding characteristics of Finnish cooking. Many of the country's dishes seem to have originated in the hands of men, or were cooked with men in mind. Take *vorshmack,* a dish that was a favorite of Finland's national hero, the late Field Marshal Carl Gustaf Mannerheim. *Vorshmack* consists of ground mutton, beef and salt herring, and it is redolent of garlic and onions. Its aggressive flavor compels the admiration of almost everyone who tries it. It is especially delicious when wolfed down late at night with beer and perhaps a *ryyppy* or two, Finnish for a shot of icy vodka. Milder by far but no less masculine is another Finnish favorite, pork gravy; also falling definitely into the category of man's food are the Finnish breads like black sour rye and such sturdy vegetables as rutabagas, whether cubed and cooked plain, or with pork or mutton, or shredded and eaten raw, or mashed and cooked slowly in a casserole *(page 151).*

Much Finnish cooking suggests the outdoors, the pleasures of the campfire. There are, for example, all the many invigorating ways Finns have of preparing the fresh fish available to them directly from any of their countless lakes or from the Baltic Sea, which curves like a sickle around the southern half of the country. They salt fish or eat it raw, or smoke it by wrapping it

Flowers and food—inseparable on most Scandinavian tables—are displayed side by side in Helsinki's waterfront market.

in layers of newspaper and setting it down in embers to smolder. Sometimes they spear it on a stick and cook it over an open fire, or pin it to a board and bake it in front of flames, or put it in an iron pot, on top of peeled potatoes, to steam in a mist of sea water.

In Finland, soup is often the subject of culinary discussions among men —each remembering his favorite and how *he* made it. It is said that in the northern part of the country a man needs to eat three bowls to get the flavor, three more to fill up. Certainly there could hardly be a more masculine soup than lake fish cooked with potatoes and dill and a large chunk of buttered black bread floating on top, or one more direct than salmon soup made with clean, clear water from a Lapland stream. For that matter, if you are looking for a blunt, outspoken dish, look no further than slaughter soup—the kidneys, liver, heart and meat of an animal, chopped up, boiled with carrots and potatoes, and served with little barley and wheat dumplings flavored with blood. Almost as though to compensate for such ruggedness, there is a delicate soup, *kesäkeitto,* made from summer vegetables—carrots, sugar peas, cauliflower florettes, tiny potatoes and spinach—picked at their absolute peak of freshness and simmered in a creamy base *(page 150).* This soup is much favored by Finnish women, who think they are dieting when they eat it—but with their consciences thus eased, usually go on to finish the meal with several small pancakes and strawberry jam.

137

Finnish cucumbers, sometimes a foot or more in length, are frequently cut into sections to be weighed and sold.

A romantic intensity pervades Helsinki's waterfront market, where, in observance of a dealer's birthday, a rose may be stuck into a heap of potatoes, or where a scale, polished to an almost liquid appearance of brightness *(opposite)*, can transform ripe tomatoes into a juicy mirage.

Finnish thirsts, like appetites, seem to fall in the masculine range. Beer continues to be brewed in many houses, and depending upon how long it is left to age, it can attain varying degrees of potency. Powerful hard liquors are produced domestically, and these are supplemented by large imports of spirits. In the consumption of Cognac, which they buy from the French, the Finns are in the front rank; though they number only four and a half million souls, they consume as much Cognac as many countries of 40 million. But to counterbalance their high intake of alcohol, they are also great milk drinkers, downing nearly 300 liters (80 gallons) per person each year—a world record. Much of this is consumed sour, either as *viili* or *piimä*, two Finnish favorites. *Viili* is eaten, *piimä* drunk. *Viili* comes in two varieties —"long" or "short," depending on the size of the curd and the bacteria used as a culture. When at its best, the long *viili* should be so elastic—or so say the Finns—as to require cutting with a scissors.

If Finnish food can be considered virile, it can also be called primitive— in the best sense of the word. Finns appreciate basic flavors, the taste of things as they are. Porridges and gruels stirred from whole grain are still enormously popular, and some are eaten as desserts. The traditional Easter dish throughout much of the country continues to be *mämmi*, a pudding made with rye flour, rye malt, molasses and bitter orange peel. This is cooked in an unusual way, successively boiled, whipped and baked. *Mämmi* is served with sweet cream, and in the past used to be spooned from the

birchbark baskets in which it was baked. Another festive cereal dish, much appreciated by Finns, is *pito-ja-joulupuuro*, barley porridge made with whole grain; it is simmered so long (five hours at least) that the lactose in the milk with which it is cooked undergoes a chemical change that turns the porridge a reddish color. Great care must be taken all this while to see that "the bishop does not come to visit"—meaning that the bottom does not blacken and burn. Such porridge is served with rose-hip or raisin purée. Still another barley porridge is *talkkuna;* when dipped in melted butter, it is a reminder that porridge was, indeed, the forerunner of bread. *Talkkuna* is best when the flour used in its preparation is milled from grain cooked beforehand in seasoned water and then browned in the oven or sauna.

Finns, unsurprisingly, love the tang of wild food. They are great hunters and fishermen, and in their woods can be found everything from bear to Virginia deer, the latter sprung from stock presented by a group of Minnesota Finns in the 1930s. In November, the month we were there, some 30 bears had been shot, and their meat appeared on several menus. Apparently more a novelty than a delicacy, in taste and texture, it was like a cross be-

Three-year-old Tuomas Vuorikoski receives instructions from his mother in the exacting art of picking wild mushrooms. Most Finns grow up to be experts in such matters, but for those with gaps in their knowledge the Helsinki cooking school where Mrs. Vuorikoski teaches is willing to identify any strange species.

tween tough, day-old pot roast and a turkey drumstick. In their pursuit of the burbot, an ugly lake fish that yields a magnificent caviar and makes an excellent winter soup, Finns are willing to brave temperatures many degrees below zero to angle for it through the ice. They rate burbot caviar and reindeer tongue as the two greatest delicacies of Northern Europe.

Because Finns appreciate the taste of game birds, some go so far as to modify the bland flavor of chicken (a bird they began to eat only in this century) by rubbing its carcass inside and out with chopped pine needles and juniper berries and then letting it hang and ripen a couple of days before roasting. And in keeping with their enjoyment of strong, natural flavors, they eat many of their meats with lingonberries, barely sugared, or with sour dill pickles, which come in crocks packed between layers of oak, cherry or black currant leaves.

Like their neighbors the Swedes, the Finns are inveterate pickers of mushrooms and berries. As early as April or May, when the snows have melted, the crinkle-capped morels make their appearance on the pine heaths. These are followed in the summer and autumn by more than 50 other varieties of

Making a *kalakukko,* Miss Kyllikki Heikkinen heaps fish and pork on rye dough, in which she will bake them.

After baking five hours, the *kalakukko* is opened. The contents are dished out and eaten with the buttered crust.

edible mushrooms, including some considered poisonous elsewhere but not by the Finns, who boil and eat them with no ill effect. Mushrooms have many uses in the Finnish kitchen; they go into soups, gravies and stews, are pickled or fried *(page 151)* and sliced into salads *(page 156).* A raw mushroom salad can convey the taste of the woods; it has an earthy sting and a touch of aspen to it.

Berries play an important part in the Finnish diet—all too often they are practically the only source of vitamins in this Northern land where fresh vegetables frequently cannot be had. Beginning in early summer and continuing into the fall, the berry harvest goes on, with crop after crop reduced to juice, jam or conserves. Raspberries or strawberries are made into snows of beaten egg white and whipped cream *(page 155),* or thick puddings called *kiisseli.* Sometimes they are eaten plain, with sugar and cream and perhaps, *piimä.* Occasionally this method of eating raspberries is varied by pouring them into a soup bowl, tossing in cubes of black bread, sprinkling sugar on top and dousing the whole with sweet cream. Blueberries, of which there are always considerable quantities, wind up in gigantic tarts, crisscrossed by bands of dough, and some are dried and set aside, later to be used in making a sweet soup, which is considered by some Finns to be a particularly efficacious stomach remedy.

The most abundant of the berries are the lingonberries that flourish in the forests. Although lingonberries resemble cultivated cranberries in flavor and appearance, they are only about one quarter the size and have an attractive underlying resinous or pinelike taste. Because of their acid content, they will keep over the winter in water alone, without benefit of any preservatives; this characteristic explains why, in the past, a thin layer of lingonberries was used as an effective seal on top of fruit conserves. In addition to being eaten with meat, lingonberries are used in several desserts, including a baked pudding made with rye flour, and one pudding that is not cooked at all, but whipped and whipped and whipped into a cool pink foam. *Vatkattu marjapuuro,* as this last is called, can also be prepared from American cranberry juice *(page 154)* as a light ending to a summer meal.

Larger than lingonberries but not nearly so big as our own variety, Finnish cranberries grow wild in different parts of the country and are much appreciated for their fresh, dry taste. Ripening in late autumn, they give off a fine aroma in the frozen swamps; however, they are often left until spring for harvesting, since a season under the snow reduces their acidity and helps to soften them. Cranberries figure importantly in the production of several Finnish liqueurs.

Delicate fruits for an exquisite liqueur

The rarest of the Finnish berries, the *mesimarja* (honeyberry), comes from the Arctic bramble, a plant that favors burned-over areas. The fruits are small and delicate, rather like tiny raspberries, and mature under the midnight sun; they succumb easily to frost and in some years they never ripen at all. Much of the crop, which needs hundreds of pickers to gather it, goes into the manufacture of an exquisite liqueur also called Mesimarja, which was once a favorite in Russian court circles.

Another fruit of the far North belonging to the raspberry family is the orange-yellow Arctic cloudberry, a rich source of vitamin C. Although it is found and enjoyed elsewhere in Scandinavia, a measure of the affection in which the Finns hold it is the fact that only they have given it five different names. The cloudberry can be important to Lapp families, who supplement their income by gathering the fruit. Picking it is hard work, necessitating much trudging to and from the swamplands, but the profits can be high. The berries sell for about 50 cents a pound, and a diligent family might pick 2,000 pounds during the season. The pleasure most Finns take in this juicy berry must have something to do with the experience of picking it for oneself ("with the fragrance of the early morning dew rising from the ground"), for it does have large, woody pits and these require a great deal of gnashing. The easiest way to get the flavor, which some people have likened to burnt caramel, is to drink the delicious golden liqueur distilled from Arctic cloudberries and sold under several Finnish labels.

The Finns' appreciation of nature comes to its fullest expression in summer, during the crayfish season. Wherever these tiny fresh-water relatives of the lobster can be found, wire cages are put down in the lakes to catch them, and for a couple of months the fun goes on. A regular ritual has sprung up around the cooking and eating of crayfish, and summer would not be summer without a crayfish party held outdoors under a full moon and a string of paper lanterns, with a blue-black lake breathing quietly on the shore. Enjoyment comes close to being bliss when the party is preceded by a sauna and a plunge in the lake, with guests arriving at table in relaxed after-sauna clothes, their skin still bearing traces of the fragrant scent of the birch whisks with which they strike themselves in the sauna to stimulate circulation.

Joys of a messy meal

Like lobsters, crayfish turn a bright red when boiled; one by one the live crayfish are dropped into the pot and cooked about seven minutes *(page 153)*. The water in which they take their final swim is heavily salted and flavored with fresh dill and dill crowns, the yellow flowering part of the herb; some people also add vinegar, sugar, garlic and beer. But the key step in cooking them is to let the crayfish steep in this dill solution for several hours or overnight. They are usually eaten cold, with toast and butter, vodka, beer or white wine. Purists try to observe the rule that with every crayfish tail a drink be taken—and since anywhere from 10 to 20 crayfish are normally consumed by each guest, these parties can become rollicking affairs.

In addition to contributing to the merriment of the evening, the alcohol helps to remove any inhibitions that might spring from the noisy, sloppy business of eating crayfish. First the tips and the movable parts of the claws are clipped off and the juice is sucked out; then the larger part of the claw is broken open to yield the fine white meat. And finally the tail meat is removed from its armor, placed on toast and a pinch of chopped dill is sprinkled on top. Because crayfish water will stain clothing, paper bibs and paper tablecloths are generally used—and fingerbowls are never far from hand.

The Swedes—who love crayfish every bit as much as do the Finns—say that the crayfish party belongs to them, that it is a basically Swedish institution. The Finns just as adamantly claim it for themselves. But who can actually say to whom it belongs or with whom it originated? The histories of

Sweden and Finland are inextricably twined, as are those of Russia and Finland; for more than 600 years Finns lived under the Swedish crown, for another 100 years under the Russian czars. And as a result, Finland's cooking is a mélange, an exciting blend of influences from both West and East. All the pleasures of the *smörgåsbord* can be found here—and then some. So much in fact are Swedish influences a part of daily living that Finns think of this groaning table as their own too, and they have a special name for it, a word that seems to sputter indignantly with umlauts—*voileipäpöytä*. In their minds, there is no such thing as Swedish meatballs: "Why should they be called Swedish when we eat them all the time?"

When questioned about the Russian origins of their beef stroganoff, their borsch (a cold beet soup), and their blinis, buckwheat pancakes raised with yeast and eaten with burbot caviar, chopped onions and sour cream, the Finns are a little less defensive. Some are likely to say that none of these taste as good in the Soviet Union—and with that they give a knowing smile. And even if blinis are conceded to be Russian, the Finns cover them with their own caviar, the peach-colored roe of the ugly burbot, and they insist that it is superior to the beluga caviar.

Russian influences via Karelia

Perhaps the greatest single influence on the Finnish kitchen has come from the province of Karelia, which now lies almost entirely within the Soviet Union. Its cooking is still going strong—in Finland—because the Karelians themselves, some 400,000 in all, chose to leave homes, businesses and professions behind, rather than remain in Russian territory; today they live throughout Finland. For centuries Karelia was the point of entry for many dishes out of the East, and some of these bear the unmistakable stamp of Russia. For example, the traditional Karelian Easter dessert is not *mämmi*, but the Russian *pasha*, a cheesecake.

Among the most fascinating of the Karelian foods are the *piirakka* (from the Russian *pirog*), pasties or pies. These can be easily carried about in their crusty packages of dough and even be frozen in the snow, which must have something to do with their continuing popularity. Today lumbermen still take them into the forest to eat for lunch.

The commonest *piirakka* is one made in the shape of a boat; it has a thin rye crust, with crimped edges, folded over a rice filling in such a way that the filling shows as a white slit down the middle. Often Karelian pasties, hot from the oven, are served with egg-butter, made by stirring chopped hard-boiled egg into fresh, soft butter. They may be eaten as a kind of hors d'oeuvre or, more traditionally, with meat dishes.

Pasties can take various shapes and be cooked according to various methods. Some are no more than three or four inches long; others are as big as briefcases. Some are deep-fried; others are made with a puff-paste crust and salmon, meat or shredded cabbage. And some are even sweet—round tarts with yeasty crusts spread with lingonberries or a deliciously sour cheese mixed with sugar, raisins and vanilla.

The most famous of these pasties comes not from Karelia, but the province of Savo in central Finland. It is the *kalakukko*, a remarkable dish if ever there was one; it can weigh up to 11 pounds and take five hours to bake.

144

Continued on page 149

A Sauna before Supper

The Finns are different from the other Scandinavians —and not least because they take the sauna, the 175° F. (or hotter) almost dehydrated air bath that relaxes mind and body and produces a feeling of clean serenity. The pleasure of the sauna is often extended by a post-bath snack and drink or even a supper of Finnish specialties. These often include salty fish to replace the body salt that is lost in the extreme heat. Naturally, the eating ritual is best when practiced in beautiful surroundings—such as a handsome modern home—in this case that of Aarne Ervi, one of Finland's brilliant young architects.

While the women sip drinks, the men take an after-sauna plunge. Below are the birch whisks Finns use in the sauna to stimulate circulation and to shake water on hot stones to keep some moisture in the atmosphere.

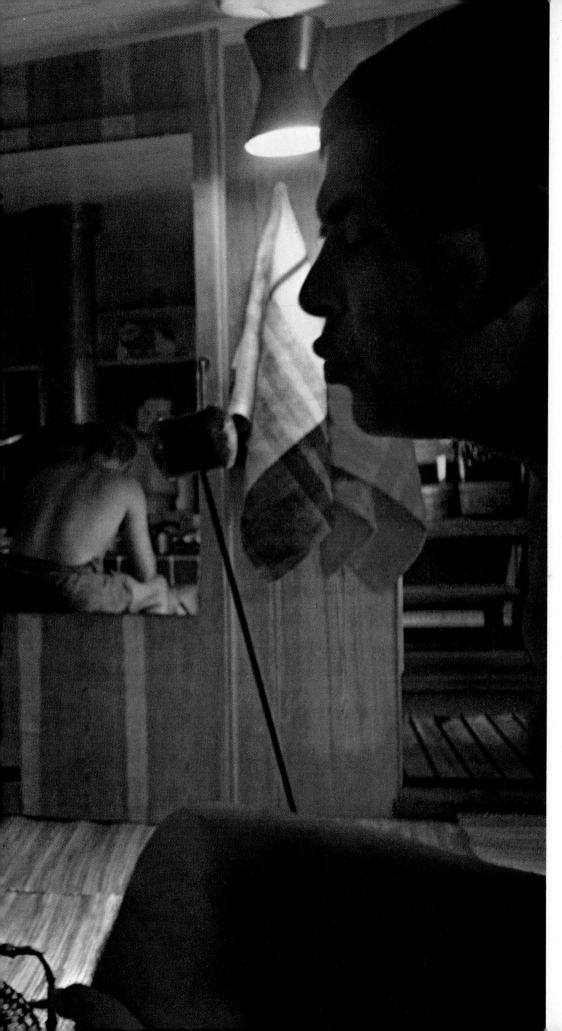

After their swim, the men eat pork-and-mutton sausages grilled over an open fire in the dressing room of the sauna. On the wooden tray can be seen Karelian *piirakka*, rice-filled pasties with a thin rye crust. The mugs hold a mild, thirst-quenching beer called *kalja*, which the Finns brew at home from water, malt, sugar and yeast.

The name, meaning "fish fowl," perhaps reflects the fact that this pasty has a shape rather like that of a bird, trussed and ready for the oven. I saw a *kalakukko* being made, and much later that day had the experience of eating it. A great ball of rye dough was rolled out to a half-inch thickness; this was strewn with a half dozen or so tiny fresh-water fish called *muikku*, a relative of the salmon. These had been cleaned, but not deboned. Some salt was added and on top of the *muikku* were placed strips of fat pork; then more fish and more pork were piled on, and at last the dough was pulled up over the filling, tightly sealed and sculpted with a moistened knife.

At serving time, several rings of crust were sliced from the domed top of the *kalakukko*, and I was invited to spoon some of the contents onto my plate. Over the crust I obediently sloshed some melted butter and I consumed it with the fish and pork as a kind of bread. Not until afterward did it occur to me to wonder what had happened to the fish bones; it turned out that they had melted away in the heat of the oven.

A somewhat less elaborate version of the *kalakukko* is the *patakukko*—pot fowl. It has the same fish and pork filling, but is baked in a casserole under a rye crust. The unlikely combination of fish and meat cooked together is one the Finns are quite fond of, and it crops up in a number of other dishes. Shoemaker's casserole consists of cubed pork simmered with salted whitefish; some whitefish may be added even to pork gravy.

Dishes touched with a dash of poetry

Finnish cooking makes heavy use of the oven. *Patakukko* and *kalakukko* are but two of many popular baked dishes. Liver-and-rice casserole (*maksalaatikko*) is a great favorite (*page 151*) that lends itself readily to the American kitchen. Still another is the Karelian hot pot (*karjalanpaisti*), a stew made with mutton, pork and veal, a little water, a little allspice and nothing more. It may be cooked as long as six hours. During this time, the three kinds of meat not only become tender enough to cut with a fork, but they blend their individual flavors to create an unusual taste. As its name would indicate, this is one of those sturdy, practical dishes of Karelia; it was devised to make use of the oven's heat after the week's baking was done.

Like many other things in Finland, the baking oven came out of the East more than a thousand years ago and well in advance, apparently, of its adoption in most of Western Europe. That the Finns have leaned heavily on it ever since is indicative of their consistent attitude toward cooking. The good old dishes, the tried and true, are still available for everyone to eat. Plain though these may often be, they are all of them touched with poetry. Finns who leave their country, never to return, remember their food and the good, strong taste of it until they die. Those who go back on a visit are likely to come away with some dill in their luggage or a little piece of cloth dipped in *piimä,* then dried to use as a starter for making the Finnish sour milk at home. And even those Finns who will never leave Finland and who eat Finnish food every day can be made nostalgic by mere mention of the ancient specialties. I remember the faraway look in the eyes of one Finn as he described a smooth, rich custard baked from beastings, the thick, creamy milk of a cow that has just calved. "I feel almost sick," he said, "from the yearning of it."

Opposite: With the late evening sun exploding through the pine trees, architect Ervi's guests raise their vodka glasses and break into song. Waiting in the foreground is the after-sauna supper: smoked, poached salmon to be eaten with a creamy-smooth egg-mustard sauce, sauna-cured leg of lamb, baked white potato pudding, vegetables, salads, and herring dishes sprinkled with clippings of fresh dill.

Kesäkeitto
SUMMER VEGETABLE SOUP

The vegetables of early summer are prized in Finland, because the season is so brief. This light yet hearty soup is a favorite luncheon or late-supper main course, and the shrimp may be added as a touch of luxury on special occasions.

To serve 6 to 8

4 small carrots, cut into ¼-inch
    dice (1½ cups)
¾ cup fresh green peas
1 small head cauliflower, separated
    into ½-inch buds (1 cup)
2 new potatoes, cut into ¼-inch
    dice (½ cup)
½ pound fresh string beans, cut in
    ¼-inch strips (½ cup)
4 small red radishes, halved
¼ pound fresh spinach, washed,
    drained and finely chopped (2 cups)
2 teaspoons salt
2 tablespoons butter
2 tablespoons flour
1 cup milk
1 egg yolk
¼ cup heavy cream
½ pound medium-sized shrimp,
    cooked and cleaned (optional)
¼ teaspoon white pepper
2 tablespoons finely chopped fresh
    parsley or dill

Select the youngest, freshest vegetables that you can find. Wash, scrape or cut them to the sizes specified in the ingredients list. Then, except for the spinach, place all of the vegetables in a 2- to 3-quart pot, cover with cold water and add the salt. Boil uncovered for 5 minutes, or until the vegetables are just tender. Add the spinach and cook another 5 minutes. Remove the pan from the heat and strain the liquid through a fine sieve into a bowl. Set the vegetable stock and the vegetables aside in separate bowls.

Melt 2 tablespoons of butter in the pan over moderate heat. Remove from the heat and stir in the flour. Slowly pour in the hot vegetable stock, beating vigorously with a wire whisk, and then beat in the milk.

In a small bowl, combine the egg yolk and cream. Whisk in 1 cup of the hot soup, 2 tablespoons at a time. Now reverse the process and slowly whisk the warmed egg yolk and cream mixture back into the soup. Add the reserved vegetables to the soup and bring to a simmer. As soon as it comes almost to a boil, reduce the heat, add the cooked shrimp, and simmer uncovered over low heat for 3 to 5 minutes, or until the shrimp and vegetables are heated through. Taste and season the soup with the white pepper as well as additional salt if necessary. Pour into a soup tureen and sprinkle with finely chopped parsley or dill.

Uunissa Paistettu Hauki
BAKED PIKE STUFFED WITH CUCUMBERS AND RICE

To serve 4 to 6

3 quarts boiling salted water
⅔ cup rice
1 large cucumber, peeled, seeded
    and coarsely chopped
1¼ teaspoons salt
2 hard-cooked eggs, coarsely chopped
2 tablespoons butter
½ cup finely chopped onions
½ cup finely chopped parsley
¼ cup finely chopped chives
⅛ teaspoon white pepper
1 to 3 tablespoons heavy cream
8 tablespoons (1 quarter-pound stick)
    butter
6 tablespoons dry bread crumbs
3- to 3½-pound pike, cleaned and
    scaled, with the backbone removed
    but the head and tail left on (or
    substitute mackerel or sea bass)
½ cup boiling water

Cook the rice uncovered in 3 quarts of boiling salted water for about 12 minutes, or until it is still slightly firm. Drain it thoroughly in a large colander and set it aside to cool.

In a small bowl, toss the chopped cucumber with the ¼ teaspoon of salt. Let it sit for at least 15 minutes, then drain and pat dry with paper towels. In a small saucepan, melt the 2 tablespoons of butter and in it cook the chopped onions and cucumbers for about 6 to 8 minutes, until they are soft and transparent but not brown. Transfer them to a large mixing bowl and add the chopped eggs, cooked rice, parsley and chives. Season with the remaining teaspoon of salt and ⅛ teaspoon white pepper, and moisten the mixture with 1 tablespoon of heavy cream, adding more if the stuffing seems too dry. Mix together lightly but thoroughly.

Wash the fish inside and out under cold running water and dry it thoroughly with paper towels. Fill the fish with the cucumber-rice stuffing, close the opening with small skewers, and crisscross kitchen string around the skewers as you would lace a turkey.

Preheat the oven to 350°. In a baking dish or roasting pan attractive enough to bring to the table and large enough to hold the fish comfortably, melt the ¼ pound of butter over moderate heat. When the foam subsides, place the fish in the baking dish, raise the heat, and cook the fish for about 5 minutes, until it is a golden brown. Carefully turn over the fish with 2 large wooden spoons or metal spatulas and brown the other side. Sprinkle the top with bread crumbs and then turn the fish over again and sprinkle the other side with the crumbs. Pour ½ cup of boiling water around the fish and bring it to a simmer on top of the stove. Bake uncovered in the middle of the oven for 30 to 35 minutes, or until the fish feels firm when pressed lightly with a finger. Serve the fish directly from the baking dish.

NOTE: In Finland, 1 cup of finely chopped cooked spinach, squeezed dry, is often substituted for the cucumber in the stuffing.

Maksalaatikko
LIVER-AND-RICE CASSEROLE

To serve 6 to 8

Cook the rice in 4 quarts of briskly boiling salted water for about 12 minutes. When the rice is still slightly firm when tasted, drain it thoroughly in a colander and set it aside.

In a heavy 6- to 8-inch frying pan, melt the 2 tablespoons of butter over moderate heat. When the foam subsides, add the onions and cook them for 3 to 5 minutes, or until they are soft and transparent but not brown. Remove from the heat and set aside.

Preheat the oven to 350°. In a large mixing bowl, gently combine the approximately 3 cups of cooked rice, milk and lightly beaten eggs. Add the cooked onions, crumbled bacon, raisins and corn syrup, and season with the salt, pepper and marjoram. Stir in the ground liver and mix thoroughly.

With a pastry brush or paper towels, spread a 2-quart casserole or baking dish with the tablespoon of butter and pour in the liver-rice mixture. Bake uncovered in the middle of the oven for 1 to 1½ hours, or until a knife inserted in the center of the casserole comes out clean. Serve hot, accompanied by lingonberries or cranberry sauce.

4 quarts boiling salted water
1 cup white
    long-grain rice
2 tablespoons butter
1 medium onion, finely chopped
    (⅓ cup)
2 cups milk
2 eggs, lightly beaten
¼ cup cooked and crumbled lean
    bacon (about 4 slices)
½ cup raisins
2 tablespoons dark corn syrup
2 teaspoons salt
¼ teaspoon white pepper
¼ teaspoon ground marjoram
1½ pounds calf or beef liver, finely
    ground
1 tablespoon butter

Länttulaatikko
RUTABAGA CASSEROLE

To serve 8

Preheat the oven to 350°. Place the 8 cups of diced rutabagas (or diced turnips) in a 4- to 6-quart stainless-steel or enameled saucepan. Pour in enough cold water to just cover the vegetables, add 1 teaspoon of salt and bring to a boil. Lower the heat and simmer, partially covered, for 15 to 20 minutes, or until the rutabagas offer no resistance when pierced with the tip of a sharp knife.

Drain the rutabagas and place them in a sieve set over a small bowl. Force them through the sieve by rubbing them with the back of a wooden spoon. In another bowl, soak the bread crumbs in the heavy cream for a few minutes. Stir in the nutmeg, 2 teaspoons of the salt and lightly beaten eggs, then add the puréed rutabagas and mix together thoroughly. Stir in 2 tablespoons of the soft butter.

Spread a 2- to 2½-quart casserole with the remaining 2 teaspoons of soft butter and put the rutabaga mixture in the casserole. Dot with the butter bits and bake uncovered for 1 hour, or until the top is lightly browned.

2½ pounds (about 2) rutabagas,
    peeled and cut into ¼-inch dice
    (8 cups), or substitute 2½ pounds
    white or yellow turnips, peeled
    and diced
3 teaspoons salt
¼ cup dry bread crumbs
¼ cup heavy cream
½ teaspoon nutmeg
2 eggs, lightly beaten
2 tablespoons plus 2 teaspoons soft
    butter
2 tablespoons butter, cut into tiny
    bits

In the luminous velvety twilight of a
Northern summer six young Finns,
armored in bibs and armed with special
knives, sit eating a messy, merry meal
of cold boiled crayfish *(right)*. Picnics
like this one take place in summer,
the only time crayfish are available,
and follow a traditional ritual. In the
decanter is cold vodka, a swig of
which (a glass, some purists say)
must precede the first morsel of
crayfish and hot buttered toast. In the
tall glasses is cold beer, a long pull
of which may follow the crayfish. By
wisely spacing his crayfish a man
might eat 15 or 20 and still walk home.

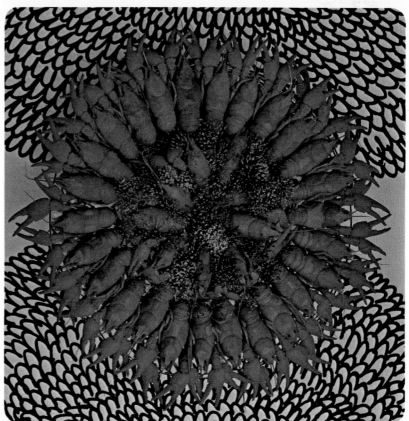

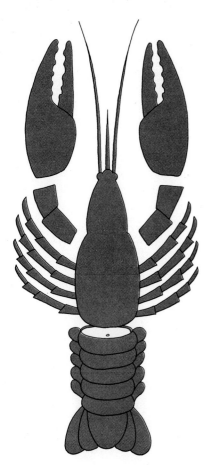

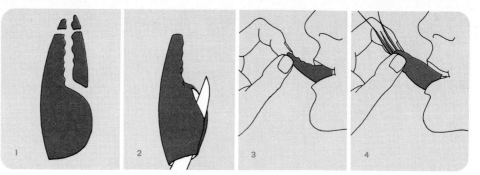

THE ART OF EATING A CRAYFISH, FINNISH STYLE

1 A stylized crayfish is shown at left: detach claws, cut off tips and the movable part of the claw.
2 With a sharp knife cut through the larger part of the claw shell to release the meat.
3 Suck what meat you can from the claw. Loud slurping noises are considered part of the fun.
4 Detach body from tail and suck the juices (there won't be any meat) from the body shell.

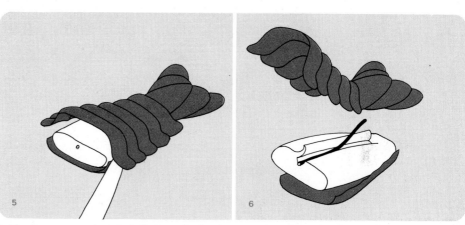

5 Neatly cut open the tail shell along the line between the top and bottom shell.
6 Remove the stringlike digestive tract, place meat on toast and eat. It is the best part.

Keitetyt Ravut
DILL-FLAVORED CRAYFISH

Scandinavian crayfish are small—about 3 inches in length—and are similar to the fresh-water crayfish of the Midwestern, Southern and Western United States. The Finns are extremely fond of these delicate shellfish and easily eat 10 to 20 apiece—usually accompanied by chilled vodka.

To serve 3 to 4

3 quarts cold water
¼ cup salt
3 tablespoons dill seed
3 large bunches fresh dill
30 live fresh-water crayfish

GARNISH
1 bunch fresh dill
Toasted white bread

In a 6- to 8-quart kettle, combine the water, salt, dill seed and 2 of the bunches of fresh dill tied with a string. Bring to a boil over high heat and boil briskly, uncovered, for 10 minutes. Meanwhile, wash the crayfish carefully under cold running water. Drop them, a few at a time, into the rapidly boiling water. When all of the crayfish have been added, cover the kettle tightly and boil about 6 or 7 minutes.

Line a 3- to 4-quart bowl with the sprigs of the third bunch of fresh dill. Remove the crayfish from the kettle with a slotted spoon and arrange them in the bowl over the dill sprigs. Strain the stock over the crayfish through a fine sieve, and let them rest in the liquid until they have reached room temperature. Then cover the bowl loosely with plastic wrap and refrigerate for at least 12 hours; they may marinate as long as 2 days if you wish. To serve, drain the crayfish of their liquid, pile them high on a platter and garnish with fresh dill. Although they can be served cold, the crayfish are at their best if they are allowed to reach room temperature. Serve with toast.

To serve 6 to 8

3 cups bottled or canned cranberry
    juice
6 tablespoons sugar
½ cup uncooked Cream-of-Wheat

Vatkattu Marjapuuro
WHIPPED BERRY PUDDING

In a 1½- to 2-quart saucepan, bring the cranberry juice to a boil over moderate heat. While the juice boils, sprinkle in the sugar, a little at a time, and then slowly add the Cream-of-Wheat, stirring briskly with a wooden spoon. Reduce the heat and simmer for 6 to 8 minutes, stirring occasionally, until the mixture becomes a thick purée.

With a rubber spatula, transfer the purée from the saucepan to a large mixing bowl. Use an electric mixer for the next step. (Although it is possible to make *vatkattu marjapuuro* with a wire whisk, it is scarcely practical; an hour of vigorous whisking might be required.) Beat with the mixer set at the highest speed for about 10 or 15 minutes, or until the pudding has doubled in volume, becomes a delicate pink color and is light and fluffy. Pour into a large serving bowl or into individual dessert bowls, and serve as soon as possible.

NOTE: If you wish to make this dessert with a nontart juice such as apple, strawberry or raspberry, add a tablespoon of lemon juice.

1 When the whipping begins, the rough-textured pudding is a deep red.

2 After a few minutes the mixture turns a bit lighter, but is not yet finished.

3 The completed berry pudding, whipped at high speed for 10 to 15 minutes, is a delicate pink like this, light yet stiff enough to stand in peaks.

154

Omenalumi
APPLE SNOW

With a large, balloon whisk, beat the egg whites and the pinch of salt in a large mixing bowl (preferably of unlined copper) until they begin to foam. Gradually add the sugar and continue to beat vigorously until the whites are stiff enough to form unwavering peaks when the beater is lifted out of the bowl. (A rotary or electric beater may be easier to use, but the whites will not rise so voluminously nor have so fine a texture.)

In a separate bowl, combine the applesauce and lemon juice. Stir a heaping tablespoon of the beaten egg whites into the applesauce to lighten it. Then, with a rubber spatula, gently fold in the rest of the whites, using an under-over cutting motion rather than a rotary motion. Turn the apple snow into a serving bowl and sprinkle the top with cinnamon.

NOTE: The Finns serve apple snow as soon as it is made, but it can be frozen effectively in ice-cube trays and served as an ice.

To serve 6 to 8

4 egg whites
Pinch of salt
1/2 cup sugar
2 cups tart applesauce, freshly made, canned or bottled
1/2 teaspoon lemon juice
1/8 teaspoon cinnamon

Mansikkalumi
STRAWBERRY SNOW

With the back of a large spoon, rub the fresh or thoroughly defrosted frozen strawberries through a fine sieve into a small mixing bowl. Stir into this purée the 1/2 cup of sugar, a little at a time.

Using a balloon-type wire whisk, beat the egg whites and salt vigorously in a large bowl (preferably of unlined copper) until the whites are stiff enough to form unwavering peaks when the beater is lifted out of the bowl. With a gentle under-over cutting motion rather than a stirring motion, use a rubber spatula to fold first the strawberry purée and then the whipped cream into the egg whites. Pour the strawberry snow into an attractive serving bowl, or individual dessert bowls, and decorate with the whole strawberries. This dessert can be served at once, or it may be refrigerated for a few hours and served later in the day.

To serve 6 to 8

2 cups fresh, hulled strawberries or substitute 2 ten-ounce packages frozen whole strawberries, thoroughly defrosted and drained
1/2 cup sugar
4 egg whites
Pinch of salt
3/4 cup heavy cream, stiffly whipped
12 to 16 whole strawberries, fresh or frozen

Pinaattiohukaiset
SPINACH PANCAKES

In a large mixing bowl, combine the milk, salt, nutmeg and flour and then stir in the melted butter. (Or, if you prefer to use an electric blender, all of these ingredients can be mixed at once at medium speed.) In a separate bowl, combine the eggs and sugar and stir this into the batter. Gradually add the chopped spinach.

With a pastry brush or paper towel, coat the bottom of a heavy 10- to 12-inch skillet with about a teaspoon of soft butter and set the skillet over moderately high heat. When the pan is very hot, drop 2 tablespoons of the batter onto the skillet and with a spoon or spatula, spread it out evenly to form a 3-inch disk. Cook the pancakes—3 or 4 at a time—for 2 to 3 minutes on each side, or until they have browned lightly. Keep them warm on a heated platter covered loosely with aluminum foil. Add more butter to the skillet as it becomes necessary while cooking the remaining pancakes. Serve the spinach pancakes as a vegetable course—accompanied, if you like, by lingonberries.

To serve 6 to 8

1 1/2 cups milk
1 teaspoon salt
1/8 teaspoon nutmeg
1 cup flour
2 tablespoons unsalted butter, melted
2 eggs
1/2 teaspoon sugar
1/2 pound freshly cooked spinach, squeezed dry and finely chopped, or substitute 1 nine-ounce package frozen chopped spinach, thoroughly defrosted, squeezed dry, and again chopped
1 to 2 tablespoons butter, softened

PASTRY

2¼ cups flour

1 teaspoon salt

12 tablespoons chilled unsalted butter,
cut into ¼-inch bits

1 egg

½ cup sour cream

1 tablespoon soft butter

MEAT FILLING

4 tablespoons butter

¾ cup finely chopped mushrooms
(about ¼ pound fresh mushrooms)

3 pounds finely ground meat (beef,
pork, ham, lamb or veal or a
combination of any of these), or
4 cups cooked ground or finely
chopped meat

2 tablespoons all-purpose flour

⅓ cup finely chopped onions

¼ cup finely chopped parsley

1 cup freshly grated Cheddar, Swiss
or Gruyère cheese

½ cup milk

1 egg combined with 2 tablespoons
milk

To serve 4

½ pound fresh mushrooms, in ⅛-inch
slices

1 cup water

1 tablespoon lemon juice

¼ cup heavy cream

1 tablespoon grated onion

Pinch of sugar

½ teaspoon salt

⅛ teaspoon white pepper

Lettuce leaves

Lihamurekepiiras
MEAT LOAF IN SOUR-CREAM PASTRY

SOUR CREAM PASTRY: Sift the flour and salt together into a large chilled bowl. Drop the ¼-inch bits of butter into the bowl. Working quickly, use your fingertips to rub the flour and butter together until they have the appearance of flakes of coarse meal. In a separate bowl, mix together the egg and sour cream and stir into this the flour-butter mixture, working with your fingers until you can gather the dough into a soft, pliable ball. Wrap in wax paper and refrigerate 1 hour. Cut the chilled dough in half and roll out each half to rectangles of 6 by 14 inches each, setting aside any scraps.

Butter the bottom of a jelly-roll pan with 1 tablespoon of soft butter. Lift 1 sheet of the pastry over the rolling pin and unroll it into the pan, or drape the pastry over the rolling pin, lift it up and unfold it into the pan.

MEAT FILLING: Melt the 4 tablespoons of butter in a 10- to 12-inch skillet. When the foam subsides, add the chopped mushrooms and cook them over moderate heat, stirring frequently, for 6 to 8 minutes, or until they are lightly colored. If you are using ground raw meat, add it to the skillet and cook, stirring occasionally, for another 8 to 10 minutes, or until the meat loses its red color and any accumulated liquid in the pan cook completely away. Stir in the flour. Scrape the meat mixture from the skillet (or the mushrooms and already cooked meat) into a large mixing bowl and stir in the chopped onions, parsley, cheese and milk. Now gather this meat mixture into a ball and place it in the center of the dough in the pan. With your hands, pat the meat into a narrow loaf extending lengthwise down the center of the dough from one end to the other. Lift the second sheet of pastry over the pin and gently drape it on top of the meat loaf; press the edges of the 2 sheets together. Dip a pastry brush into the egg-and-milk mixture and moisten the edges of the dough. Press down on the edges all around the loaf with the back of a fork (the tines will seal the edges securely). With a fork prick the top of the loaf in several places to allow steam to escape.

Preheat the oven to 375°. Gather together into a ball all of the excess scraps of dough and roll it out to a thin rectangle. With a pastry wheel or small, sharp knife, cut this dough into long, narrow strips. Brush the loaf with more of the egg and milk mixture and crisscross the pastry strips over the top of the loaf in an attractive pattern. Now brush the strips with the milk and egg mixture and set the jelly-roll pan in the center of the oven. Bake for 45 minutes, or until the loaf has turned a golden brown. Serve thick slices of the hot meat loaf, accompanied by a bowl of cold sour cream and a side dish of lingonberries.

Sienisalaatti
FRESH MUSHROOM SALAD

In a 1-quart enamel, glass or stainless-steel saucepan, bring the water and lemon juice to a boil. Add the sliced mushrooms and cover the pan. Reduce the heat and simmer gently for 2 to 3 minutes. Then remove from the heat, drain the mushrooms in a sieve, and pat them dry with paper towels. In a 1-quart bowl, combine the heavy cream, grated onion, sugar, salt and pepper. Add the mushrooms and toss lightly in the dressing until they are well coated. Serve as a salad, on crisp, dry lettuce.

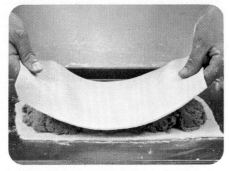

1 To make *lihamurekepiiras*, shape the meat mixture into a loaf on a sheet of dough.

2 Cover with the second sheet of dough and press the edges together.

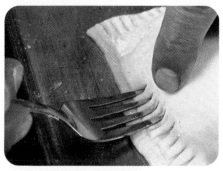

3 With a fork, seal the edges to make a tight, decorative border.

4 Decorate the loaf with strips of dough and brush with the egg-milk mixture.

Hot *lihamurekepiiras*, its golden pastry crust crisp and flaky, is garnished with parsley sprigs and served with a dollop of sour cream.

To make 5 quarts

2 large lemons
½ cup plus 5 teaspoons granulated
  sugar
½ cup brown sugar
5 quarts boiling water
⅛ teaspoon active dry yeast
15 raisins

Sima
LEMON-FLAVORED MEAD

With a small, sharp knife or rotary peeler, carefully peel off the yellow skins of the lemons and set them aside. Then cut away the white membranes of the lemons and discard them. Slice the lemons very thinly. In a 6- to 8-quart enameled or stainless-steel bowl, combine the lemon slices, lemon skins, the ½ cup granulated sugar and the brown sugar. Pour the boiling water over the mixture, stir, and let it cool to tepid. Then stir in the yeast. Allow the *sima* to ferment, uncovered, at room temperature for about 12 hours. To bottle, use 5 one-quart bottles with tight covers or corks. Place 1 teaspoon of sugar and 3 raisins in the bottom of each bottle. Strain the *sima* through a sieve and pour the liquid into the bottles. Close the bottles tightly and let stand at room temperature 1 to 2 days, until the raisins have risen to the surface. Chill the bottles until ready to serve.

To make 14 to 16 crullers

2 tablespoons lukewarm water
½ package (1½ teaspoons) active
  dry yeast
1 cup lukewarm milk (110° to 115°)
2 eggs
1½ teaspoons sugar
½ teaspoon salt
2 cups flour
Vegetable oil for deep-fat frying
Confectioners' sugar

Tippaleivät
MAY DAY CRULLERS

Put the 2 tablespoons of lukewarm water into a small bowl and sprinkle in the yeast. Let it stand 2 or 3 minutes, then stir until the yeast is dissolved. Set the bowl in a warm, draft-free place (such as an unlighted oven) for 3 to 5 minutes, or until the yeast bubbles and the mixture doubles. Now stir in the milk. In a large bowl, stir the eggs and sugar to combine them. Pour in the yeast mixture and, stirring briskly, add the salt. Add the flour, ½ cup at a time, beating vigorously until a soft batter is formed. Cover with a kitchen towel and set in a warm place (again, the unlighted oven) for 1 hour, or until the batter has doubled in bulk, but do not let it stand longer.

Pour enough oil into a deep-fat fryer or heavy 10- to 12-inch skillet to reach a depth of about 2 inches, and place over medium-high heat until the oil is very hot. Spoon 1 cup of the batter into a pastry bag fitted with a ¼-inch plain tip. Holding the bag upright, squeeze the batter into the hot fat in a 3- to 4-inch circle, moving the bag in a circle to build a "bird's nest" of 2 or 3 rings more or less atop one another. Deep-fry 2 or 3 crullers at a time, turning them over with a spatula or tongs after about 1 minute, or when they are a golden brown. Fry the other side, then remove with a slotted spoon and drain on paper towels. When the crullers are cool, sift the confectioners' sugar over them and serve with coffee or *sima (above)*.

When the oil in the skillet is very hot, twirl the batter into it from a pastry bag, forming several bird's nest shapes.

After the bottom edges begin to show brown, flip the crullers over with a spatula or tongs and brown the other side. The crullers (*right*) are drained and sprinkled with sugar. Finns serve them with *sima*, homemade mead.

VIII

Baking Refined to a Fine Art

Even if the Scandinavians did not enjoy a well-deserved reputation as good all-around cooks, they would still be entitled to culinary fame as bakers. Why this should be so has to do not only with the ingredients used and skills acquired in making baked goods over the centuries, but—through an interesting quirk—with coffee. Coffee is *the* beverage of Scandinavia, consumed morning, noon and night, after meals and in between as well. The Icelanders claim that they drink more of it than any other people in the world, and the Swedes rank themselves second, trailed by the Danes. Now coffee is never so good as when something really good is eaten with it, as the Scandinavians long ago recognized. The amount of baking they do today seems in direct proportion to the amount of coffee they drink. Their pastry shops and coffeehouses, called *konditorier*, are so numerous that hardly ever is city air without its little trace of yeast odor.

With the heartiest appetites of all, the Danes are not above having pastries with their breakfast coffee, again with their midmorning coffee and again after a *smørrebrød* lunch. Even those who forgo these sweets earlier in the day are bound to have one or two during a coffee hour held late in the afternoon or in the evening. At such times it is charming to see the Danish woman's solicitude for her husband: not only does she pour his coffee, she puts cream and sugar in it for him—then stirs it. And to round out her own pleasure in the coffee ritual she may follow his example and light up a cigar.

A great many of the baked goods of Scandinavia seem actually to have been designed with coffee in mind. Few are of the delicate, tea-time type: they are mouthfuls, rather than morsels. And they are rich not in a cloying

Only in Sweden is there a flower-crowned cake like this (actual height about 24 inches). A specialty of Skåne, the *spettekaka* (cake made on a spit) is produced by beating sugar and scores of eggs for hours on end, and baking the result in front of an open fire. So complicated is its preparation that today the cake is made primarily by commercial bakers.

way, but in a way that tempts by making "just one more" seem possible. They are all made with butter, and lots of it, and some are cream-filled or cream-covered. Their flavors are low-key—gentle dustings of cinnamon and cardamom—and common to many is the taste of nuts—and one nut in particular, the almond. The way chocolate is used elsewhere, almonds are used here. They are finely ground and mixed into cookie batters; they are slivered and strewn over pastries; they are combined with sugar, butter and milk and baked on top of the cake the Swedes call a *toscatårta (page 168)*. And when pounded to a paste, almonds take on a variety of other uses such as marzipan, whose bittersweet taste is one of the most pervasive flavors in Scandinavia. A little marzipan may be insinuated into Danish pastry, or quantities of it rolled out thinly and wrapped around cake as a kind of icing. Blended with jam, marzipan is used as a cookie filling; mixed with flour, as a cookie itself. Molded into little pigs and other forms, it is eaten as a sweet or employed as a decoration. And come Shrove Tuesday in Sweden, it is eased into a hollowed-out bun filled with whipped cream.

The best place to see and sample the baked goods of Scandinavia is at that adjunct of all well-run households, the coffee table. More than just a piece of furniture, it is an institution, a gathering spot, a focus for family activities. Here families meet during winter in common defense against the climate. I recall the members of a large Danish family too busy with jobs and school to eat together very often, but certain, at 9 o'clock each night, to gather around an oval table in the parlor and exchange the news of the day over coffee. In summer, they would carry the table to the garden and sit there all through a long Sunday afternoon, soaking up the sun, while hornets drawn by the sugar icing formed a menacing circle around the pastry.

In the not so distant past all the edible ornaments of the coffee table were homemade, and to some extent they still are. Though more pastry is being bought these days it equals the home product in quality for a simple reason —commercial bakers in Scandinavia still have home-bakers to compete against. In the old days in Sweden custom prescribed that for an occasion such as a birthday, which no Swede is ever too old to celebrate, the housewife had to bake at least seven kinds of cookies, in addition to several cakes and pastries; but in these busy and calorie-conscious days she can be forgiven if she cheats a little and buys some of the things she needs, or bakes not seven different kinds of cookies but turns one dough into seven different shapes. In Finland, the custom was to serve guests seven items in all—always a braided yeast cake known as *pulla;* a pound cake; an elaborate filled cake; and four kinds of butter cookies. Guests usually began with the yeast cake and a couple of cookies; then, with a second cup of coffee, they ventured on to the pound cake and two or three cookies more, while making certain to reserve enough room for a piece of the filled cake and a third cup of coffee. And anyone worth his manners was certain, with the fourth cup, to sample all the items missed before. This elaborate coffee table was always spread early enough in the afternoon to allow appetites to revive by evening.

The bounty of today's coffee table offers an interesting insight into the nature of Scandinavian hospitality, for the less well off the family, the more lavish the spread is likely to be. Danes in modest country homes, for example, would be embarrassed if they could not lay out for guests at a birthday party or coffee party some buttered buns; *sandkage,* or pound cake; a giant Danish pastry in the shape of a pretzel (the baker's sign in Denmark and Norway); a prune tart; a crown of meringue fluffed all over with whipped cream and studded with strawberries; an apple cake; a layer cake; and an assortment of cookies, blond with butter and shimmering like a diamond display with sparkles of crushed sugar.

While such a party requires a great deal of advance preparation, more often than not the coffee table comes into use at a moment's notice, for in Scandinavia unexpected company is always expected. Before the advent of the home freezer, housewives lived under a sword of Damocles. They were required to have something freshly baked on hand to offer their friends, perhaps some pastry in the cupboard, a cake in the refrigerator, and certainly several kinds of cookies stashed away in a tin box. Now, the freezer has gone a long way toward making their plight easier by allowing them to do much of their baking well in advance of the arrival of their guests.

Unexpected company has done more than anything else to bring cookie baking to a high art in Scandinavia. There are no cookies anywhere else quite so good. They are what cookies should be—crisp enough to snap without crumbling, yet so delicately constituted that they all but dissolve and trickle away in the mouth. Some of their crispness can be attributed directly to the amount of butter used, but credit must also be given to a mysterious ingredient called salt of hartshorn. This predates baking powder as a rising agent by several centuries, and once was made from the antlers of a deer, hence its name. Now it is produced chemically, and can be bought as *aqua ammoniae* (ammonium carbonate). Many people still use it. Salt of hartshorn makes their cookies crisper and lighter than does ordinary baking powder. Although the hartshorn emits an odor of ammonia during baking, the results are more than worth any crinkling of nostrils it may cause; moreover, the cookies will not bear a trace of the smell.

Flavorsome and elaborate confections

Some idea of how seriously the Danish housewife takes the threat of unexpected company can be gained from the fact that her cookie recipes usually yield 12 dozen or more flavorsome morsels. When she begins her preparations for Christmas, in anticipation of the steady stream of visitors she will receive, she will think nothing of turning out 300 *brune kage (page 193)*, a favorite brown spice cookie. And for the *brune kage* to be really good she may start on them a full two weeks in advance of baking day, so that the ingredients will have all that time to meld their flavors in the batter. A final test of her excellence will be how thin she can make them. A Danish girl in America whose mother sent her a box of fragile *brune kage* as a Christmas remembrance was shocked to find only cookie dust inside—but her nostalgia prompted her to pour it out and dab it up with moistened fingertips.

In cakes, as in cookies, the challenges for a Scandinavian housewife are numerous. But it should be said at the outset that a cake in Scandinavia can be quite a different thing from a cake in the United States. There is, for example, the *kransekage* (literally, wreath cake) made almost completely from marzipan. This towering confection, some two and a half feet tall, is built up in concentric rings, with zigzag pipings of white sugar icing all around. A favorite at birthdays or weddings in Norway and Denmark, the *kranse-*

kage is difficult to make and is most often baked by professionals, who finish it off with a couple of crisscrossed national flags on top and a flurry of bonbons wrapped in cellophane and fixed to the sides with burnt caramel.

If *kransekage* exceeds a housewife's ambitions, a *lagkage* (layer cake) most certainly does not, although it is no simple thing either. In Scandinavia a layer cake means at least three, and usually more, layers baked thin and crisp and piled one on top of the other, with thick latherings of cream or custard in between. One, called Othello cake in Denmark, consists of a layer of pastry, a layer of creamy vanilla custard, a layer of almond macaroons, another layer of vanilla custard and yet another layer of pastry, surmounted by more custard and an additional and final layer of pastry glazed with chocolate icing. And around the sides whipped cream is smoothed.

A Danish recipe for a *lagkage* to end all layer cakes calls for a half pound of butter, a half pound of ground almonds, a half pound of sugar and three cups of flour. The measures for the filling are equally extravagant—a pint of cream, a half pint of milk, eight egg yolks, sugar and vanilla. But what is amazing about the cake is not so much its richness but the way it is treated after it has been assembled. It is put in a cool place, or in the refrigerator, and then, almost as though it were alive, fed from time to time by administering cream to its absorbent layers. The woman to whom this recipe belongs remembers how her family used to make expectant trips to the cool cellar, where the cake was kept, and poke holes into it—wells into which they poured the so-called filling cream.

Not all cakes in Scandinavia are so unabashedly rich. There is the Danish *sandkage (page 168)*, a kind of pound cake that got its name from the grainy texture imparted to it by the potato flour that is still often used in its preparation. It is baked in a loaf shape and served unadorned by any topping, but for all its unpretentiousness, it must be golden with eggs and butter. In the old days a sand cake batter that had not been beaten for at least an hour, and that did not include a dozen eggs, was looked down upon. Mercifully, standards have been lowered somewhat since then. Opinions as to what constitutes a good sand cake vary. Some people like it dry, some moist, others slightly underbaked. In Finland, a similar cake, *kermakakku,* is made with sour cream and delicately spiced with cinnamon and cardamom or ginger; it is so light it seems to be reaching for the sky *(Recipe Booklet)*.

While many of the baked goods of Scandinavia are found in identical or similar form in each of the countries, there is one whole category of baking in which the Danes hold a uniquely superior position—pastry. No one else can make pastry as good as the kind they can—none quite so light or with so many tissue-thin layers. The rest of the world calls this Danish pastry, but the Danes call it *wienerbrød,* Vienna bread, which might seem like excessive modesty on their part, but in fact is not. Its origins are indeed Viennese. About one hundred years ago the bakers of Copenhagen went on strike, demanding cash wages instead of the traditional room and board. The employers retaliated by firing the Danish bakers and importing Germans and Austrians to replace them. It was not long before Viennese pastry became popular, for no Dane had ever used the Viennese method of folding butter into the yeast dough. When the Danish bakers, pragmatic fellows, finally returned to their jobs, they copied the techniques of the Viennese, and then, being Danes, went on to improve the pastry by adding jam and other kinds of filling to it. Danish pastry became so famous abroad that its praise was sung even in Austria.

For the Danes pastry is not something to be made from a recipe only; it must be made with feeling as well—all the little insights that years of experience have yielded and for which there are often no words. They proceed cautiously, painstakingly—making sure that the temperature of the dough and the butter are the same, chilling the dough between rollings to keep the butter from oozing out, allowing the dough to rise in a warm place, holding back on the fillings. But other variables also come into play. The flour the Danes use differs from American flour. During the baking Danish flour holds up better, thus preventing the collapse of the paper-thin layers so essential to the pastry's character. Danish butter is also different, for it is made from cultured, rather than sweet, cream and since this butter has a lower water content, it is more malleable and easier to roll out. Even climate comes into play; mild summers assure that temperatures will never be so high that a crust forms on the dough as it is rising, or worse, that the butter melts out of it.

But in spite of these differences, Danish pastry made in an American home can perfectly well compare with that made in Denmark. It assuredly will not be like the pastry that is commonly called Danish in the United States, for which Danes who know it have a word—cement. The recipes and procedures outlined in words and pictures on pages 174-179 have been especially worked out for this book with the aim of achieving Danish standards of excellence despite the difference in available ingredients.

Ingrained though the coffee-and-cake habit of the Scandinavians may now be, it is, as eating patterns go, a relatively new one, for it did not start until the 16th and 17th Centuries, when coffee and sugar were introduced to the North. But long before these cakes originated there was of course bread, and in Scandinavia bread is still one of the most varied of foods in shape, texture and consistency *(page 172)*. Even a bread made from a single grain can be entirely different from place to place or country to country. Take rye bread. In eastern Finland it is a thick, moist loaf; in western Finland it will be flat and hard and have a hole through the middle. In Denmark it is a brown, dense brick, which, when sliced an eighth of an inch thin, functions as the buttered underpinning for the open-face sandwich. And in Sweden rye bread is something else again—sweet more often than sour.

Many Scandinavian breads are hard rather than soft. Often they do not take loaf forms but range instead from flat, shinglelike rectangles only a couple of inches square to disks the size of wheels. They may be made without leavening, as was the first bread of the area, or raised with sour dough as in the Middle Ages. Some breads are cooked on iron griddles or baked in wood-burning ovens, and a few, harking back to the prehistoric past, are baked directly in the embers. Others are twice-baked to dry them out, and still others are allowed to dry out naturally—the vestigial hole piercing many breads of this type dating from the time when bread used to be strung on stakes and suspended from the ceiling.

What is exciting about the bread of Scandinavia is that the past survives and is perpetuated through it. In fact, in bread can be read much of the social history of the region from the Viking days onward. The sugar in many of Sweden's loaves suggests how much this commodity meant to the coun-

Hot from the oven, crusty loaves of Finnish sour rye cool off on boards before being strung along overhead poles to dry out. Mrs. Hilda Ahola, a farm wife, bakes as many as 150 such loaves at a time, enough to last her family a couple of months. She makes the hole in the bread by punching through the dough with a cow's horn.

try's poor: when they finally were able to afford sugar, the peasants included it even in the dough for their humble bread. Throughout much of Scandinavia white bread continues to be called French bread, an admission of the debt bakers and, for that matter, cooks of the area owe to culinary methods imported from France. The role climate played in shaping foods down through the centuries is to be seen in the grains still used—oats, barley, buckwheat and above all rye, all of which flourish where the weather is damp and cool. And again the climate's influence can be detected in the number and types of crisp breads consumed throughout the area. These are dry for the simple reason that they used to be made from grain that often had to be harvested before the short Northern growing season gave it a chance to ripen fully. To store grain that was still green would have caused it to spoil, so it was ground and immediately baked into bread. The bread in turn was stored—hung from rafters or put away in chests. When harvests failed and there was no longer any preserved bread on hand to eat, people stripped the inner bark from trees, pulverized it and baked it into loaves. Bark bread was eaten as late as the 19th Century during famines.

The bread of Scandinavia (of which this array is but the smallest sampling) takes a variety of forms—from hard, stippled wheels, like the Swedish *knäckebröd* at far left, to plump rounds, ovals, rectangles and braided twists. The little loaf with the hole in it used to be made frequently in northern Sweden from a mixture of batter and pig's blood and then suspended over stoves to dry out; in the spring, it would be boiled in salt water to be eaten with fried pork fat and onions. Today it is baked only on special occasions.

Inevitably, much superstition came to surround the growing of precious grain, the milling of flour and the baking of bread. Three straws from the harvest were baked into the bread, and if a loaf containing these straws cracked during storage, it was read as an omen that the harvest to come would be poor. To invite God's blessing, the sign of the Cross was made over the grain itself, over the dough, in front of the oven and over the baked bread. But lest the devil be tempted, singing during baking was prohibited. And on certain days, Sundays, Mondays and Thursdays, no bread could be baked at all. If a loaf revealed a fissure when cut open, death lurked nearby. A loaf with a candle in it, or weighted with mercury, when floated on the water could be counted on to find the body of a drowned person. And by some imagined miracle, leftover Christmas bread eaten on Easter Day provided protection against disease, snake bites and other catastrophes.

The superstitions surrounding bread have vanished, but the reverence and the deep appreciation for it are still there. No well-laid table is without its bread basket in which three, four or more varieties are stacked, leaning against each other like cards in a deck, each breathing forth its own special goodness.

Sandkage
SAND CAKE

To make one 8-inch round cake

2 teaspoons unsalted butter, softened
1 tablespoon dry bread crumbs
16 tablespoons (2 quarter-pound sticks) unsalted butter
1 cup sugar
4 eggs, at room temperature
1 tablespoon brandy
1 teaspoon vanilla
1 teaspoon grated lemon rind
2 cups all-purpose flour
1 tablespoon cornstarch
¼ teaspoon salt
2¼ teaspoons double-acting baking powder

Preheat the oven to 350°. With a pastry brush or a paper towel, lightly spread the bottom and sides of an 8-inch tube pan (including the inner cone of the pan) with the 2 teaspoons of soft butter. Sprinkle the bottom and sides of the pan evenly with bread crumbs, turn the pan over and tap out any excess crumbs.

Cream the ½ pound of butter and sugar together with an electric mixer set at medium speed or by beating them against the sides of a bowl with a wooden spoon until very light and fluffy. Now beat in the 4 eggs, 1 at a time, making sure that each one is thoroughly incorporated before adding another. Then beat in the tablespoon of brandy, teaspoon of vanilla and teaspoon of grated lemon rind. Should the mixture appear to be curdling, beat it very hard until it becomes smooth again. Sift the flour, cornstarch, salt and baking powder together into a mixing bowl and add them to the butter-egg mixture all at once. Beat vigorously until the ingredients are all absorbed, but no longer.

Pour the batter into the prepared tube pan. Rap the pan once sharply on the table to eliminate any air pockets, and bake in the center of the oven for 50 to 60 minutes, or until the top is golden brown and springy when lightly touched. Run a knife around the edge of the cake to loosen it from the pan; then place a wire cake rack on top of the cake and invert the two. Set another rack on top of the cake and again invert, so that the top of the cake is now facing up. Serve at room temperature.

Mazarintårta
MAZARIN CAKE

To make one 8-inch round cake

PASTRY
8 tablespoons (1 quarter-pound stick) unsalted butter, softened
1½ teaspoons sugar
¼ teaspoon salt
2 egg yolks
1⅓ cups all-purpose flour

FRANGIPANE FILLING
8 tablespoons (1 quarter-pound stick) unsalted butter, softened
1 cup almond paste, at room temperature
2 eggs, lightly beaten
1 teaspoon grated lemon rind
2 teaspoons flour

1 tablespoon butter, softened
Confectioners' sugar

TO MAKE THE PASTRY, cream the butter and sugar together by using an electric mixer set at medium speed or by beating them against the side of a bowl with a wooden spoon until light and fluffy. Beat in the salt and the egg yolks, 1 at a time. Now beat in the flour and mix well. Flour your hands lightly and shape the pastry into a ball. Wrap in wax paper and chill for at least 30 minutes.

TO MAKE THE FRANGIPANE, cream the butter by using an electric mixer set at medium speed or by beating it against the side of a bowl with a wooden spoon until it is light and fluffy. Beat in the almond paste, 2 table-spoons at a time, and then beat in the lightly beaten eggs. Continue to beat until the mixture is very smooth, then stir in the grated lemon rind and flour. Set aside.

Preheat the oven to 325°. Place the chilled dough on a floured board or pastry cloth. Dust a little flour over it and roll it out—from the center to within an inch of the far edge. Lift the dough and turn it clockwise, about the space of 2 hours on the clock; roll again from the center to the far edge. Repeat—lifting, turning, rolling—until you make a circle 11 or 12 inches in diameter and about ⅛ inch thick. Butter the bottom and sides of an 8-inch false-bottomed cake pan with the tablespoon of softened butter.

Roll the pastry over the pin and unroll it over the pan, or drape the pastry over the rolling pin, lift it up and unfold it over the pan. Gently press the pastry into the bottom and around the sides of the pan, being careful not to stretch it. Roll the pin over the rim of the pan, pressing down hard to trim off the excess pastry. With a rubber spatula, spread the filling on top of the pastry.

Place the cake pan in the center of the oven for 45 to 50 minutes, or until the pastry is golden brown and the filling is set. Let the cake cool a little in the pan, then set the pan on a large jar or coffee can and slip down the outside rim. Slide the cake onto a platter, sprinkle with confectioners' sugar, and serve at room temperature.

Toscatårta
ALMOND-TOPPED CAKE

To make one 8-inch round cake

CAKE
2 teaspoons unsalted butter, softened
1 tablespoon dry bread crumbs

1 cup all-purpose flour
1 teaspoon double-acting baking powder
¼ teaspoon salt
2 eggs
⅔ cup sugar
½ teaspoon vanilla
¼ cup milk
4 tablespoons unsalted butter, melted

ALMOND TOPPING
2 tablespoons unsalted butter, softened
¼ cup sugar
1 tablespoon flour
2 tablespoons milk
⅓ cup sliced blanched almonds
½ teaspoon vanilla

Preheat the oven to 350°. With a pastry brush or a paper towel, spread the bottom and sides of an 8-inch round pan with 2 teaspoons of soft butter, then sprinkle with bread crumbs. Turn the pan over and tap out any excess crumbs.

Sift the flour, baking powder and salt together in a mixing bowl. In another large bowl, beat the eggs with a wire whisk, rotary or electric beater until they are well blended. Slowly beat in the sugar and vanilla and continue to beat until the mixture falls back into the bowl in a lazy ribbon when the whisk or beater is lifted out.

With a rubber spatula, fold the flour mixture and milk alternately into the eggs and sugar by first adding about ⅓ of the flour, then a little milk, then another ⅓ of flour, the remaining milk, and last, the remaining flour. (Fold by using a slow under-over motion rather than a rotary motion.) Before the last of the flour has been folded into the batter, add the melted butter. As soon as there is no further trace of either flour or butter, pour the batter into the prepared pan. Be careful not to overfold. Rap the pan sharply on the table once to remove any air pockets.

Bake the cake in the center of the oven for 30 to 40 minutes, or until the cake is golden brown and is springy when touched lightly. Test further by inserting a toothpick into the center of the cake; it should come out dry and clean.

Meanwhile, prepare the almond topping. Combine the butter, sugar and flour in a small pan and stir together briefly with a wooden spoon. Add the milk and cook over low heat, stirring constantly, for 2 or 3 minutes, until the mixture is smooth and thick. Remove from the heat and stir in the almonds and vanilla. Set aside.

Preheat the broiler to its lowest level. When the cake is done, carefully run a knife around the edge to loosen it from the pan; then place a wire cake rack on top and invert the two. Set another rack on top of the cake and again invert; the top of the cake is now facing up. With an icing spatula or spoon, spread the topping lightly and evenly over the hot cake. Place the cake, still on its rack, under the broiler, about 3 inches from the heat. Broil 3 to 5 minutes, until the top is golden brown and bubbling. Check constantly to be sure that the topping does not burn. Serve the toscatårta while it is still warm.

1 To make apple muffins, divide the dough into 12 pieces and press these into the cups of a muffin tin.

2 After the cups are lined, fill them with the chopped apples and apricot preserve. Top with slivered almonds.

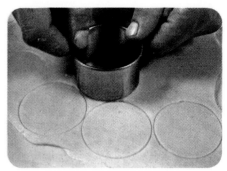

3 Roll the remaining dough out thinly and cut it into circles with a cookie cutter or wine glass.

4 Place a circle of dough on top of each of the filled cups. The circles should just fit the cups.

5 Press the edges of the dough together to seal them. When baked (*right*), the muffins are golden brown.

Makes 12 muffins

5 tablespoons unsalted butter
½ cup sugar
1 egg
1½ cups all-purpose flour
¼ teaspoon baking powder

FILLING
1½ cups applesauce

ALTERNATE FRUIT FILLING
2 tablespoons unsalted butter
2 tart cooking apples, peeled, cored and diced finely (about 2 cups)
¾ cup apricot preserves
Slivered almonds
Confectioners' sugar

Äppelformar
APPLE MUFFINS

Cream the butter and sugar together by using an electric mixer set at medium speed or by beating them against the sides of a bowl with a wooden spoon until light and fluffy. Beat in the egg. Sift the flour and baking powder together and add to the butter mixture, using your fingertips to blend all the ingredients into a dough. Shape into a ball, wrap in wax paper and chill for at least 1 hour.

Preheat the oven to 350°. The *äppelformar* are made in muffin tins of 12 cups, each of which is 2 or 2½ inches in diameter. Lightly oil or butter the cups. Cut off ⅓ of the dough, rewrap it and replace it in the refrigerator. Divide the remaining dough into 12 pieces and firmly press each piece into the bottom and sides of the cups with your fingers. The dough lining should be about ¼ inch thick. Fill each cup with 2 tablespoons of applesauce. Roll out the remaining chilled dough to a ⅛-inch thickness and using a 2- or 2½-inch cookie cutter or glass, cut the dough into 12 circles the same diameter as the muffin cups. Moisten the edges of the muffin tops with cold water and pinch them together with the edges of the filled muffins, sealing them completely. Bake for 30 to 35 minutes. Loosen the muffins with a knife and let them cool in the cups. Use a narrow spatula or knife to lift them out. Sprinkle with confectioners' sugar before serving.

ALTERNATE FRUIT FILLING: Melt the butter in an enameled or stainless-steel saucepan over moderate heat and add the finely diced apples. Cook 1 or 2 minutes, shaking the pan to coat the apples in the butter. Line the muffin cups with dough, as above, and fill each almost full with the apples. Top each with 1 tablespoon of apricot preserve and a sprinkling of slivered almonds. Cover with the muffin tops and bake as above.

Operatårta
CREAMY LAYER CAKE

To make 1 cake

Preheat the oven to 400°. Spread an 11-by-16-inch jelly-roll pan with 1 tablespoon of the soft butter and line the pan with a 22-inch strip of wax paper, letting the wax paper extend over the narrower ends of the pan. Similarly spread the wax paper with the remaining soft butter, then sprinkle it with the 2 tablespoons of flour and tip it from side to side to be sure the surface is evenly covered. Knock out any excess flour.

In a large mixing bowl (preferably of unlined copper), beat the egg whites with a large balloon whisk, rotary or electric beater until they form soft peaks. Gradually beat in the sugar, 1 tablespoon at a time, and continue to beat vigorously until the egg whites form stiff, unwavering peaks. Place the egg yolks in another large mixing bowl and stir them gently for a minute or so; then stir in the vanilla. With a rubber spatula, mix a heaping tablespoon of the beaten egg whites into the yolks, then pour the mixture over the remaining egg whites in the bowl and sprinkle with the cornstarch and flour. Fold all of the ingredients together gently, using an under-over motion rather than a rotary motion. When the egg whites are no longer visible, pour the mixture into the already prepared jelly-roll pan and spread it out evenly and gently with a rubber spatula. Bake for 10 to 12 minutes, or until the cake is a light golden brown. Remove the pan from the oven, loosen the sides of the cake with a metal spatula or knife and, using the ends of the wax paper as handles, lift it out of the pan. Turn it over onto wax paper to cool and carefully peel off the original wax paper.

While the cake is cooling, prepare the pastry cream. In a 1½- to 2-quart enameled or stainless-steel saucepan, vigorously beat the ¼ cup flour and ½ cup of the light cream into a smooth paste with a wire whisk. Then gradually beat in the rest of the cream, salt and sugar. Cook over moderate heat, still beating vigorously, for 1 or 2 minutes, or until the mixture is thick and smooth. Remove from the heat.

In a small bowl combine ¼ cup of the hot sauce with the egg yolks. Then slowly pour this mixture in a thin stream into the pan, whisking constantly. Cook over low heat for 1 or 2 minutes, stirring all the time, but do not let it boil. Remove from the heat and stir in the vanilla, and then the softened gelatin. Set the pastry cream aside to cool.

When the spongecake has cooled to room temperature, slice it crosswise into 3 equal parts (each measuring 11 by 5 inches). Place 1 layer on a flat serving platter and spread ¼ of the cooled pastry cream over it with a spatula or spoon. Place the second layer of cake on top and spread with another ¼ of the pastry cream. Top with the remaining cake and spread the top and sides with the remaining pastry cream. With your fingertips or a piece of wax paper, gently press the sliced almonds into the pastry cream all around and on top of the cake. Chill for at least 2 hours before serving.

SPONGECAKE
2 tablespoons soft butter
2 tablespoons flour
4 egg whites
¼ cup sugar
4 egg yolks
½ teaspoon vanilla
¼ cup sifted cornstarch
¼ cup sifted flour

PASTRY CREAM
¼ cup flour
2 cups light cream
¼ teaspoon salt
¾ cup sugar
8 egg yolks
2 teaspoons vanilla
1 package powdered unflavored gelatin, softened for 3 minutes in ¼ cup cold water

¾ cup sliced blanched almonds

Suomalaisleipä
FINNISH BREAD

To make 1 loaf

4 packages active dry yeast
3 teaspoons dark brown sugar
1¼ cups lukewarm water
1 tablespoon melted butter
1½ teaspoons salt
2 cups all-purpose flour
1½ cups rye flour
1 tablespoon soft butter

Sprinkle the yeast and 1 teaspoon of the brown sugar over ½ cup of the luke-warm water. Be absolutely sure that the water is lukewarm—neither too hot nor too cool to the touch. Let the mixture stand for 2 or 3 minutes, then stir it to dissolve the yeast completely. Set the cup aside in a warm, draft-free spot (such as an unlighted oven) for 5 to 7 minutes, or until the mixture has begun to bubble and has almost doubled in volume.

Pour the yeast mixture into a large mixing bowl, add the remaining ¾ cup of lukewarm water, and, with a wooden spoon, mix in the remaining 2 teaspoons of brown sugar, the melted butter, salt, white flour and 1 cup of the rye flour. When the mixture forms a smooth dough, gather it into a ball, cover the bowl loosely with a kitchen towel and let it rest at room temper-ature for about 10 minutes.

Transfer the dough to a floured pastry cloth or board and knead it by pulling the dough into an oblong shape, folding it end to end, then press-ing it down and pushing it forward several times with the heels of your hands. Turn the dough slightly toward you and repeat the process—pulling, folding, pushing and pressing. Continue to knead, using the extra ½ cup of rye flour to sprinkle over the dough and pastry board or cloth if either becomes sticky.

When the dough is elastic and smooth, gather it into a rough ball and place it in a large, lightly buttered bowl. Dust the top of the dough lightly with flour, cover it again with the kitchen towel and let it rest in the warm, draft-free spot (the oven, again) for about 45 minutes, until it has doubled in bulk and no longer springs back when it is poked with a finger.

Preheat the oven to 375°. With a pastry brush or paper towel, lightly spread a cookie sheet with the tablespoon of soft butter and sprinkle it with flour, tipping the sheet to coat it evenly. Turn it over and tap it on a hard surface to knock off any excess flour. Punch the dough down with your fist, and knead it again briefly on the pastry board. Shape it into a round, flat loaf about 9 or 10 inches in diameter, and set on the cookie sheet. Bake 1 hour, or until the bread has a dark-brown crust and a toothpick or skewer inserted in its center comes out dry and clean. Remove to a cake rack to cool, and serve, if possible, while still warm.

The Pick of the Danish Pastries

A hot, bubbling stream of coffee cascading into a cup, a trayful of freshly baked Danish pastries—this is the stuff of which pleasure is made. And the pleasure can be combined with a marvelous feeling of accomplishment, for pastries as buttery, as flaky and as airily light as these can be made at home. They need loving care and deep appreciation. Making them is a challenge, but the job is rendered easier by the step-by-step photographs on pages 175-177, which detail the complete process from dough to oven for the five varieties of pastry shown on the opposite page. The recipes are on pages 178-179.

172

Makes 2 cakes or about 2 dozen pastries

½ cup lukewarm water
2 packages active dry yeast
½ cup sugar
5 to 6 cups unsifted all-purpose flour
   or 6 to 7 cups granulated flour
½ cup cold milk
1 tablespoon sweet butter
2 whole eggs
1 teaspoon salt
¼ teaspoon ground cardamom
1 teaspoon vanilla
1 pound unsalted butter, chilled

Wienerbrød
DANISH PASTRY DOUGH

Pour the lukewarm water into a small bowl and sprinkle the yeast and 1 teaspoon of the sugar over it. Let the mixture stand for 2 or 3 minutes, then stir it to dissolve the yeast completely. Set the bowl in a warm, draft-free place, such as an unlighted oven, for 8 to 10 minutes, or until the yeast bubbles and doubles in bulk.

Place 4 cups of all-purpose flour (or 5¼ cups of granulated flour) in a large mixing bowl. Make a well in the center and add the yeast mixture, the cold milk, 1 tablespoon of butter, 2 eggs, salt, cardamom, vanilla and the remaining sugar. With your fingers, mix the ingredients together until a soft dough is formed, then shape into a ball and place it on a floured pastry cloth or board. To knead the dough pull it into an oblong shape, fold it end to end, then press it down and push it forward several times with the heels of the hands. Turn dough slightly toward you and repeat the process—pulling, folding, pushing and pressing. Continue kneading until the dough is smooth and elastic. This will take at least 10 minutes. Sprinkle the dough with flour, wrap in aluminum foil and refrigerate for 30 minutes.

Meanwhile, remove the butter from the refrigerator and let it soften to the point where it is neither too hard nor too soft; it should hold the impression of a finger. If the butter is in the shape of a brick, place it on a sheet of wax paper lightly dusted with flour, dust with more flour and cover with another sheet of wax paper. With a heavy rolling pin, roll the butter into an 8-by-12-inch rectangle, ¼ inch thick. Cut it in half, making 2 sheets, each a 6-by-8-inch rectangle. Wrap both halves in wax paper, and place in the refrigerator. If the butter has become very soft while rolling it, chill until it is again as firm as when you began rolling it, but it should not become hard. If the butter is in quarter-pound sticks, slice each quarter in half lengthwise. Place 4 of the pieces side by side on wax paper dusted with flour, dust with more flour and cover with another sheet of wax paper. With a heavy rolling pin, roll the butter into a rectangle 6 by 8 inches in size and ¼ inch thick. Repeat with the remaining butter.

Liberally sprinkle a pastry board or cloth (of canvas or heavy muslin) with flour. Roll the chilled dough out on the floured surface into a 9-by-18-inch rectangle, ⅛ inch thick. Place one sheet of butter across the center of the dough and bring the end of the dough farther from you over the butter, sealing it along the sides with your fingers. Place the other sheet of butter on top and bring the other half of the dough over that, again sealing the butter in. Dust with flour, wrap in aluminum foil and chill 20 minutes.

Turn the dough around so that the narrow side faces you. Roll out the dough to an 8-by-18-inch strip. Fold both narrow ends in to meet at the center, then fold in half, making 4 layers. Wrap again in foil, chill another 20 minutes, and repeat the procedure—with the narrow side toward you, roll it out, fold it in 4 layers, then chill for 20 minutes. Remove from the refrigerator, roll into an 8-by-18-inch rectangle again, and finally fold it in half. Wrap in foil and chill 2 to 3 hours (or overnight) before using.

To make the butter cake *(page 179),* use half the dough. To make the pastries *(page 178-179),* use a quarter of the dough for each recipe. Even if you choose to use all the dough for only 1 type of pastry, cut it into quarters to facilitate handling.

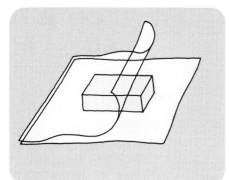

1 Place the butter on floured wax paper and cover with another sheet of wax paper.

2 Keeping butter under top sheet, roll out into an 8-by-12-inch rectangle.

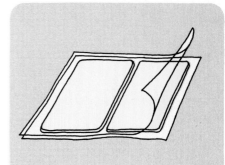

3 Cut butter in half, wrap in wax paper and chill in refrigerator.

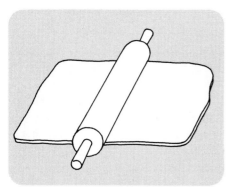

4 Now roll out the dough to make a rectangle of about 9 by 18 inches.

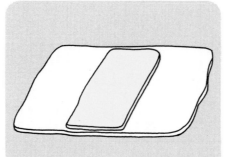

5 Place one half of the rolled butter in center of the rolled dough.

6 Fold over half the dough. Seal edges (here left open for illustration).

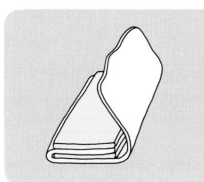

7 Place other half of butter on top and fold second half of dough over that.

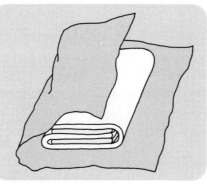

8 Sprinkle the dough with flour, wrap in aluminum foil and chill.

9 Now roll out the dough to form an 8-by-18-inch rectangle.

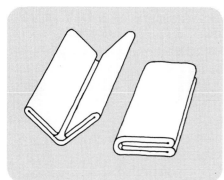

10 Fold both ends to the center. Then fold one half over the other, making four layers. Chill 20 minutes and repeat steps 9 and 10. Then roll out again, fold in half and chill for 2 or 3 hours.

A sliced section of the butter-rich dough shows the layers of the rollings. When baked it will produce a light, flaky, delicious pastry.

Step-by-Step to the Best in Danish Pastry

The four baked pastries and the cake shown in the making on these pages are all confected from the Danish pastry dough whose preparation is presented on the preceding page. Each pastry recipe calls for a quarter of the dough. The cake recipe alone calls for one half of it. (The dough is most easily handled in quarter parts.) A floured pastry board or a muslin or canvas pastry cloth are the best working surfaces. The cloth is helpful, as several of the pictures show, in rolling up the dough or in flipping one side over the other because it can be lifted and used to ease the dough along. But on the floured board the flat surface of a narrow spatula will prove just as useful in making the dough behave. Because of the chilling and rechilling, making the basic dough takes time and is exacting, but not difficult. The results are worth the time and effort; these are the finest Danish pastries to be found outside Denmark itself.

ENVELOPES
1 Cut rolled-out dough into 4-inch squares and fold.

2 Folds are from corners to the middle, where gentle finger pressure seals them.

COCKS' COMBS
1 Cover one half of a sheet of dough with frangipane.

2 Fold the other half over, seal edges closed with your fingers, then trim the edges.

SNAILS
1 Cover filling with wax paper and roll into dough.

2 Use pastry cloth to help roll dough up into a long, fat cigar shape.

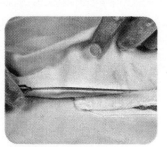

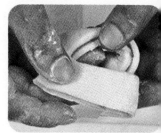

APRICOT SLIPS
1 Cover one half of a sheet of dough with apricot preserve.

2 Using pastry cloth to help, flip over the other half so that both sides meet.

3 Cut into 2-by-5-inch strips and make a 3-inch slit lengthwise in each strip.

4 Tuck one end of each strip under, and pull up and out through its slit.

BUTTER CAKE
1 Press a circle of dough snugly into a cake pan.

2 Spread a butter-sugar mixture over half a 14-by-14-inch sheet of dough.

3 Now fold unspread half of dough over spread half; seal edges with your fingers.

4 After cutting the folded dough into 2-inch strips, roll up each strip.

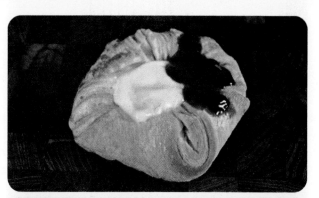

3 Fill the center of each folded square with a tablespoon of pastry cream.

4 Add a dab of red currant jelly and bake to produce the delicacy at right.

3 Cut the folded dough into six 2½-inch strips. Make 3 slits ¾ through each strip.

4 Bend strips slightly. The baked pastry (right) has been sprinkled with sugar.

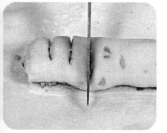

3 Make 2 half cuts and then a full cut ½ inch apart along the roll's length.

4 Gently spread each section apart a little. The baked pastry is at right.

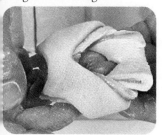

5 Gently press the slip down with your hands, slightly flattening it.

6 Brush with egg white and sprinkle with sugar; then bake the pastry (right).

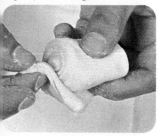

5 Take a flap of dough at one end of each roll, tuck under, and press gently to secure.

6 Set rolls on the dough in the pan, bake, and spread butter cake with icing (right).

To make 5 pastries

¼ Danish pastry dough *(page 174)*
⅓ cup pastry cream *(page 171)*
2 tablespoons red currant jelly
1 tablespoon soft butter
2 tablespoons flour

Spandauer
ENVELOPES

Preheat the oven to 400°. On a floured surface, roll the dough into a 4-by-20-inch rectangle. With a pastry wheel or small, sharp knife, trim the ragged edges of the dough and cut the rectangle into 5 parts, making 4-by-4-inch squares of dough. Fold in each corner to meet in the center, and press down the points to seal them. Place a heaping tablespoon of pastry cream in the center of each envelope and top with a teaspoon of red currant jelly. With a pastry brush or paper towel, grease a cookie sheet with 1 tablespoon of butter and sprinkle it with flour, tapping off any excess. Place the *spandauer* on the sheet and set in the middle of the oven for 10 minutes. Reduce the heat to 350° and bake 15 minutes, until the pastries are a light gold. With a wide spatula, transfer them to a wire cake rack to cool.

To make 6 pastries

FRANGIPANE FILLING
3 tablespoons unsalted butter
6 tablespoons almond paste
1 teaspoon flour
⅛ teaspoon grated lemon rind

¼ Danish pastry dough *(page 174)*
1 egg white combined with 1 teaspoon
    water
Granulated sugar
1 tablespoon soft butter
2 tablespoons flour

Hanekam
COCKS' COMBS

To make the frangipane filling, cream the butter by using an electric mixer set at medium speed or by beating it against the side of a bowl with a wooden spoon. When light and fluffy, beat in the almond paste, a little at a time, and then the flour and grated lemon rind. Preheat the oven to 400°. On a floured surface, roll the dough into a 10-by-15-inch rectangle. With a pastry wheel or small, sharp knife, cut off its ragged edges. Spread a thin layer of the frangipane lengthwise over half of the dough. Fold the other side over, seal the edges with your fingers and cut into 2½-inch strips. Now cut 3 slits ¾ of the way into each strip, and bend the strips slightly so that they form a crescent. With a pastry brush or paper towel, grease a cookie sheet with 1 tablespoon of butter and sprinkle it with flour, tapping off any excess. Set the pastries on the sheet and brush each strip with the egg white and water mixture. Sprinkle with sugar and bake 10 minutes. Reduce the heat to 350° and bake another 10 minutes. Remove from the oven and, with a wide spatula, transfer the pastries to a wire cake rack to cool.

To make 8 pastries

¼ Danish pastry dough *(page 174)*
1 egg white mixed with 1 teaspoon
    water
3 tablespoons sugar combined with
    1 tablespoon ground cinnamon
2 tablespoons dried black currants,
    soaked in 2 tablespoons Cognac
    or rum and drained
1 tablespoon soft butter
2 tablespoons flour

Snegle
SNAILS

Preheat the oven to 400°. On a floured surface, roll the dough into a 9-by-16-inch rectangle. Brush lightly with the egg white and water mixture, then sprinkle with the chopped nuts, the cinnamon-sugar mixture and the currants. Place a sheet of wax paper on top and gently press the topping into the dough with a rolling pin. Peel off the wax paper and roll up the dough lengthwise, forming a 16-inch-long tight roll. Make 2 slits ½ inch apart, penetrating only ¾ of the way into the roll. Then cut all the way through the roll ½ inch past the partial cuts. (Each pastry will thus be 1½ inches long and have 2 slits in it.) Gently spread open each pastry until it resembles a fan. Lightly grease a cookie sheet with 1 tablespoon of butter and sprinkle it with flour, tapping off any excess. Place the fans on the sheet and bake 10 minutes, then lower the heat to 350° and bake another 15 minutes. Remove from the oven and with a wide spatula transfer the fans to a wire cake rack to cool.

Abrikossnitte
APRICOT SLIPS

Preheat the oven to 400°. Cook the apricot preserve in a 1-quart enameled or stainless-steel saucepan over low heat, stirring almost constantly, until it has reduced to about 6 tablespoons. Set aside to cool.

On a floured surface, roll the dough into a 10-by-18-inch rectangle. With a pastry wheel or small, sharp knife, trim away its ragged edges. Using a spatula or the back of a spoon, spread half of the dough lengthwise with the apricot preserve. Carefully fold over the other half of the dough to form a long envelope. Dust the top with flour, place a sheet of wax paper on top, and, with a rolling pin, roll the dough gently to press in the filling. Peel off the wax paper and cut through the dough at 2-inch intervals, making 9 pastries 2 by 5 inches in size. With a small, sharp knife, make a 3-inch slit in the center of each pastry, leaving 1 inch unslit on either side. Bend one uncut end of the strip under the slit and, with your finger, push it up through the pastry to make a bow-tie-like shape. Lightly grease a cookie sheet with 1 tablespoon of butter and sprinkle it with flour, tapping off any excess flour. Set the pastries on the cookie sheet and brush them with the egg white and water. Sprinkle with sugar and bake 10 minutes. Reduce the heat to 350° and bake another 15 minutes. Remove from the oven and, with a wide spatula, transfer to a cake rack to cool.

To make 9 pastries

½ cup apricot preserve, rubbed through a sieve
¼ Danish pastry dough *(page 174)*
1 egg white combined with 1 teaspoon water
Coarse sugar
1 tablespoon soft butter
2 tablespoons flour

Smørkage
BUTTER CAKE

Cut off ⅓ of the dough and replace the other ⅔ in the refrigerator. On a floured pastry cloth or board, roll the small piece of dough into an 11- or 12-inch circle. Place the bottom of an 8- or 9-inch false-bottomed cake pan over the dough and with a sharp knife, cut the dough around the pan into a circle slightly larger than the pan (the dough tends to shrink when cut). Press the circle of dough into the bottom of the cake pan until it fits snugly, and brush with the egg white and water mixture.

Preheat the oven to 350°. Roll out the remaining ⅔ of dough into a 14-by-14-inch square. Cream the 4 tablespoons of butter and the sugar by using an electric mixer set at medium speed or by beating them against the side of a bowl with a wooden spoon. Beat in the almond extract and spread this mixture over half of the dough. Fold over the other half so that the two ends meet. With a small, sharp knife, cut the dough at 2-inch intervals, making 7 strips each 2 by 7 inches in size. Roll up each strip lengthwise and tuck the flap under the roll. Stand up 6 of the rolls (tucked end under) around the border of the dough in the pan, and stand the last roll in the middle. Bake in the center of the oven for 45 minutes, or until the top is golden brown.

Meanwhile, make the icing. In a large mixing bowl, beat the egg white to a froth by hand or in an electric mixer, and then beat in the sugar, salt and lemon juice. Continue to beat until the mixture is light and fluffy and forms soft peaks when the beater is removed from the bowl. (If the icing in the bowl is covered with plastic wrap, it can be kept at room temperature for several days.) Remove the cake from the oven and while it is still warm, brush the entire surface with the icing.

To make an 8- or 9-inch round cake

½ Danish pastry dough *(page 174)*
1 egg white combined with 1 teaspoon water
4 tablespoons unsalted butter
¼ cup sugar
2 teaspoons almond extract

ICING
1 egg white
1½ cups sifted confectioners' sugar
Pinch of salt
1 teaspoon lemon juice

To make 12

2 eggs
⅓ cup superfine sugar
3 tablespoons flour
2 teaspoons soft butter
1 tablespoon flour
1 cup chilled heavy cream
1 tablespoon sugar
1 teaspoon vanilla
16 to 18 fresh strawberries or ¾ cup
    lingonberries

Fyllda Strutar

PASTRY CONES FILLED WITH WHIPPED CREAM AND BERRIES

Preheat the oven to 400°. In a large bowl, beat together the eggs and sugar until thick and pale yellow, about 5 minutes. Stir in the flour, a little at a time, and mix until smooth. Grease a cookie sheet with the 2 teaspoons of soft butter and sprinkle it evenly with flour. Turn the sheet over and tap it lightly against a table or counter to knock off any excess flour.

Place 2 tablespoons of the batter on the cookie sheet and with the back of a large spoon or a rubber spatula, spread the batter out to form a thin circle about 4½ inches in diameter. (Do not place more than 3 or 4 circles on the sheet; they dry out rapidly after having been baked and must be relatively moist if they are to be successfully formed into cones.) Set the cookie sheet in the middle of the oven and bake 3 to 4 minutes, or until the circles are a pale gold around the edges. Quickly lift a circle loose from the cookie sheet with the flat of a metal spatula. Holding the circle gently in both hands, fold the two sides toward the center to form a cone. Stand the cone up in a water glass and let it remain there for 1 to 2 minutes, until it has dried and holds its shape. Now quickly shape the remaining baked circles, replacing the cookie sheet in the oven for a minute if the pastry has cooled too much and become brittle. Stir the batter before subsequent spreadings to make sure it is well mixed, and grease and flour the cookie sheet for each batch you prepare.

The *strutar* can be baked several days in advance and kept crisp in airtight containers. Just before you are ready to serve the cones—as a dessert or confection—whip the chilled cream with a wire whisk, rotary or electric beater in a large chilled bowl until it thickens. Add the sugar and vanilla and continue to beat until it is firm enough to hold its shape. Spoon the whipped cream into the cones (or pipe it in with a pastry bag) and top each with a strawberry or a few lingonberries. A traditional, practical way of serving the cones is to place a tall glass in the center of a round bowl. Stand up 1 cone in the glass, then surround it with the others, leaning them against the glass.

NOTE: Forming the cone takes practice and some dexterity *(see pictures below)*. For a simpler, equally delicate dessert—a pastry sandwich—prepare the batter as above. Then place 1 tablespoon of batter on the prepared cookie sheets and spread it into a 2-inch circle. Bake a dozen or so circles at a time, for 4 to 5 minutes, lift them from the sheet with a metal spatula, and let them cool on a cake rack. When ready to serve, spread the whipped cream over half of the circles and cover them with the remaining circles.

Start *strutar* by spreading
2 tablespoons of batter in a
circle on the cookie sheet.

Remove the baked circle
from the sheet by lifting it
off with a spatula or knife.

Shape the circle around one
thumb to form a cone and
set in a glass *(right)*.

Displayed in slender vases, the completed *fyllda strutar* are a decorative asset
when ready for serving—filled with helpings of flavored whipped cream
and topped with fresh red strawberries or bittersweet lingonberries.

IX

Christmas: Antidote to Darkness

The Norwegian Christmas coffee table, shown in its most opulent splendor, may include 10 different kinds of traditional cookies and five different types of cake. The cigar-shaped cookies are called *krumkaker* and are made with special irons engraved with religious and seasonal patterns.

Deccember is the darkest time of year in Scandinavia, when the nights are longest and the greater part of winter still stretches bleakly ahead. The only proper refuge from the darkness is home; here comfort is assured, and plants on the window sills and cut flowers in profusion on tables do their utmost to dispel the gloom. But all this would be to little avail if Christmas were not approaching toward the end of the month. Christmas is the Scandinavians' antidote to darkness, their way of breaking winter's hold. Nowhere is it celebrated quite so warmly—or with so much light and food—as in this northern corner of Europe.

The climax of the season is not Christmas Day but Christmas Eve—and perhaps this too has to do with darkness. Coming to dinner through blue-black streets, having the door of welcome thrown open and the yellow light suddenly stab out into the dark—all this belongs to Christmas in Scandinavia. Then there is the embracing warmth of the living room, the chatter on the way to the dining room, the table under the coppery glow of candle-light. On Christmas Eve the big meal of the season—the biggest, richest, most lavish meal of the year—is eaten. And after dessert, the plates of cookies and cakes are passed from hand to hand and the coffeepot is emptied, refilled and emptied again.

But the feasting by no means ends with Christmas Eve. The next day there is a cold buffet to conquer, and on the 26th and 27th, when calls are paid on friends, still more food must be ingested. The nibbling can go on as long as the season lasts—and to many in Scandinavia, Christmas is not officially over until January 13, Saint Canute's Day.

At Christmastime Scandinavians brighten their homes and trim their trees with distinctive ornaments. Typical are the straw yule goat, star, paper angel and starburst shown above. Below, carrying a small Christmas tree, is Scandinavia's Santa Claus. He plays the same jolly role at Christmastime as he does in other nations.

During this period, all the many food traditions of the Scandinavians come to the fore—and Scandinavian hospitality expands. National differences melt away in the good feeling that prevails throughout the area, and in an overlapping of Christmas customs, the Scandinavians can seem like one people instead of several. There is an often-repeated saying that the Christmas spirit must not be allowed to leave the house. And the only sure way to guarantee that it will not, so the belief goes, is to offer every visitor, even the stranger who comes to the door, some little tidbit to eat. No one would be so witless as to refuse—and thus break the spell and carry the Christmas spirit away with him.

I have had the good fortune of celebrating two Christmases in Copenhagen. They remain firmly imprinted on my memory as pinnacles of contentment. The first was marked by a small family dinner in the apartment of an elderly retired couple living on a tiny pension. Despite their limited means, they had roast duck *and* roast pork to eat, and nothing would do but that I put away double portions of each, two helpings of apple cake for dessert, and before the evening was out, as many kinds of cookies as could be ringed around my coffee cup. My second Danish Christmas exceeded the first one by far, probably because as a GI up from Germany on a three-day pass and thousands of miles away from home, I was an object of pity. On a round of visits to friends I had so much food offered to me and I ate so much of it (had to, lest I take the Christmas spirit away with me) that on the 24-hour train ride back to Frankfurt, I developed not the slightest appetite, nor was I the least bit hungry the next morning. Settling into my bunk at night I felt the way a bear must feel when, fat from its autumn feasting, it curls down in its cave for a winter's sleep.

Echoes of childhood

Perhaps the most remarkable thing about Scandinavian Christmas is that it is, in every respect, an old-fashioned Christmas. Here—and real—are all the ingredients that elsewhere go into the fabrication of a nostalgic Christmas scene: the snow piled up on the rooftops and yeasting out over the eaves, the bowl of hot punch, *glögg (page 194),* sending up wreaths of steam and flame, the gingerbread houses and the gingerbread men and

women, the Christmas tree with flickering candles on it and with children dancing around it, singing carols and hymns. To confront such a tree for the first time is to have some chord of memory struck, to recall an image from Hans Christian Andersen's "The Fir Tree," read aloud a long time ago by someone . . . by whom? A teacher? Mother? "From its branches . . . hung little nets cut out of colored paper, and each net was filled with candies. Gilded apples and walnuts hung in clusters as if they grew there, and a hundred little white, blue, and even red, candles were fastened to its twigs. Among its green branches swayed dolls. . . . And up at its very top was set a large gold tinsel star. It was splendid, I tell you, splendid beyond all words!"

In its signs and symbols and in its foods, Scandinavian Christmas seems to hover somewhere between this century and the last. Its roots are agricultural; they go back to the days when most people lived in the country. Many ornaments are made of straw, a reminder of how straw used to be spread on the farmhouse floor, sometimes to a depth of four feet, to suggest the manger, and how the whole family would all but nest in it, taking their meals there, running and charging around in the straw in pursuit of the Christmas games.

Gifts for all God's creatures

The farm animals, too, shared in the festivities as they munched extra rations of their favorite feed. And the little Christmas elf, the *nisse*, who many people believed lived in the barn, was always provided a bowl of porridge on Christmas Eve; the *nisse* still has his place in the festivities, and his image cut out of paper still figures importantly as a decoration. Nor were the birds forgotten. On the farms it was the custom to put out grain for them; today a golden sheaf of oats or wheat hangs on many a balcony or terrace—an invitation for the birds to come join in the feast.

Because Scandinavian Christmas is so special, a great deal of time must be spent preparing for it, and this too is part of its aura. As early as the first Sunday in December, the Christmas decorations are gotten out and gone over; those beyond repair are thrown away and new ones made, familiar ones refurbished. (Some of these are generations old, originally woven and

Oranges studded with cloves in fancy patterns and hung from shelves are popular Christmas decorations, as are paper hearts and red tulips. Below is the *nisse*, a barn elf. A benevolent creature, he can be mischievous unless he is well treated—as he has been here, eating the porridge set out for him at Christmas in the company of the family cat.

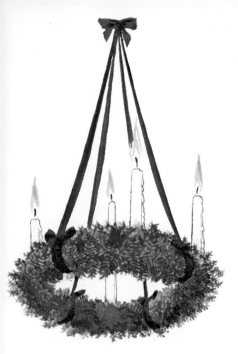

The Advent wreath contains four candles for the four weeks of Advent. Each is lit on its own Sunday until by Christmas all four are blazing.

Fortified by a glass of nonalcoholic beer, a Scandinavian boy triumphantly finds the almond hidden in the rice porridge served to the family members on Christmas Eve. Because the prized almond turned up in his portion he wins the marzipan pig shown below.

strung together by young hands now grown bony and wrinkled.) In the days that follow the house is cleaned, the shopping done, the candles bought. From ovens issue hundreds of cookies, yellow with butter or dark with syrup and redolent of cloves and ginger—*pebernødder* in Denmark, *pepparkakor* in Sweden. Into boiling fat are dropped the brandy-flavored ribbons of dough that appear throughout Scandinavia under different names —*klejner, klener, klenätter*—but everywhere are consumed with equal zest. Cakes are baked, some like large fruit buns *(page 194),* others swollen twists of yeast dough, still others really nothing more than sops, or sponges, for butter. In the air it is possible to smell Christmas, and such clouds of steam and heat pass up from stoves and ovens to the chilly heavens that precipitation in the form of fragrant snow would seem an inevitable result by Christmas Eve.

At Christmas people want the traditional foods, the ones they had in childhood, and they see to it that they get them. Where but in Scandinavia could such a fuss still be made over rice porridge? Few are the homes that would be without it on Christmas Eve—with sugar and cinnamon sprinkled over it and a pat of butter spreading out into a sunburst on top. Buried in one of the earthenware bowls arranged at the place settings will be a single blanched almond, which to the finder can mean marriage in the year to come, or other great good fortune, and which in Denmark at least brings its own immediate reward—a piece of candy or a marzipan pig with a red ribbon tied around its neck.

Today many of the most complicated of the old Christmas foods are bought ready-made, but there are women who still insist on cooking everything themselves and seemingly will stop at nothing to do so. For as the Swedes say, "If we're going to have fattening Christmas food, it had better be good." To be sure, only the stalwart continue to prepare their own pig's head. For this the housewife will steel herself and follow the commands of her recipe: "Clean and scrape the head and singe the bristles. Brush the teeth clean. Keep the mouth open with a stick so that an apple can be placed there when ready for serving. . . ."

The spirit of Christmas past

If all these preparations for Christmas sound time-consuming, they are nothing compared to what they were a century ago when Scandinavia was still dominated by a storage economy and most people still lived on farms. The Swedes have assembled a complete picture of Christmas in those days through the personal reminiscences of people who lived then. This oral record—much of it gathered over the years through questionnaires sent out to old people—is one of the treasures of the Nordiska Museum in Stockholm, and has served as the basis for a lively book (available in English) called *Christmas in Sweden 100 Years Ago.* In this book there is a charming account of the holiday fever by a woman called Mother Bengta Nilsson, born in 1844 in Skåne. "People started their preparations for Christmas in October," she recalls. "They slaughtered as many as twenty to thirty sheep at the bigger farms, and eight to ten at the smaller ones. At Martinmas [November 11] it was the turn of the geese. When they had finished with the geese, the pigs were killed and an ox or large cow was

186

slaughtered at the same time. They made masses of brawn [a pressed pork roll], sausages and black puddings. The walls and ceiling of the pantry . . . were crammed to overflowing with jars, pans and barrels filled with all sorts of provisions, such as honey, butter, lard, and goose fat. There were also big firkins of red whortleberry preserve, as well as large ventilated cheese cupboards. . . ."

A loaf to be admired

But that was only the beginning. She goes on to recount how next the beer was made, the aquavit distilled ("several hundred gallons so there would be enough for the whole year"), the candles dipped, and "then came the big wash, which lasted for several days"—and what a soaking and wringing of clothes and linen that involved. In the week before Christmas the baking was done. Loaves could weigh up to several pounds apiece, and as many as 60 to 70 pounds might be baked to serve the appetites of a family of six. In most homes something called a show-bread also was baked. This was a round loaf made only of water and flour, but beautifully decorated with dough figures and glazed all over; it was not to be eaten, but treasured and admired before finally being crumbled and strewn across the land to assure a good harvest. Often the different kinds of breads and cookies baked were amassed on the Christmas table in towering piles, one pile for each member of the family, with perhaps an orange or an apple sitting supreme on top.

At the place of every member of a Swedish family seated around the Christmas breakfast table is a *julhög*, or yule pile. The one shown here has a coarse rye bread on the bottom, next a fine wheat bread strewn with sugar and chopped almonds, a saffron bun containing raisins, a heart-shaped brown cookie and a big red apple.

While the oven was still hot from the Christmas baking, the meat would be roasted—"neck and spareribs of pork and legs and breast of mutton . . . geese and large eels. . . ." And on Christmas Eve, after "the furniture, walls and ceiling had been scoured with sand and pea-straw brushes and then rinsed with water and well dried with linen rags," straw was sprinkled on the floor, colorful wall-hangings were put up, some with Biblical scenes woven into them or painted on them, and a fine, homespun cloth was spread on the table. "In the middle of the table we placed a wooden platter, large as a trough, piled high with all sorts of tasty food, such as meat, Christmas ham, pigs' trotters, meat sausage, leg of mutton, mock brawn, collared brawn. . . ." But this was not the meal proper—only the overture, so to speak. "We began with bread and butter, with which we ate goose drippings and as many kinds of sausages and other delicacies as we could stuff down. The beer and aquavit were passed round constantly. Then came a dish of browned cabbage. We boiled several large white cabbages the day before . . . and pounded them in a firkin until they were as fine as porridge. Then we browned them in butter and added thick cream and a few pepper-corns. After the cabbage, we had lye-cured fish and mustard sauce, and this was followed by buckwheat porridge served with milk and cream." When the porridge had been eaten, "we had dessert. This consisted of various kinds of cake, such as puff-paste twists . . . sugar chips and almond patties. After the meal we sang and played Christmas games."

That was Christmas in Sweden one hundred years ago. How is it cele-brated today? Not so differently. The idea is still, as everywhere in Scandi-navia, to "eat Christmas, drink Christmas and play Christmas." And the foods are as plentiful and fattening as ever. Actually the Christmas celebra-

Wearing a crown of candles and escorted by her brother and sisters, the eldest daughter of a Swedish family carries coffee and saffron-colored Lucia buns *(below)* to her parents on the feast of Saint Lucia, December 13.

tions get off to a somewhat earlier start in Sweden these days than they did in the past. A custom once restricted to the western part of the country has been widely adopted all over, and now, on the morning of December 13, Saint Lucia's Day, little girls in long white dresses, wearing crowns of lingonberry greens studded with candles, come to their parents' beds bearing trays of saffron yeast buns and coffee.

In all Swedish homes a lightly salted ham will be served on Christmas Eve, usually with tart homemade applesauce and often with red cabbage. This will be part of the *smörgåsbord,* and on the table will be all the other Christmas specialties—liver paste, roast spareribs, sausages sweet with marjoram and thyme, some boiled, others sliced and fried, brawn and a great deal more, and inevitably, pickled herring and herring salad. The *smörgåsbord* is never so good—never so pleasant and so cozy—as when laid out in the kitchen, on a sideboard draped with an enormous tablecloth that can be pulled up over all the nonperishable items to protect them until the next time around.

The Christmas ham, like the *smörgåsbord,* must be a big one—big enough to yield as many between-meal snacks as family appetites, always large at this time of year, may dictate. Often a large, sharp knife is kept in place beside it with this in mind. The ham is usually boiled first, then baked under a delicate crust of breadcrumbs and pungent mustard mixed with sugar and egg. The ham—massive and important on its platter—wears a paper ruff at its bony end. The water in which the ham has cooked, and in which the sausages for the *smörgåsbord* also may have been boiled, is saved for a family ceremony known as *doppa i grytan,* dipping in the pot. Into this broth everyone dips a piece of *vörtbröd,* a type of rye bread, and consumes it out of hand and sopping wet—perhaps mostly for the sake of nostalgia. The ritual harks back to the days not so long ago when even the tiniest bit of nourishment—in the most abundant of years and at this most abundant time of year—could not be wasted. To many in Sweden, Christmas would not be Christmas without "dipping in the pot."

A meal paying homage to tradition

Two other requisites of Swedish Christmas are *lutfisk,* the sun-dried, lime-cured ling, a relative of the cod, and the rice porridge mentioned earlier. How long Swedes have thus been eating these two simple foods as part of their Christmas celebration no one knows, but the custom of having *lutfisk* dates back at least four centuries to Catholic Sweden, to what was then the fast, rather than the feast, of Christmas. *Lutfisk* is always served with a white sauce, melted butter, green peas, boiled potatoes and lots of freshly ground black pepper and mustard. The rice-porridge dessert is a humble but fit ending to a meal that pays homage to the past.

The Christmas customs of the other Scandinavians are in many ways like those of the Swedes, and all have a rustic tinge to them. Rice porridge has its place on the tables of the Norwegians, Finns and Danes, and with the exception of Denmark, so does *lutfisk.* And pork—in one form or another—crops up everywhere, either on Christmas Eve or Day. The Norwegians make a main dish of *ribbe,* great chops of pork with the massive rib bones attached, roasted to a brown turn in the oven. These they serve with caraway-flavored sauerkraut, into which they stir some pan drippings to give the vinegar-tart cabbage "the real Christmas flavor." The Finns share with the Swedes the taste for ham, but they may bake theirs in a rye-dough crust, and they forgo the traditional Swedish accompaniment of red cabbage for their own turnip pudding.

To my mind, the most delicious of the Christmas Eve dinners is the Danish. Invariably—or at least in big households—it consists of a rotund goose, red cabbage, sugar-browned potatoes and lingonberry sauce. Filled with apples and prunes and roasted slowly to ensure its absolute tenderness, the goose gradually takes on some of the flavor of the fruit stuffing *(page 190)*. The cook will sometimes leave the door of her oven ajar during the last few minutes of roasting time to allow the skin to become crackly, and this can be so good that strips of it will be as avidly sought at table as the meat itself. The same wise cook often discards the stuffing, especially if the goose fat has made it greasy, and arranges around the steaming bird a garnish of halved, poached apples, their centers filled with port-soaked prunes or with red blobs of currant jelly.

Most Danes begin Christmas dinner with rice porridge, but more and more of them are getting away from this. Instead, they substitute at the end of the meal a dessert they have given the French name *ris à l'amande*, a light, fluffy rice pudding into which whipped cream and chopped almonds are folded for a marvelous contrast of textures *(page 192)*. Onto the *ris à l'amande* often goes a cherry sauce, but a little Cherry Heering can be even better.

Making merry round the tree

This was the meal—and the dessert—the second Christmas I spent in Copenhagen. Recalling it now and the wine-instilled merriment of my friends at table fills me with warmth and longing. After dinner was over, it was our pleasant duty to link hands and dance around the Christmas tree in the middle of the living room, and then to sit down and take coffee and brandy by candlelight. Well toasted by a peat fire that had died to a crumbling ash, we went to bed after midnight, unmindful of the damp chill of our bedrooms, and we woke in the morning late, not caring about the darkness pressing through the windowpanes. Another day of feasting lay ahead, to be followed by yet another—and winter seemed a long time and a long distance away.

In Scandinavia Christmas disappears when the last of the candles burns itself down into a hardened puddle of wax. By then the worst of winter can be said to be behind, and the days—imperceptibly at first—begin to brighten. People seem now almost to lean toward the spring, to strain toward it. I remember how some went out into their gardens in the winter months to pick branches and put them in water to force the buds open, and I remember how tulips, well in advance of their season, began to fill up vases, and how hyacinths and other bulbs were brought out of their dark closets and put down upon the window sills to sprout. And from this early contact with the new, as yet unborn, season there came a yearning for—and talk of—the foods of spring, the strawberries, the tiny shrimp, the first salmon, all the sweet, clean-tasting delicacies of Scandinavia. So it has always been, and so it will always be.

With joined hands, a family dances around a Christmas tree all ablaze with real candles. On the coffee table are coffeepot and cups, cream and sugar, and a bowl filled with holiday cookies.

To serve 8 to 10

8- to 10-pound young goose
½ lemon
Salt
Freshly ground black pepper
2 cups apples, peeled, cored and
    coarsely chopped
2 cups presoaked dried prunes, pitted
    and chopped
1 large onion, peeled and quartered

Gaasesteg med Aebler og Svedsker
ROAST GOOSE STUFFED WITH APPLES AND PRUNES

Preheat the oven to 325°. To prepare this classic Danish Christmas dish, first wash the goose under cold running water. Pat it thoroughly dry with paper towels, then rub the bird inside and out with the cut side of half a lemon. Lightly salt and pepper the inside, and stuff the cavity with the coarsely chopped apples and prunes and the onion quarters. Close the opening by lacing it with skewers or by sewing it with heavy white thread. Fasten the neck skin to the back of the goose with a skewer and truss the bird securely so that it will keep its shape while cooking.

Roast the goose on a rack set in a shallow open pan for 3 to 3½ hours (about 20 to 25 minutes to the pound). As the goose fat accumulates in the pan, draw it off with a bulb baster or large kitchen spoon. Basting the goose itself is unnecessary.

To test whether the bird is done, pierce the thigh with the tip of a small, sharp knife. If the juice that runs out is still somewhat pink, roast another 5 to 10 minutes. If the juice is a pale yellow, set the finished bird in the turned-off oven with the door ajar for about 15 minutes to make it easier to carve.

Transfer the goose to a large heated platter and remove the string and skewers. Scoop out the stuffing and discard it. The fruits and onion will have imparted their flavor to the goose but will be far too fatty to serve.

Traditionally, poached apples stuffed with prunes *(page 192)* are served with the Christmas goose. Red cabbage and caramelized potatoes *(below and page 191)* complete the Christmas menu in Denmark.

To serve 6

1 medium head red cabbage, 2 to
    2½ pounds
4 tablespoons butter, cut into small
    pieces
1 tablespoon sugar
1 teaspoon salt
⅓ cup water
⅓ cup white vinegar
¼ cup red currant jelly
2 tablespoons grated apple

Rødkaal
BRAISED RED CABBAGE

Wash the head of cabbage under cold running water, remove the tough outer leaves, and cut the cabbage in half from top to bottom. Lay the flat sides down on the chopping board, cut away the core and slice the cabbage very finely. There should be approximately 9 cups of shredded cabbage when you finish.

Preheat the oven to 325°. Combine the butter, sugar, salt, water and vinegar in a heavy stainless-steel or enameled 4- to 5-quart casserole. When it comes to a boil and the butter has melted, add the shredded cabbage and toss thoroughly with two wooden spoons or forks. Bring to a boil again, cover tightly and place in the center of the oven to braise for 2 hours. There is little danger that the cabbage will dry out during the cooking, but it is a good idea to check on the liquid level occasionally. Add a little water if it seems necessary.

About 10 minutes before the cabbage is finished, stir in the jelly and grated apple, replace the cover and complete the cooking.

The piquant taste of red cabbage will improve if, after it has cooled, it is allowed to rest for a day in the refrigerator and then reheated either on top of the stove or in a 325° oven. In any case, serve hot, as an accompaniment to a stuffed loin of pork or goose to complete the traditional Danish Christmas dinner.

Brunede Kartofler
CARAMELIZED POTATOES

To serve 8

24 small new potatoes
½ cup sugar
8 tablespoons (1 quarter-pound stick)
   unsalted butter, melted

Drop the unpeeled potatoes into a pan of boiling water and cook 15 to 20 minutes, or until they offer no resistance when pierced with the tip of a sharp knife. Let them cool slightly; then peel them.

Melt the ½ cup of sugar in a heavy 10- to 12-inch skillet over low heat. Cook slowly for 3 to 5 minutes, until the sugar turns to a light-brown caramel. Stir constantly with a wooden spoon and watch the sugar closely; the syrup changes color very rapidly and burns easily. It must not become too dark or it will be bitter. Stir in the melted butter, and add as many potatoes as possible without crowding the pan. Shake the pan almost constantly to roll the potatoes and coat them on all sides with the caramel. Remove the hot, caramelized potatoes to a heated serving bowl and repeat the procedure until all the potatoes are coated.

Drop the boiled new potatoes into the hot caramelized sugar and butter. Shake the pan gently to make sure that all the potatoes are thoroughly coated. Golden in its caramel coating *(below) brunede kartofler* is a fine Christmas dish.

Halve Aebler med Svedsker

POACHED APPLE HALVES STUFFED WITH PRUNES IN PORT WINE

To serve 8

16 medium prunes
2 teaspoons sugar
⅔ cup port wine
8 baking apples, ½ pound each
1 cup sugar
1 quart cold water

In an enameled, stainless-steel or ovenproof glass bowl, combine the wine, sugar and prunes. Marinate the prunes in this mixture for at least 6 hours, then preheat the oven to 350°. Bake the prunes in their bowl, uncovered, for about 30 minutes, or until they are tender but not falling apart.

Meanwhile, prepare the poached apples. Pare the apples and cut them in half vertically. Scoop out the cores as neatly as possible with a small, sharp knife. In a 2- to 3-quart enameled or stainless-steel saucepan, combine the sugar and water, bring to a boil, and boil steadily for 2 or 3 minutes. Then lower the heat and add the apple halves, 8 at a time. Simmer for 10 minutes, until they are tender but not too soft. Transfer the poached apples to a heated platter with a slotted spoon and poach the remaining apples. Drain the baked prunes of all of their liquid and place 1 prune in each apple half.

To prepare these in advance, cover with plastic wrap and refrigerate. Just before serving, place the prune-filled apples on a lightly buttered cookie sheet, cover with foil and bake 10 minutes in a preheated 400° oven. Serve with roast goose, or duck, as part of the traditional Danish Christmas dinner.

Ris à l'Amande

RICE AND ALMOND DESSERT

To serve 6 to 8

1 quart milk
3½ tablespoons sugar
¾ cup long-grain white rice
¾ cup blanched and chopped almonds
¼ cup sherry
2 teaspoons vanilla
½ pint chilled heavy cream

Bring the milk to a boil in a 2-quart saucepan and add the sugar and rice. Stir once or twice, then lower the heat and simmer uncovered about 25 minutes, or until the rice is quite soft but not mushy. (Cooking time for rice varies, but a sure test is to rub a grain between the thumb and forefinger; if there is no hard kernel in the center, the rice is done.) Pour the finished rice immediately into a shallow bowl to cool it quickly, and then add the chopped almonds, sherry and vanilla.

Whip the heavy cream in a chilled bowl with a wire whisk or hand or electric beater until it thickens and holds its shape softly. Fold it into the tepid rice mixture, turn the pudding into a serving dish and chill before serving.

A cold cherry or raspberry sauce or a spoonful of cherry liqueur is often served on top of this modern version of an ancient Christmas porridge.

Mor Monsen's Kaker

MOTHER MONSEN'S CAKES

To make about 2 dozen small cakes

2 teaspoons unsalted butter, softened
1 pound unsalted butter, softened
2 cups sugar
4 eggs
2 cups flour
1 teaspoon vanilla
½ cup finely chopped blanched almonds
¼ cup dried currants

Preheat the oven to 375°. With a pastry brush or paper towel, spread a 12-by-18-inch jelly-roll pan with 2 teaspoons of butter. Cream the butter and sugar together by beating them against the side of a bowl with a wooden spoon or by using an electric mixer set at medium speed. When light and fluffy, beat in the eggs, 1 at a time. Then beat in the flour and vanilla. Spread the batter evenly onto the pan, sprinkle the surface with the almonds and currants and bake 20 to 25 minutes, until the surface is a light gold. Remove from the oven and let the cake cool in the pan. With a sharp knife, cut into small triangles or squares.

These cakes, frequently served at Norwegian Christmases, can be made 2 weeks before the feast, but they must then be wrapped in aluminum foil or placed in an airtight tin and stored in a cool place.

Brune Kager
LITTLE BROWN CAKES

Heat the corn syrup, brown sugar and butter in a heavy saucepan until the sugar is thoroughly dissolved. Do not let it boil. Remove from the heat and let it cool. Meanwhile, sift the baking soda, flour and powdered cloves together into a large bowl. Add the cardamom, grated lemon peel and the lukewarm syrup and knead the dough well by pressing it down with the heel of your hand, turning it, folding it over and pressing again. Continue kneading for 5 to 10 minutes, until the dough is smooth and shiny. Wrap in wax paper and set aside in a cool place for at least 2 hours.

Preheat the oven to 400°. On a lightly floured surface, roll the dough into a sheet ⅛ inch thick, then with a cookie cutter or small wine glass cut it into 2-inch rounds. Grease a cookie sheet and lay the cookies on it about an inch apart. Lightly press 1 almond into the center of each and bake 5 or 6 minutes, or until they are a light gold. Cool the *brune kager* on the cookie sheet. The cookies can be stored for several weeks in tightly sealed tins.

To make about 6 dozen cookies

½ cup dark corn syrup
5 tablespoons dark brown sugar
4 tablespoons unsalted butter
½ teaspoon baking soda
1½ cups flour
1 teaspoon powdered cloves
1¼ teaspoons ground cardamom
1¼ teaspoons grated lemon peel
3 ounces whole blanched almonds

Spritsar
SPRITZ RING COOKIES

In a large mixing bowl, cream the butter and sugar together with an electric mixer set at medium speed or by beating them with a wooden spoon until light and fluffy. Then add the egg yolks and almond extract. Sift the flour and salt together and add it a third at a time to the creamed mixture, beating it well after each addition with a wooden spoon.

Preheat the oven to 400°. Place the dough in a pastry bag fitted with a small star tip. Force the dough out onto an ungreased cookie sheet in S or O shapes about 2 inches in diameter. Bake for 10 or 12 minutes, or until the cookies are a light gold. Immediately remove them to a cake rack with a wide spatula. The cooked *spritsar* can be stored for several weeks in tightly sealed tins.

To make 6 dozen

16 tablespoons (2 quarter-pound sticks) unsalted butter, softened
¾ cup sugar
2 egg yolks
1 teaspoon almond extract
2½ cups all-purpose flour
¼ teaspoon salt

Jødekager
JEWISH CAKES

Cream the butter and sugar together by using an electric mixer set at medium speed or by beating them with a wooden spoon until light and fluffy. Beat in the egg. Sift together the flour, salt and baking powder and beat into the creamed butter, ½ cup at a time. Continue to beat until thoroughly mixed. Then form into a ball, wrap in wax paper and chill for several hours.

Preheat the oven to 400°. Divide the chilled dough in thirds. On a lightly floured pastry board, roll out each third of dough into a circle about ⅛ inch thick. Using a 2- or 3-inch cookie cutter, cut the dough into rounds. Gather up the excess dough, roll it out again, and cut out additional rounds. Lay the rounds side by side on a lightly greased cookie sheet, and, with a pastry brush, spread the tops lightly with the beaten egg white. Then sprinkle with the cinnamon-sugar mixture. Bake 2 sheets of cookies at a time in the center of the oven for about 8 minutes. Remove from the oven and, with a spatula, immediately transfer the cookies to a cake rack. Let them cool thoroughly before storing them in airtight tins.

To make about 3 dozen cookies

16 tablespoons (2 quarter-pound sticks) unsalted butter
¾ cup sugar
1 egg
2½ cups flour
½ teaspoon salt
1 teaspoon baking powder
1 egg white, lightly beaten
¼ cup cinnamon and ¼ cup granulated sugar combined

To make 1 large loaf

2 packages active dry yeast
¼ cup sugar
½ cup lukewarm milk (110° to 115°)
¼ teaspoon salt
½ teaspoon vanilla
½ teaspoon grated lemon rind
2 eggs, lightly beaten
½ teaspoon ground cardamom
3 to 4 cups flour, all-purpose
1 cup mixed candied fruits (lemon, orange, cherry, pineapple)
1 tablespoon flour
8 tablespoons (1 quarter-pound stick) unsalted butter, softened

To serve 20 to 25

2 quarts dry red wine
2 quarts muscatel
1 pint sweet vermouth
2 tablespoons Angostura bitters
2 cups raisins
Peelings of 1 orange
12 whole cardamoms, bruised in a mortar with a pestle or by covering with a towel and crushing with a rolling pin
10 whole cloves
1 piece (about 2 inches) fresh ginger
1 stick cinnamon
1½ cups (12 ounces) aquavit
1½ cups sugar
2 cups whole almonds, blanched and peeled

Julekage

DANISH CHRISTMAS FRUIT LOAF

Sprinkle the yeast and 1 tablespoon of the sugar over the lukewarm milk. Let the mixture stand in the cup for 2 or 3 minutes, then stir gently to dissolve them. Set in a warm place, perhaps in an unlighted oven. When the yeast begins to bubble in about 8 to 10 minutes, stir it gently, and with a rubber spatula, transfer it to a large mixing bowl. Stir in the salt, vanilla, lemon rind, eggs, cardamom and the remaining sugar. Then add 3 cups of flour, a little at a time, stirring at first and then kneading with your hands until the dough becomes firm enough to be formed into a ball.

Shake the candied fruits in a small paper bag with 1 tablespoon of flour. (The flour will prevent the fruits from sticking together and enable them to disperse evenly throughout the dough.) Now add the fruits and the softened butter to the dough and knead for about 10 minutes, adding more flour, if necessary, to make the dough medium-soft. The finished dough should be shiny and elastic, and its surface blistered. Shape into a ball and place in a large buttered bowl. Dust the top lightly with flour, cover with a kitchen towel and set it in a warm, draft-free spot (again, an unlighted oven is ideal). In 45 minutes to 1 hour the dough should double in bulk and leave a deep depression when two fingers are pressed into the center.

After removing the dough, preheat the oven to 350°. Punch the dough down with your fists and knead again quickly. Shape it into a fat loaf and put it into a lightly buttered 1½-quart loaf pan. Cover again with the towel and let the dough rise in a warm spot for 15 to 20 minutes until it is almost double in bulk.

Bake the *julekage* in the center of the oven for 45 minutes. Remove the loaf from the pan and let it cool on a cake rack. It will keep well for 2 or 3 weeks if wrapped well in aluminum foil and refrigerated.

Professorns Glögg

THE PROFESSOR'S GLÖGG

In a 6- to 8-quart enameled or stainless-steel pot, mix together the dry red wine, muscatel, sweet vermouth, bitters, raisins, orange peel and the slightly crushed cardamoms, whole cloves, ginger and cinnamon. Cover and let the mixture stand at least 12 hours so that the flavors will develop and mingle. Shortly before serving, add the aquavit and the sugar. Stir well and bring it to a full boil over high heat. Remove at once from the heat, stir in the almonds and serve the hot *glögg* in mugs. In Sweden, a small spoon is placed in each mug to scoop up the almonds and raisins.

ALTERNATE: To make a simpler *glögg*, divide the quantities of spices in half and mix them with 2 bottles of dry red wine. Leave it overnight, then stir in ¾ cup of sugar and bring almost to a boil. Remove from the heat, stir in 1 cup of whole, blanched and peeled almonds, and serve hot.

Opposite: A Danish holiday dinner is depicted here; it is a dinner that can be prepared in the United States as well, from the recipes on the preceding pages. On the bottom shelf are red cabbage and sugar-browned potatoes; on the middle shelf, a roast goose stuffed and garnished with prunes and apples. On top, at center, is *ris à l'amande*, a light, fluffy rice pudding, blended with chopped almonds and decorated with cherries; and last, but not least, a trayful of the sweet, crisp cookies known as *brune kager* and *Jødekager*. The Christmas tree is decorated with traditional Danish ornaments of glass and paper under a shower of tinsel.

Glossary

AEBLESKIVER (EH-bleh SKEE-vor): Danish doughnuts prepared in a special skillet

AGURKESALAT (ah-GOOR-keh sa-LAHT): cucumber salad, Danish

AKVAVIT (ah-kva-VEET), (aquavit in English): "water of life," a liquor made from the distillation of potato or grain spirits, popular throughout most of Scandinavia

ÄPPEL-FLÄSK (EHP-pel flesk): a dish of apples, onions and Canadian-style bacon, eaten in Sweden and Denmark

ÄPPELFORMAR (EHP-pel FOR-mar): Swedish apple muffins

ÄPPELKAKA (EHP-pel KAW-ka): Swedish apple cake

ÄRTER MED FLÄSK (EHR-ter med flesk): Swedish yellow pea soup

ASIER (ah-see'yor): sweet-sour pickled cucumber garnish, Danish

BERGENS FISKESUPPE (BEHR-gensk FEES-keh SOOP-peh): Bergen fish soup

BETASUPPE (BEH-ta SOOP-peh): Norwegian mutton soup

BIFF À LA LINDSTRÖM (BEEF ah-lah leend-STREWM): hamburgers à la Lindström, a Swedish specialty

BLODBUDDING (blohth-BOOD-ding): "blood pudding," a Danish dish of animal blood, barley, flour, sugar and seasonings baked as a pudding or used as sausage filling

BLODFERSK (blewd-fehrshk): "blood-fresh," an expression used by Norwegians to denote freshness of fish

BÖCKLING (BEUH-kling): Swedish name for smoked Baltic herring

BRÄNNVIN (BRENN-veen): "burned" wine, another name for aquavit

BRUNA BÖNOR (BREW-na BURN-oor): browned beans, Swedish

BRUNEDE KARTOFLER (BROO-neh-theh kar-TOF-ler): sugar-browned potatoes, Danish

BRUNE KAGER (BROO-neh KAH-gher): "brown cakes," Danish

BRYNT POTATIS (brewnt po-TAW-tiss): browned potato wedges, Swedish

DANNEBRØG (dah-neh-breugh): Danish flag

DOPPA I GRYTAN (DOHP-pa ee grew-TAN): "dipping in the pot," a family custom in Sweden, dipping rye bread in the broth of the ham and sausages cooked for the Christmas *smörgåsbord*

DYRESTEK (DEW-reh stehk): venison steak, roasted, Norwegian

FÅGELBO (foh-gull-boo): "bird's nest," chopped lettuce or parsley, onions, pickled beets, capers, and finely chopped anchovies arranged in concentric circles around raw egg yolk, a dish from the Swedish *smörgåsbord*

FÅRERULL (foh-ruh-RUL): larded and spiced mutton roll, Norwegian

FÅR I KÅL (for ee KOHL): stew of mutton and cabbage eaten in Norway

FÄRSRULADER (FEHRSH-roo-LAH-der): finely minced veal, mixed with various ingredients and rolled around a core of thinly sliced leeks, Swedish

FENELÅR (feh-neh-LOR): Norwegian dried, salted and smoked mutton

FISKEPUDDING (FEESS-keh POOD-ding): fish pudding, Norwegian

FJORD (f'yor): a narrow inlet of the sea between high banks or rocks

FLAESKEAEGGEKAGE (FLES-keh-eg-geh-KAH-gheh): bacon and egg cake, Danish

FLAESKESTEG MED SVAER (FLES-keh-stegh meh sver): roast pork with crackling, Danish

FLØTEVA VAFFEL (FLUH-teh-va vahf-fel): Norwegian sour-cream waffles

FORLOREN SKILDPADDE (for-LOR-en skeel-PAHD-deh): "mock turtle," a festive Danish dish made from calf's head

FRIKADELLER (FREE-ka-DEL-ler): a famous Danish dish of finely ground pork, veal, bread crumbs, and onions shaped into cakes and sautéed in butter

FRUKTSOPPA (FROOKT-sohp-pah): fruit soup, Swedish

FYLLDA STRUTAR (FILL-da strew-TAR): pastry cones filled with whipped cream, Swedish

GAASESTEG MED AEBLER OG SVEDSKER (GOH-seh-stegh meh ehb-lor oh SVEHS-kor): Danish roast goose.stuffed with apples and prunes

GAMMELOST (GAHM-mehl-OOST): "old cheese," a Norwegian cheese prepared from sour rather than fresh milk

GLASMÄSTERSILL (GLAHSS-mes-ter-SEEL): "glassblower's herring," a Swedish dish of herring pieces pickled in a glass jar with spices, carrots, onions, vinegar and sugar

GLÖGG (glewg): hot punch served in Scandinavia during the winter, particularly for Christmas

GRAVLAX (grawv-LAHKS): a Swedish specialty of raw salmon cured with pepper, dill, sugar and salt and served with mustard-dill sauce

GRAVLAXSÅS (GRAWV-lahks-SOHS): *gravlax* sauce (mustard-dill)

GRØNLANGKAAL (GRURN-lung-KOHL): kale in cream sauce, Danish

HAKKEBØF (HAHK-keh-BOHF): "hacked" or chopped-beef patties, a favorite in Denmark

"HÁVAMÁL" (HAH-vah-MAHL): the Viking code

HIMMELSK LAPSKAUS (him-melsk laps-kewss): "heavenly potpourri," fresh fruit and nuts with brandied egg sauce, Norwegian

HOVDESSERT (HOHV-des-SEHR): meringues with chocolate sauce, Swedish

HUSMANSKOST (HEWSS-mahns-KOHST): everyday eating of the past in Sweden, the most native dishes today

HYGGE (hewg-geh): Danish word meaning to make comfortable or at home, or to feel at home

INLAGD SILL (EEN-lah'gd SEEL): Swedish pickled herring

JANSSONS FRESTELSE (yahn-SOHNS FRESS-tel-SEH): "Jansson's Temptation," an anchovy and potato casserole popular in Sweden

JØDEKAGER (yeuh-thuh-kah-gher): Jewish cakes, a Danish Christmas cookie

JULEKAGE (YOO-leh-KAGH-gheh): Christmas fruit loaf, Danish

KAERNEMAELKSKOLKSKAAL (KEHR-neh-MELK-skolk-skol): Danish cold buttermilk soup

KALAKUKKO (KAH-lah-kook-ko): "fish fowl," a Finnish pasty of rye dough filled with tiny fresh-water fish, somewhat bird-shaped

KALJA (KAHL-yah): a Finnish home-brewed, nonalcoholic beer

KALOPS (KAH-lohps): chunks of beef simmered with allspice and bay leaf, a Swedish dish

KARJALANPAISTI (KAHR-yah-lahm-PIE-stee): "Karelian hot pot," a Finnish stew of mutton, pork and veal

KARRYSALAT (KAR-rew-sa-LAHT): curried macaroni salad, Danish

KAVIARTOPP (KAH-v'yar-TOHP): "caviar mound," cod roe in dill dressing from the Swedish *smörgåsbord*

KEITETYT RAVUT (KAY-teh-tewt RA-voot): boiled crayfish, Finnish

KERMAKAKKU (KEHR-ma-kahk-koo): sour cream poundcake, Finnish

KESÄKEITTO (KEH-sah-KAYT-tuh): a Finnish summer soup of vegetables simmered in a creamy base

KIISSELI (KEES-sel-lee): Finnish word for a thick pudding

KLEJNER (KLEIN-awr): Danish dessert of brandied flavored strips of dough, deep-fat fried

KLENÄTTER (kleh-NET-ter): Swedish dessert identical to the *klejner* of Denmark

KLENER (KLEH-ner): spelling of klenätter in the Skåne area of Sweden

KLIPPFISK (kleep-feesk): codfish salted and dried on cliffs in the open Nordic air

KNÄCKEBRÖD (knek-ke brewhd): "break bread," Swedish flat bread

KOKT LAMM MED DILLSÅS (kookt lahm meh dill-SOHS): boiled lamb in dill sauce, Swedish

KOLDE BORD (KOL-luh BOR): Danish "cold table," resembling the Swedish *smörgåsbord* but differing in certain specialties and the appearance of more salads and the makings for open-face sandwiches

KONDITORI (kohn-dee-toh-ree): pastry shop

KRANSEKAGE (KRAHN-seh-KAH-gheh): "wreath cake," a Danish and Norwegian cake made largely of marzipan

KRUMKAKER (KROOM-kahk-er): "rolled cookies," a Norwegian Christmas cookie

LAGKAGE (lahg-kah-gher): layer cake

LANGOUSTE (lawn-GOOST): spiny lobster

LÄNTTULAATIKKO (LAHNT-too-laa-teek-ko): Finnish rutabaga casserole

LEFSER (LEFF-ser): Norwegian holiday bread, thin and saucer-shaped, which is eaten buttered and sugared and folded like a handkerchief

LEVERPOSTEJ (LEH-ver poh-STY): liver paste or pâté, Danish

LIHAMUREKEPIIRAS (LEE-hah-moo-reh-keh-PEE-rahs): Finnish meat pie with sour-cream crust

LÖJROM (loy-room): roe from tiny Swedish fresh-water fish served on hard-cooked egg halves with chopped onion

LÖKDOLMAR (LUHK-dohl-MAR): Swedish stuffed onion rolls

LUTEFISK (LOO-teh-FEESK) (Norwegian); or **LUTFISK** (LOOT-feesk) (Swedish): a dish made from dried fish, usually cod, which is soaked in lye prior to cooking

MADMOR (mahth-MOR): "food mother," a title used in the past for a Danish farm wife

MAKSALAATIKKO (MAHK-sah-laa-teek-ko): Finnish liver and rice casserole

MÄMMI (MAM-mee): a Finnish rye pudding made with molasses, flavored with bitter orange and served with cream

MANSIKKALUMI (MAHN-seek-ka-LOO-mee): Finnish strawberry-snow dessert

MAZARINTÅRTA (ma-sa-REEN-TOR-ta): Swedish mazarin cake

MESIMARJA (MESSY-mar-ya): Finnish honeyberry, fruit of the Arctic bramble

MØRBRAD MED SVEDSKER OG AEBLER (mor-brath meh SVEHS-kor oh EHB-lor): pork loin stuffed with prunes and apples, Danish

MUIKKU (MWEEK-koo): tiny fresh-water fish in Finland related to the salmon

NATTMAT (naht-mawt): "night food" offered just before a party breaks up in Sweden

NISSE (NISS-seh): Christmas elf

NYPONSOPPE (NEW-pon-SOHP-pa): Swedish fruit soup made of rose hips served with almonds and whipped cream

ØLLEBRØD (UH-luh-BROHTH): a thick Danish soup made of sweet beer and stale rye crusts

OMENALUMI (OH-meh-na-LOO-mee): Finnish apple-snow dessert

OPERATÅRTA (OO-peh-ra-TOR-ta): creamy layer cake, Swedish

OSTKAKA (OOST-kaw-kah): a Swedish cheesecake much like a pudding which is baked in a mold

OXRULADER (OKS-roo-la-der): piquant beef rolls, Swedish

PAALAEG (poh-LAYGH): "something laid on," that which is put on buttered bread to make the Danish open-face sandwich

PAISTETUT SIENET (PYE-steh-toot SEE-yen-ett): fried mushrooms, Finnish

PASHA (PAH-sha): cheesecake of Russian origin eaten in Finland

PATAKUKKO (PAH-tah-kook-ko): "pot fowl," a Finnish casserole of small fresh-water fish and salt pork baked under a rye crust

PEBERNØDDER (PEH-ber-NUEH-dor): Danish "pepper nuts," a variety of Christmas cookie

PEPPARKAKOR (PEH-par-kah-koor): Swedish gingersnap cookies

PERICUM (peh-REE-koom): a yellow meadow flower of Denmark

PERSILLESOVS (per-SEEL-leh-SOHS): parsley sauce, Danish

PIIMÄ (pee-ma): sour milk drunk in Finland

PIIRAKKA (PEE-rahk-kah): Finnish word for pasties or pies, from the Russian word *pirog*

PINAATTIOHUKAISET (PEE-natt-tee-yo-hoo-KYE-sett): spinach pancakes, Finnish

PINNEKJØTT (PEE-neh-SHUTT): salt-cured mutton chops, steamed on peeled birch twigs in Norway

PIROG (pee-ROGH): Russian for pasties from which came the Finnish *piirakka*

PITEPALT (pee-teh-palt): potato dumplings stuffed with pork from the north of Sweden

PITO-JA-JOULUPUURO (PEE-to-ya-YO-loo-poo-roh): whole-grain barley pudding cooked in milk and served with rose-hip or raisin purée in Finland

PLÄTTAR (pleh-tar): pancakes, Swedish

POSTEJ (poh-STY): Danish for paste or pâté

POTKAS (poht-KASS): Swedish word for pot cheese

PULLA (POOL-lah): a Finnish braided yeast cake

PUSS PASS (pooss-pass): Norwegian stew of mutton, carrots, potatoes and cabbage

PYTT I PANNA (PEWT ee PAHN-nah): "tidbits in a pan," diced potatoes and meats with onions and parsley served with raw egg yolk or fried egg in Sweden

RAKØRRET (RAH-ker-ret): trout that has been salted down and cured, a Christmas favorite in Norway

RÅRAKOR (roh-rah-koor): lacy Swedish potato pancakes

REKESAUS (REH-keh-SOHS): Norwegian shrimp sauce

RIBBE (REEB-beh): rib pork chops, a Norwegian Christmas specialty

RIS À L'AMANDE (REE ah-lah-mahnd): Danish rice pudding with whipped cream and chopped almonds served with cherry sauce

RØDGRØD MED FLØDE (rohth-GROH meh FLUH-theh): "red gruel" with cream, a Danish pudding of thickened raspberry and currant juices eaten with sweet cream

RØDKAAL (rurth-kohl): Danish red cabbage

ROMFROMAGE (rohm-froh-mahj): a Danish dessert of whipped cream, beaten eggs and sugar with rum and liquored cherries

RØMMEGRØT (rohm-meh-greht): a special Norwegian porridge made with sour cream, milk and flour and served with cinnamon and crunchy sugar

RULLEPØLSE (ROO-luh-PUL-seh): spiced and larded meat roll of veal, beef or lamb served in Denmark

RYYPPY (REWP-pee): Finnish for a shot of icy vodka

SANDKAGE (sahnd-KAH-gheh): "sand cake," a specialty of Denmark

SIENISALAATTI (SEE-yen-ee-sa-LAAT-tee): Finnish mushroom salad

SILL (seel): Swedish designation of herring other than that from the Baltic

SILLGRATIN (SEEL-gra-TEEN): *sill* herring and potato casserole, Swedish

SILLSALLAD (SEEL-sa-LAHD): *sill* herring salad, Swedish

SIMA (SEE-ma): Finnish lemon-flavored mead

SKYR (skeer): curdled milk, formerly known by that name over most of Scandinavia, now found only in Iceland

SLOTTSSTEK (sloht-stehk): Swedish royal pot roast

SMÅ KÖTTBULLAR (smo SHIRT-bool-lahr): small Swedish meatballs

SMÄLTSILL (smohlt-seel): "melted" *sill* herring, Swedish

SMÅVARMT (smo-VAHRMT): "small warm," the hot part of the *smörgåsbord*

SMÖRGÅSBORD (smur-gohs-BOARD): "bread and butter table," a large variety of hot and cold dishes arrayed on a table, a tradition which was fully developed in the 1880s in Sweden. Traditionally accompanied by aquavit

SMØRREBRØD (smur-er-BREWTH): "buttered bread," Danish open-face sandwiches

SNAPS (snahps): aquavit

SPANDAUER (spun-DOW-er): spandauers, a Danish pastry

SPARK (spahrk): Swedish chair toboggan

SPEKEMAT (SPEH-keh-MAHT): Norwegian salt-cured meats

SPEKESKINKE (SPEH-ker-SHEEN-keh): ham cured in brine, a kind of Nordic prosciutto

SPETTEKAKA (SPEHT-teh-KAH-kah): a towering cake of eggs and sugar from southern Sweden specially baked on a spit

SPINATSUPPE (speen-AHT-SOOP-peh): spinach soup, Norwegian

SPRÄNGD (spraing'd): "burst" or cured, used in reference to meat which has been set in brine prior to cooking in Sweden. The Danes use the same expression for this process

SPRITSAR (spreet-sar): Swedish spritz ring cookies

STABBUR (STAHB-ber): a wooden storehouse built on stilts in Norway to keep a year's supply of food so that a farm could survive independently if necessary

STEGT KYLLING (stehkt SHEWL-ling): braised chicken, Danish

STEGT RØDSPAETTE (stehkt rohths-peh-teh): fried plaice, Danish

STEKT MARINERT MAKRELL (stehkt ma-ree-NEHRT mock-RELL): grilled marinated mackerel, Norwegian

STRÖMMING (STRUM-ming): Swedish term for Baltic herring

SUOMALAISLEIPÄ (SOO-wo-ma-lice-rooeys-LAY-pa): Finnish yeast bread

SURSTRÖMMING (SEWR-STRUM-ming): fermented Baltic herring, a specialty of Sweden

SVARTSOPPA (SVAHRT-SOHP-pah): "black soup," a famous dish of Skåne in Sweden, prepared from goose and pig's blood, spices, and other seasonings

SYLTEDE RØDBEDER (SEWL-teh-theh ROHTH-beh-thor): pickled beets, Danish

SYR (syr): milk which has been kept for months before eating in Norway and Sweden

TAK FOR MAD" (tahk for mahth): "thanks for the food" in Danish

TALKKUNA (TALK-koo-nah): a thick Finnish porridge made of barley and dipped in melted butter before eating

TETTE MELK (TEH-teh MELK): milk in which Norwegians place leaves of the *tette* meadow plant to preserve the milk and start a specially flavored culture

TIDBID (teed-beeth): Danish light snack

TIPPALEIVÄT (TEEP-pah-leh-vat): Finnish May Day crullers or birds' nests

TORRFISK (torr-feesk): stockfish

TORSK MED EGGESAUS (torshk meh EG-geh-sowss): boiled cod with egg sauce, Norwegian

TOSCATÄRTA (TOH-ska-TOR-ta): an almond-topped Swedish cake

TYKMAELK (tewk-melk): "thick" or sour milk in Denmark

UUNISSA PAISTETTU HAUKI (OO-nees-sah PYE-stet-too HOW-kee): Finnish baked, stuffed pike

VANILJSÅS (va-neel'-sohs): vanilla sauce, Swedish

VARM KRABBSMÖRGÅS (vahrm KRAHB-smer-gohs): hot crab-meat canapés, Swedish

VÅRSMÖRGÅSAR (VOHR-smer-goh-SAR): Swedish spring sandwiches

VATKATTU MARJAPUURO (VAHT-kaht-too MAHR-ya-POO-ro): fluffy whipped berry pudding, Finnish

"VELBEKOMME" (vell-beh-kohm-meh): "if you please" or "may it become you well," said in the nature of a blessing in Denmark

VIILI (vee-lee): thick sour milk eaten in Finland

VOILEIPÄPÖYTÄ (VOY-LAY-pa-PUH-ew-tah): Finnish *smörgåsbord*

VORSHMACK (vor-shmahk): a dish of ground mutton, beef and salt herring cooked with garlic and onions, eaten in Finland

VÖRTBRÖD (vurt-brewd): a type of Swedish rye bread

WIENERBRØD (VEE-ner-BROHTH): "Vienna bread," the Danish appellation of their own Danish pastry

Recipe Index: English

NOTE: An R preceding a page refers to the Recipe Booklet. Size, weight and material are specified for pans in the recipes because they affect cooking results. A pan should be just large enough to hold its contents comfortably. Heavy pans heat slowly and cook food at a constant rate. Aluminum and cast iron conduct heat well but may discolor foods containing egg yolks, wine, vinegar or lemon. Enamelware is a fairly poor conductor of heat. Many recipes therefore recommend stainless steel or enameled cast iron, which do not have these faults.

Recipe Index: Scandinavian

General Index
Numerals in italics indicate a photograph or drawing of the subject mentioned.

Credits and Acknowledgments

The sources for the illustrations in this book are shown below. Credits for the pictures from left to right are separated by commas, from top to bottom by dashes.

All photographs by Richard Meek except:
4—Top and bottom right Charles Phillips. 8—George Silk. 13—Map by Lothar Roth; base map by Ginn and Company, Boston, Massachusetts; illustrations by Otto van Eersel. 18, 19—Howard Sochurek. 35—James Whitmore. 39—Marvin E. Newman. 102—Marvin E. Newman 112, 113—Top Bob and Ira Spring from Freelance Photographers Guild. 119—Drawing by Matt Greene. 120—Charles Phillips. 124—Charles Phillips. 129—National Museum of Finland, Helsinki. 134—Carlo Bavagnoli. 145—Bottom Dale Brown. 152—Carlo Bavagnoli. 153—Drawings by Matt Greene. 154—Charles Phillips. 157—Top Charles Phillips (4). 158—Charles Phillips. 170—Charles Phillips. 175—Drawings by Matt Greene, photograph by Charles Phillips. 176, 177—Charles Phillips. 180—Charles Phillips. 184 through 189—Drawings by Erik Blegvad. 191—Charles Phillips.

For their help in the production of this book the editors wish to thank the following: *in Denmark,* Mrs. Gerda Andersen and Mrs. Gudrun Winkel, Ekkodanmark, Copenhagen; Mrs. M. Astor and Mrs. Rosalie Holmes, The Federation of Danish Dairy Associations, Aarhus; Miss Alice Bruun, Danish Ministry of Fisheries, Copenhagen; Henning Bensdtsen and Niels Hansen, Bornholm; The Danish Meat Research Institute, Roskilde; Peter F. Heering, Copenhagen; Erik Høgsbro Holm and Bengt Petersen, Danish Ministry of Foreign Affairs, Copenhagen; Eyvind Knauer, Carlsberg Breweries, Copenhagen; Mr. and Mrs. Martin Maarbjerg, Copenhagen; SAS and SAS Catering, Copenhagen; Mrs. Jeanne Steinmetz, Danish National Tourist Association, Copenhagen; Flemming Wedel, Danish Agricultural Council, Copenhagen; *in Finland,* Holger Carring, Arabia Ceramics, Helsinki; Mr. and Mrs. Aarne Ervi, Helsinki; Veikko Nylund, Kuopio; Mrs. Armi Ratia, Marimekko Textile, Helsinki; Mrs. Maire Revell, Helsinki; Erkki Savolainen, Finnish Ministry for Foreign Affairs, Helsinki; Mr. and Mrs. Jorma Soiro, Helsinki; Mrs. Elinor Vuorikoski, Suurkeittio, Helsinki; *in Norway,* Audun Boysen, Norwegian Brewery Society, Oslo; Hroar Dege and Mrs. Babben Hoff, The Norwegian Food Center, Oslo; Professor and Mrs. Knut Faegri, Bergen; Tryggve Fitje, Voss Travel Association, Voss; Hansa Brewery, Bergen; Ragnar Jansen, Vinmonopolet, Oslo; Olav N. Sandven, Sandven Hotel, Norheimsund; *in Sweden,* Mrs. Harriet Albert, Royal Norwegian Ministry of Foreign Affairs, Stockholm; Bo Beijer, Stockholm; Professor Gösta Berg, Skansen, Stockholm; Olle Bornefors and Lars Lendrop, Savoy Hotel, Malmö; Mrs. Teje Colling, Nordiska Museum, Stockholm; Mr. and Mrs. Carl Gustav Holst, Stockholm; Göte Lilian, Sundet Bakery Shop, Malmö; Mats Rehnberg, Radio Sweden, Stockholm; Mrs. Birgitta Sidh, Farmers' Test Kitchens, Stockholm; Bertil Stibeck, Mora Hotel, Mora; Per-Arne Wallin, Luleå; and *in New York City,* Bonniers Inc.; Design Research Inc.; Erik Eriksen, Press Attaché, and staff of Danish Information Office, Danish Consulate General; Finnish Information Service; Frederik Lunning Showroom; Georg Jensen Inc.; Jan Holmgren; Mikko Immonen, Consul, and staff of Finnish Consulate General; Lars Langaaker, Cultural Attaché, and staff of Norwegian Information Service; John Larsen, chef, Copenhagen Restaurant; Norwegian Consulate General; Mrs. Anne Marekallio; Norsk Inc.; Nyborg & Nelson Inc.; Svend Jensen of Denmark Inc.; Swedish Consulate General; Swedish Information Service; and Mrs. T. Tallroth.

Sources consulted in the production of this book include: *Danish Home Baking* by Karen Berg; *Swedish Food* by Greta Borgstrom and Birgit Danfors; *The Great Scandinavian Cook Book* translated and edited by J. Audrey Ellison; *An Armchair Visit to Denmark,* published by Federation of Danish Dairy Associations; *Danish Food* by Grete Grumme; *The Art of Danish Cooking* and *The Art of Scandinavian Cooking* by Nika Standen Hazelton; *Take a Silver Dish* by Bodil Jensen; *Wonderful, Wonderful Danish Cooking* by Ingeborg Dahl Jensen; *The Complete Scandinavian Cookbook* by Alice B. Johnson; *The Finnish Cookbook* by Beatrice A. Ojakangas; *Finnish Cookery* by Jorma Soiro; *Droll, Danish and Delicious* by Susanne; *Norway's Delight: Dishes and Specialties* by Elise Sverdrup; *Finnish Food* by Kirsti Tolvanen; *Christmas in Sweden 100 Years Ago* and *Swedish Christmas Celebrations* by Tre Tryckare; *Swedish Baking at its Best* by Marianne Grönwall van der Tuuk; *The Oskar Davidsen Book of Open Sandwiches* by James R. White; and *Swedish Smörgåsbord* by Tore Wretman.